William Taft

Labyrinth of Desire

Labyrinth of Desire

Invention and Culture
in the Work
of Sir Philip Sidney

William Craft

DELAWARE

Newark: University of Delaware Press
London and Toronto: Associated University Presses

Associated University Presses
440 Forsgate Drive
Cranbury, NJ 08512

Associated University Presses
25 Sicilian Avenue
London WC1A 2QH, England

Associated University Presses
P.O.Box 338, Port Credit
Mississauga, Ontario
Canada L5G 4L8

The paper used in this publication meets the requirements of the American National Standard for Permanence of Paper for Printed Library Materials Z39.48–1984.

Library of Congress Cataloging-in-Publication Data

Craft, William, 1951-
  Labyrinth of desire : invention and culture in the work of Sir Philip Sidney / William Craft.
      p.   cm.
  Includes bibliographical references (p.) and index.
  ISBN 0-87413-522-2 (alk. paper)
  1. Sidney, Philip, Sir, 1554 –1586--Criticism and interpretation.
2. Literature and society--England--History--16th century.
3. Desire--In literature.   4. Invention (Rhetoric)   I. Title.
PR2343.C73 1994
821'.3--dc20   93-39886
                                                                            CIP

          OCLC: 290245712

PRINTED IN THE UNITED STATES OF AMERICA

For Anne
in whom all joys so well agree

His end . . . was not vanishing pleasure alone, but moral images and examples, as directing threads, to guide every man through the confused labyrinth of his own desires and life.

—Greville, *A Dedication to Sir Philip Sidney*

There is no art delivered to mankind that hath not the works of nature for his principal object. . . . Only the poet, disdaining to be tied to any such subjection, lifted up with the vigour of his own invention, doth grow in effect another nature, in making things either better than nature bringeth forth, or quite anew, forms such as never were in nature. . . : so as he goeth hand in hand with nature, not enclosed within the narrow warrant of her gifts, but freely ranging only within the zodiac of his own wit.

—Sidney, *A Defence of Poetry*

Contents

Preface

Fulke Greville's "labyrinth of desire" makes an engaging definition of culture. Culture is a labyrinth created by desire, desire to embrace and to avoid, desire unconscious and communal as well as intentional and individual. Writing my preface last, I am struck by the seeming contrast between Greville's image of the reader caught in the "confused" labyrinth and Sidney's of the poet "disdaining to be tied to any . . . subjection, lifted up with the vigour of his own invention." But Greville's assumption of a sharp distinction between entangled reader and unconstrained poet-guide is false—false to Sidney's work as well as to general experience.

Like Daedalus, Greville's "every man" finds himself caught in a maze of his own making but not under his full control. Sidney's poet appears differently Daedaluslike, "freely ranging within the zodiac of his own wit." The tension implicit in these two images—the human figure caught in the prisonhouse of culture, the poet soaring free on the wings of his invention—has dominated the interpretation of Sir Philip Sidney's fiction for some time now. Yet this opposition has also obscured the shape of his fiction, misrepresenting its complexity, its causes, its effects.

Greville's labyrinth and Sidney's zodiac are in fact inseparable: both poet and reader work within the maze; both can find there some exercise of critical and imaginative freedom. My thesis is that Sidney's work imitates his experience in a culture—Protestant, humanist, Tudor—that was at once constraining and liberating. Sidney's poetic invention was incited by his discovery that the codes by which his culture sought to evade the contingencies of power and desire reach an end, breaking off before the longed-for goal of conquest or escape appears. Sidney's habit as a poet was to counterfeit an image of these codes of humanist virtue and erotic control, extending their paths until their limits become clear. This feigning or counterfeiting became his principal means of criticizing the cherished constructs of his culture, including those he plainly loved and himself employed.

Sidney's feigning exposes the limits of self-sufficient, Ciceronian virtue and of self-denying but poetically empowering eros. The very multiplicity of breakdowns in plot and crises of character in his fiction implies a more complete and complex vision of human action and human art than these codes allow. Yet from what vantage point does Sidney see his own act of invention? Does he dismantle what Astrophil calls others' "inventions fine" (*AS* 1.6) to claim for his own an ideal stability and an immunity from the contingent world? The defender of poetry who laughed at the platonic stargazer fallen into a ditch would find such a claim amusing. The Protestant who recalls "our infected will" (*DP* 79) would find it sinful.

I suggest that Sidney saw within the labyrinth of culture an early Protestant and late humanist vision of invention as provoked and indeed compelled by the unfinished status of the world and of the self. As such, invention becomes a human labor undertaken in imitation of the ongoing creation of nature and God. This invention is the work of human wit "lifted up" in consciousness and mimetic power, but not lifted out of the cultural labyrinth of desire that Greville thinks Sidney's readers—with the poet's superior aid—can escape. To the contrary: invention is inspired by the labyrinth, extending and so transforming it. Instigated by the entanglements of experience, the poet makes a text whose chief value as a fictional labyrinth, says Sidney, is to provoke the invention of the reader.

As Ovid's story of Icarus makes so clear, Daedalus's art cannot lift him out of the maze of longing, chance, and death. The cautions Sidney offers about "our degenerate souls"—as well as his desire for this "too much loved earth"—show that he knew and felt this constraint (*DP* 82, 78). His particular genius was to see that the wit of poet and reader could make the frustrations of the maze a basis for invention, for counterfeiting a fictional image that reconfigures the culture that prompted it. Greville notwithstanding, Sidney found no humanly fashioned escape from the labyrinth of desire, but he discovered in it an occasion for the fullest exercise of human gifts. The study that follows explores that exercise—at once conditioned by Tudor culture and critical of it—in Sidney's major poetic texts, in his *Defence of Poetry*, and in his correspondence and explicitly political writing, placing the revised *Arcadia* at the center of interest.

Chapter 1 works out this argument in relation to Sidney's political promise, his Aristotelian and affective poetics, and his convictions as a Protestant humanist. Most modern readings of Sidney's poetry assume that he sought to construct a static ideal that shields the self from contingency and assures the stability of poetic representation. These readings tend to divide sharply between those who see Sidney's poetry rising above cultural conflict on an ideal trajectory and those who see it overwhelmed by cultural contradictions that idealism cannot resolve. But these mirror-image views belie the paradigm shift that Sidney's fiction effects. The heroic life Sidney represents (most completely in his *New Arcadia*) is not static but dynamic, an action both critical and mimetic. Sidney's poetic practice—apparent in early writing such as *The Lady of May* and *The Letter to Elizabeth* as well as his private letters—links him in purpose and method with religious and intellectual reformers like Luther, Calvin, and Montaigne: he reveals the limits in paradigms of good conduct even as he insists on the validity of inventing new ones in response to experience.

Chapter 2 explores the fashion in which the *New Arcadia* displays the humanist invention or code of justice through the education, friendship, and triumphant travels of Pyrocles and Musidorus, and then exposes the limits of its claims for heroic self-sufficiency in the erotic ruin of Amphialus. In Amphialus, the Arcadian mold of form and glass of fashion, every effort at "just" domination of others and of self leads to domination by those very forces Tudor justice was designed to control.

Chapter 3 turns to Sidney's testing of another "invention fine," set in opposition to the first: the erotic abandonment of self to the image and interest of another. Sidney found this invention variously represented in the courtly, Petrarchan, and romance literature of love, though as *Astrophil and Stella* and the revised *Arcadia* reveal, he decidedly rejected the intellectualized eros of the neoplatonists. Once again, the *New Arcadia* reveals the beauty and power of a central cultural invention, this time by contrasting its virtues with the self-destructive effects of illicit desire. But the secondary figures who form this heroic image appear helpless in their radical dependence on the beloved for self-definition, and their very status as icons of self-negating love keeps them at a distance from the main characters and from us. Rarely do they act effectively within the complexities of the main narrative.

Chapter 4 argues that in those complexities the Pyrocles and Musidorus of the *New Arcadia* are driven to the very sort of invention that defines the work of the poet. But in this case the text is themselves, in what Sidney would call "the ethic and politic [private and public] consideration" (*DP* 83). In action, and in stories and poems of their own, they attempt to "counterfeit" a new self in light of the radical breakdown experience has made in their old self-knowledge. When their counterfeiting seeks to regain their lost status as self-assured "lords of truth" (*NA* 164), when it tries to shield them from the "endless overthrow" (*NA* 136) that is the condition not only of lovers but of all within the labyrinth of earthly experience, it becomes self-deceptive—a "counterfeiting" in the modern sense of a cheat. But when their counterfeiting begins with an acceptance of their transformed lot and aims to make an "opposing imitation" of the old self in the interest of others and of their own self-knowledge, it approaches the heroic work of poetry. Sidney fashions their actions in the context of the continual reformation stressed both in the Protestantism to which he was heir and a skeptical humanism akin to that of Montaigne.

Chapter 5 defines the experience of the reader in the *New Arcadia* as one analogous to the disorientation and invention found in the two princes. Sidney's last major work of fiction is presented as the culmination of a poetry that from the start displays the same conflicts with traditional heroism, the same self-conscious attention to the fictionality of his enterprise, and the same refusal to oversimplify disturbing, unpredictable human experience. The *Old Arcadia* is read as undercutting comically the invention of justice tested "heroically" in the *New*, *Astrophil and Stella* as exploring tragically the invention of eros likewise tested in the revised *Arcadia*.

But the movement from *Old Arcadia* through the sonnet sequence to the *New* reveals more than a preoccupation with these themes. It also reveals a steady gain in Sidney's ability to make his fiction represent the experience of counterfeiting a life within the force of contingency—matter making form rather than form dictating matter. This same formal maturity enables Sidney to move the reader into the very heroic activity that the *Defence* assigns to the poet. Sidney's fiction then mediates a dialogue between text and reader that provokes questions about the Renaissance representation of gender, class, and the body as it also tests our present assumptions about the vigor of invention.

In all, I find Sidney both constrained and enabled by the Elizabethan and Continental discourse of power, love, and religious devotion. It was a discourse he made as well as one to which he was subject. Like Luther and like Montaigne, in its very volatility, in its labyrinthine paths, he finds the design of heroic life.

For much of what I have learned in writing this book, and for rescue from more than one cave of error, I owe to many a happy debt. For scholarly guidance, I am thankful first to James Devereux, S. J., my mentor at Chapel Hill, patient and demanding teacher, abiding friend. For a second education in Sidney's poetics and for keen criticism coupled with constant encouragement, I am grateful to S. K. Heninger, Jr.

Alan Hager, Margaret Hannay, Gerald Rubio, Susanne Woods, Anne Prescott, Wendy Olmsted, Jerry Mills, Anne Hall, Teresa Talouse,

Robert Ducharme, and Jeff Shulman have all read my work in one incarnation or another and made it better for their knowledge and generous suggestions. Teachers Jon Lawry, Frederick Horn, Larry Sells, George Bleasby, and Thomas Stumpf made a life built around the written word and its engagement with the world irresistible. My mother and father have encouraged me in that life with a liberality of love that makes me the most fortunate of sons.

For a fellowship that enabled me to review and revise my understanding of Sidney, I owe thanks to the Newberry Library and its splendid staff. Grants from Mount Saint Mary's College allowed me to devote more summers than I care to tally to writing this book. The Lutheran Theological Seminary at Gettysburg has provided space in which I could work and counsel about the Reformation love of grace. Before the manuscript went to Delaware Press, Judy Ott, office manager without equal, set it in clear and clean form with her usual extraordinary skill.

To Anne Craft, beloved reader and editor unsparing of her time and my ego, I owe the joy of conversation about writers and the worlds they make, and the joy of a mutual life giving birth to little worlds, ages ten and seven, made more cunningly than writers ever can.

Use of material from the following works is made by permission of Oxford University Press: Sir Philip Sidney, *The Countess of Pembroke's Arcadia (The New Arcadia)*, edited by Victor Skretkowicz (1987); Sir Philip Sidney, *The Countess of Pembroke's Arcadia (The Old Arcadia)*, edited by Jean Robertson (1973); Sir Philip Sidney, *Miscellaneous Prose of Sir Philip Sidney*, edited by Katherine Duncan-Jones and Jan van Dorsten (1973); Sir Philip Sidney, *The Poems of Sir Philip Sidney*, edited by William A. Ringler, Jr. (1962); and Michael Montaigne, *The Essayes of Michael Lord of Montaigne*, translated by John Florio (1924).

Brief section in Chapters 2 and 4 of *Labyrinth of Desire* are reprinted with changes by permission from *Studies in English Literature* 1 (Winter 1985): 45–67; other short segments are revisions of work that first appeared in *Studies in Philology* and in *Renaissance Papers*.

Labyrinth of Desire

1
Right Poetry

The truest poetry is the most feigning.
—Shakespeare, *As You Like It*

The present fervor for reading and writing about Sidney suggests that we have found a bond between his struggles and our own. Antedating the tide of middle-class realism in fiction, his lyric and narrative works display a self-conscious delight in invention and a sense of its volatility that anticipate our own obsession with the power and the limits of human making. Responding to the inadequacy of Elizabethan categories intended to manage political and erotic experience, his effort to redefine heroic action may also appeal to those who now ponder the limits of the Enlightenment self-interest that has governed our own national and private life. The poetic career spent in testing and transforming Tudor humanist assumptions about poetry and the virtuous life culminates in Sidney's revised *Arcadia*, the central though not exclusive interest of this book. It is there that the question of Sidney's place in Renaissance and Reformation culture becomes most challenging, and it is there that the vitality and achievement of his poetry become most clear.

Would-be reformers risk being judged by the same norms they have rejected as insufficient measures of experience. Martin Luther declares that souls are justified before God by the gift of faith, but cannot shake the question, Why do good works?[1] Sidney's poetic work has met with a comparable problem. Many readers of his fiction look there for a fixed ideal that assures the validity of fictional representation and offers an unchanging image of virtuous action. Seeing none, they see in the *New Arcadia's* multiplying plots and unfinished status a reprise of Sidney's political frustrations or the tragic consequence of an effort to maintain both imaginative liberty and traditional form. Yet it is the

3

task of Sidney's literary theory and practice to say that within the "zodiac of his own wit" (*DP* 78), the poet discovers no such certainty. What the poet does manifest is the vigor of invention, invention both limited and liberated by the maze of convention and experience that defined Sidney's life as courtier and poet.

Within the labyrinth of his culture Sidney found, or was compelled to find, a way in which the discovery of limitation could become the source of invention. The very inadequacy of those codes of conduct that had fueled what Astrophil calls "great expectation" (*AS* 21.5) provoked in Sidney an act of transformation. What his poetry imitates then are not the Platonic, Ciceronian, and Petrarchan paradigms of love and justice, but the shifting patterns of experience by which the partiality of these paradigms is revealed. Sidney's *New Arcadia* feigns these established paradigms or paths, pushing them to their moral and psychological endpoint, at which point new paths are drawn that more fully approach the completeness and mystery of experience.[2]

Sidney's mimetic writing, starting with *The Lady of May* and ending with the revised *Arcadia*, becomes increasingly intricate, less and less Euclidean in its efforts to depict an image of the heroic life. His narratives and lyrics continually demonstrate that a classical geometry of virtue, love, and power—in which heroic action can be drawn after a known, ideal template of human conduct—cannot accommodate the complexity of real experience. The very maze of desire and frustration so often defined by critics as a trap Sidney either escaped or languished in becomes for him a model for the shape of human invention. As I will argue below, the notion of incomplete or labyrinthine nature as a provocation for invention was not limited to Sidney. It is central to the sixteenth-century Protestant vision of divine and human invention and to Montaigne's skeptical vision of self-representation.

Sidney's most accomplished fiction does not endorse an old heroic ideal or offer a new one. *Ideal* is exactly the wrong term. By the time he began revising the *Old Arcadia*, if not before, Sidney had rejected the neoplatonic model of the psyche—with its insistent division of impure experience from intellectual vision—that would permit such a notion. The *New Arcadia* offers not an ideal but a human activity. Sidney's final fiction develops consistently from his argument in *A Defence of Poetry* that the poet's work is an action analogous to the shaping work of nature and from his representation in the first *Arcadia* and in *Astrophil and Stella* of the inadequacy of humanist and erotic designs.

The *New Arcadia* enacts its own complex vision: the ongoing invention of the heroic life in light of events that always reveal the insufficiency of cherished models of meaning—even as they suggest the image of a yet more comprehensive design. Sidney's story both represents and realizes the action it commends as heroic. Uniting *gnosis* with *praxis*, the revised *Arcadia* engages writer and reader in the poetic "work" forced upon its princes by the mysterious motions of love and politics: representing, counterfeiting, figuring forth the new life within the shifting patterns of experience.

In 1945 Theodore Spencer declared that "it is Sidney—not Spenser— who is the most central of English poets in the generation that was soon to know Shakespeare."[3] Many Sidney scholars agree, but their readings of his fiction have diverged radically, creating a gulf between estimates of Sidney's poetic response to the promises and problems of Tudor humanist culture. Rather than a debate, there now appears to be an unbridgeable distance between those who find Sidney able (sustained by this culture or unconstrained by it) to create in his poetry a stable image of the heroic life, and those who find Sidney overwhelmed by the political, moral constraints of Tudor culture or his own restless imagination.[4]

For C. S. Lewis and E. M. W. Tillyard, Sidney remains what he was in 1578 for Sidney's father: "a rare ornament of his age."[5] Tillyard finds Sidney "the most centrally Elizabethan" poet, and Lewis believes the *Arcadia* "gathers up what a whole generation wanted to say."[6] But this praise is also reductive judgment: unlike Spenser's, Sidney's poetry is a bright pool reflecting courtly ideals and fashions but never sounding any depth. The two Arcadian princes, says Lewis, "do not live in the mind"; the *Arcadia's* Elizabethan qualities appealed only "as long as that society lasted"; the charity and self-denial Sidney practiced as he died "are traits we might not have anticipated from the *Arcadia*."[7] Tillyard calls the *Arcadia* an epic but finds that it "cannot strike the notes of tragedy or prophecy."[8] This Sidney is a noble relic, like the Victorian gentleman he was once imagined to be.[9]

Fulke Greville's declaration that Sidney's purpose in *Arcadia* was moral guidance has itself guided a series of modern admirers.[10] Beginning with Edwin Greenlaw and developing further in the work of Kenneth Myrick, Jon Lawry, and A. C. Hamilton, there forms a reading of Sidney's fiction that follows Greville in assigning it great imaginative and affective power. Sidney the humanist educator-poet resolves in art if not in life the conflicts between civic virtue and private desire. In the revised *Arcadia*, love becomes the occasion for noble action, teaching and moving the reader to embrace it. Calling Greville's reading "authoritative," Hamilton appropriates the language of the *Defence* to assert that "the work brings the reader such knowledge of himself that he becomes capable of virtuous action."[11] Together with Myron Turner, Hamilton and Lawry believe that the *New Arcadia* transforms the heroic life. Possessive love and violent rebellion display the limits of aggressive masculine chivalry and glorify by contrast the patient endurance exemplified by Pamela and learned by the princes, who become "Miltonic 'new' heroes."[12] The reader becomes witness and student of a pageant in which "Love . . . is an harmonious adjunct to heroism. Like epic and pastoral when combined in a heroic poem, the brave and the fair can now envision and inhabit one world."[13]

These critics have recovered and championed a Sidney of complex moral, political, and erotic imagination. Yet several significant readers now find not a triumphant but a tragic pattern in Sidney's life and work. Trapped in the monolith of Elizabethan power and paralyzed by the ambiguity of his own rebellious desires, this Sidney produces poetry doomed to recapitulate his political-psychological frustrations. The unfinished *Arcadia* becomes a metaphor of those unresolved tensions, the broken book an apt image of his broken life. Richard Helgerson, finding Sidney "too good and serious a son to defend successfully values hostile to what he had been taught," says that Sidney's "*New Arcadia* abandons in midsentence its uncompleted attempt to erect a fictional image of heroic love."[14] Defeated politically, "Sidney tested poetry—and all that was associated with it—love, beauty, contemplation, and desire—against the humanists' standard of rational well-doing. And poetry failed."[15] Richard McCoy describes "a frustrated subaltern" facing Lawrence Stone's crisis of the aristocracy, suffering "ideological uncertainty about the legitimacy of self-assertion . . . reinforced by feelings of guilt and ambivalence. The impact of these feelings on his literature is apparent in the recurrent pattern of contradiction and irresolution."[16] McCoy's *New Arcadia* spins further and further out of Sidney's moral and poetic control until it ends in "a suspension of the action—probably the most appropriate resolution."[17] Likewise John Carey's rhetorical and structural analysis finds in the miserable Arcadian prince Amphialus a "self negation" that "takes over the work itself."[18]

Reading the two *Arcadias* through the lens of "socio-political experience," Annabel Patterson represents a Sidney similarly ineffectual: writing pastoral "covert discourse" in the *Old Arcadia*, he risks being either ignored or misread; writing romance with more openly political dimensions in the *New*, he produces work in which neither "arcane representation" nor "direct counsel" can further his aims.[19] The politically and generically hamstrung poet of these readers is as culturally limited as the noble ornament of Lewis and Tillyard: the prisoner of his age. Equipped with neither the imaginative liberty Sidney claimed in the *Defence* nor the ironic humor he habitually displays, this failed poet could well cry with Musidorus, "all I do is but to beate a rock and get fome" (*NA* 141)—and not expect us to smile.

Ronald Levao allows Sidney much more imaginative and critical liberty. Far from disabled by "informing traditions," Sidney as poet and critic "deeply explores both the world by which he is defined and the agile efforts of fiction-making to take the measure of that world."[20] Yet freed from constraints, this Sidney dances over a void. His fiction-making can only reflect itself, endlessly confirming its own powers but failing to achieve "mastery in an increasingly volatile world."[21] This failure plays itself out in the unfinished *New Arcadia*, where proliferating plots and moral complexities leave Sidney unable to control his fiction.[22] Levao's Sidney is arresting because he is not a relic, neither perfected nor confounded Tudor-humanist son. But the liberating autonomy Levao discovers in Sidney leads the poet into a trap as deep as the cultural paralysis envisioned by others—or rather into a void, where poetry, where all human culture, has no legitimate ground on which to stand. Levao has taken the question of how Sidney can reconcile his fictive powers with the yearning for an assured heroic control of life and art as far as it will go and given the right answer: Sidney can't.

But what if the question has not been rightly stated? In its current form it assumes an understanding of heroic action (and often of poetry) that belies Sidney's own efforts and those of other contemporary reformers of intellectual, artistic, and religious culture. The error lies in attributing to Sidney the very vision of heroism that his work sets out to transform. If heroism is defined in traditional humanist terms as a magnificent self-sufficiency stoically impervious to the turns of experience, it will never coincide with the inventive, revolutionary imagination in Sidney stressed by Levao. Self-assured magnanimity—modeled for us in institutes like Elyot's *Boke of the Gouernour*—can be found in Spenser's Guyon, who travels alone but "ever more himselfe with comfort feedes / Of his own vertues and praise-worthie deedes."[23] But neither the poet Sidney nor his Arcadian princes operate in Guyon's Faerie wood, where self-sufficient virtue masters passions and grace restores the exhausted but unsullied knight. In Sidney's fiction, Providence is real but mysterious, and virtue lies in inventive response to the limits of Guyon's temperate ideal.

Lewis and Tillyard find a brilliant but dated endorsement of this aristocratic ideal in Sidney; Helgerson, McCoy, and others find him deeply dissatisfied with it but temperamentally or politically unable to give it up; Levao finds Sidney asserting the liberty of human invention from it but haunted by a loss of mastery. Hamilton, Lawry, and Turner argue that Sidney modifies this old heroism with another, "Miltonic" ideal of passive, "feminine" endurance. In all these cases the achieved or desired image of the heroic life is static. But the heroic life that Sidney seeks to define and display in his poetry is dynamic—an action, like invention itself. If this is so, then Sidney's final work of fiction displays a radical *unity* of moral intent and passionate imagination.

Proceeding from a Protestant and skeptical humanist construct of human history as an act of continuous creation, Sidney found a model for heroic poetry and heroic work. Living within a far from monolithic political, religious, and aesthetic culture, Sidney became a brilliant yet fully engaged critic of that culture. In testing and extending cultural assumptions his definitive act of re-formation was the act of feigning. In ways analogous to the work of Luther and Montaigne, Sidney developed a vision of invention as an act both provoked and validated by the unfinished status of the world and of the self. Sidney's *New Arcadia* is his fullest instance and image of such critical invention, and as such a valid human work prompted by the matrix of Sidney's experience.[24]

The rest of this chapter examines the political endeavor, religious conviction, and poetics from which Sidney's fiction developed. Moving from *The Lady of May* and *Letter to Elizabeth* through the *Defence of Poetry*, with help from Sidney's correspondence, it affirms the work of invention as legitimate, though never delivered from moral doubt or political risk.

I

The disciplined path to virtue and power set for Philip Sidney by his education at Shrewsbury School, by the admonitions of his father, and by the tutelage of the Hugenot diplomat Hubert Languet shaped his political ambition and his poetics. But it did not deprive him of his critical faculties or impose ruinous limits on his imagination. Sidney did inherit the imposing brand of humanism that Professors McCoy and Helgerson emphasize, and it became—as they argue—a source of personal and political discomfiture. But the defining characteristic of Sidney's maturing humanism, a habit of mind linking him with reformist and skeptical writers on the continent, is the practice of continually reassessing and reforming the constructs of human invention. For Martin Luther the object of that habit is the church, for Michel de Montaigne the self, for Sidney the heroic life, including the poetry that represents it.

Montaigne is famous for his declaration of earthly instability: "I describe not th' essence but the passage; not a passage from age to age ... but from day to day, from minute to minute." Yet his meditation concludes with a qualification: "I may perhaps gaine-say my selfe, but truth ... I never gaine-say."[25] He ends his reflections on "The Inconstancie of our Actions" with this caution:

It is no part of a well-grounded judgement simply to judge ourselves by our exteriour actions: A man must thorowly sound himselfe, and dive into his heart, and there see by what wards or springs the motions stirre. But forsomuch as it is a hazardous and high enterprise, I would not have so many to meddle with it as doe.[26]

For Montaigne the experience of inconstancy does not negate the possibility of truth; what it does is to make necessary a heroic—hazardous and high—human activity of inquiry and reformation. A like conviction characterizes Sidney's public life and poetic theory, as analysis of his response to his humanist fathers and of his *Defence* reveals.

Following his return from the diplomatic mission of 1577, Philip Sidney complained to family and friends that his knowledge and zeal were being squandered by Elizabeth's neglect.[27] His sponsors would have agreed with Greville that Sidney was never "possessed of any fit stage for eminence to act upon."[28] Yet neither Sidney's efforts nor his estimate of their worth was crushed by this disappointment. If we look at the two most formative political relationships Sidney experienced, those with his father and with Languet, we will find confirmed Alan Hager's thesis that Sidney's "most characteristic mode of thought . . . seems to be a criticism of weaknesses in our conventional understandings or constructions of experience."[29]

Sidney habitually employs the poetic faculty of feigning to make his criticisms and to formulate alternatives. In the *Defence* Sidney chooses to illustrate the moving power of poetry with two "proofs": Menenius Agrippa's persuading the Roman people to unite with the senate through the tale of a body's parts that starved when they rejected the belly, and the prophet Nathan's convicting King David of adultery and murder through the story of the man whose lamb was stolen from him and slaughtered (*DP* 93-94). Sidney responds with similar tactics to the benevolent tyranny of parental expectation.

In his own career Sir Henry Sidney played the Tudor good soldier, but Philip showed himself disinclined to repeat the performance.[30] Highly principled like his son but more dutiful, Sir Henry served his sovereign as Lord President of Wales and as Lord Deputy in Ireland, winning respect from many contemporaries but scant reward from Elizabeth.[31] Yet the father endeavored to mold his son after his own fashion, advising the twelve-year-old Philip to "Be humble and obedient to your masters, for, unless you frame yourself to obey others—yea, and feel in yourself what obedience is, you shall never be able to teach others how to obey you."[32] It should not surprise us then to find Sir Henry twelve years later the first mythologizer of his son: Philip's brother Robert is directed to "Imitate his virtues, exercises, studies and actions; he is a rare ornament of his age, the very formula that all well-disposed young Gentlemen of our Court do form also their manners and life by."[33] No doubt such expectations could burden any son, but Sidney was not undone did by them.

In 1578 and 1579, as Sidney discovered that Elizabeth was in no hurry to advance him, he wrote *The Lady of May* and his letter opposing the marriage to Alençon.[34] Both separate him from the model of fixed, uncritical service evident in his father, and both do it—like Nathan in the *Defence*—through a poet's feigning. If Sir Henry had designs for his son, Philip's uncle the Earl of Leicester was to be the agent who realized them. A masque prepared for the entertainment of Elizabeth at Leicester's Wanstead estate, *The Lady of May* represents a double feigning: it is a fiction, patently artificial as such devices were, and it is also a criticism of Elizabeth disguised as compliment.

Both the shepherd (Espilus) who defends the pastoral life and the forester (Therion) who champions the hunters' lot allude to the frustration of virtuous action at court, as A. C. Hamilton has noted.[35] Conventional flattery and thinly veiled complaint are usually intermingled, as when old Dorcas asks,

> How many courtiers, think you, I have heard under our field in bushes make their woeful complaints, some of the greatness of their mistress' estate, which dazzled their eyes and yet burned their hearts; some of the extremity of her beauty mixed with extreme cruelty; some of her too much wit, which made all their loving labours folly? (*LM* 28)

In Rixus the barbs continue, too sharp to be missed, even as Elizabeth is distracted with every sort of praise: the rustics recognize majesty in her countenance; they make her arbiter in the Lady of May's dilemma; the learned ignorance of their would-be scholar Rombus flatters her superior wit and judgment;[36] and her anti-Catholic host worships her as if she were the Virgin Mary. The performance rushes her along on such a tide of flattery that she has no leisure to take offense.

The structure of the masque enforces another criticism, more covert but also more complete than the conventional complaints of neglect. Stephen Orgel writes that by associating the pastoral suitor Espilus with a narrow vision of love as possession—in contrast to the hunter Therion's assertion of liberty in love—Sidney criticizes the very categories of pastoral debate he has employed: Therion is not only a more active man, he is a better thinker too. There is "for Sidney . . . no dichotomy between contemplation and action: the one necessarily leads to the other."[37] If this is so, then Elizabeth is forced into making an inevitably compromising choice, since as the Lady of May implies,

in choosing between her shepherd and forester suitors, she also chooses between their ways of life: "judge whether of these two be more worthy of me, or whether I be worthy of them; and this I will say, that in
judging me, you judge more than me in it" (*LM* 30).[38]

Had Elizabeth chosen Therion, Sidney would have led her to concede
the falsehood and hypocrisy that characterized his life under her command. But contrary to Orgel, I believe her favoring the discredited
shepherd was not a fiasco for Sidney.[39] It was instead an outcome as
acceptable to him as the opposite decision, perhaps more so. Alan
Hager thinks that the queen may have purposefully chosen the well-
provided Espilus over Therion "to remind Sidney of the importance of
economic and hierarchical relationships"—to put him in his social
place.[40] Robert Stillman writes that Elizabeth's choice "destroyed the
work's unity," but he ingeniously suggests that by declining to give the
queen's "words" and "reasons" for her favoring of Espilus (*LM* 30), Sidney hints at an unjust judgment.[41]

I suggest that the masque compels the Queen to make a reductive
choice—like the choice between subservient idleness and disobedi-
ence that she has imposed on Sidney. A song in which Espilus must
sing of a victorious forest god and Therion of a defeated Pan would
only heighten the discordant judgment she has made. Sidney's point
is that of Therion's fellow forester, Rixus: the life of action "raise[s]
up the mind" (*LM* 29). To divorce mind and action, as the Queen has
done with Sidney and with others, is to lose both; it is a dehumaniz-
ing act of possessive fear—the very thing Espilus seems ready to do
with his bride. It is no accident that the most forthright, admirable figure in the masque is the Lady of May herself—she who will by the
Queen's choice be subjected to the same kind of dominance imposed
upon Philip Sidney.

Sidney obliges his uncle with the witty, elaborate compliment of
Elizabeth that Leicester must have hoped for in *The Lady of May*, but
feigning enables him to redefine the heroic life in a way implicitly critical of Elizabeth's policy. He adopted a parallel tactic in protesting the
prospective marriage with Alençon. The argument that Sidney served
as Leicester's dupe in offering advice the earl was too shrewd to give
himself does not accord with the case, nor does the assumption that
Elizabethan wrath sent Sidney running to Wilton with his political tail
between his legs.[42] That Sidney did write at the request of Leicester's
anti-Alençon faction there is no doubt,[43] but caught between his sovereign and an anxious Leicester (imprisoned briefly when Monsieur's
negotiator told Elizabeth of his secret marriage to Essex' widow), Sidney turned once more to feigning. Sidney wrote the *Letter* with no
intention of persuading the Queen: under the cover of a loyal courtier's

advice he published to English and European friends his support of the united Protestant cause Elizabeth had declined to join.

After St. Bartholomew's Day in 1577, when he watched the mass murder of Hugenots from the vantage of Francis Walsingham's Paris quarters, Sidney's devotion to a Protestant alliance against Catholic France and Spain remained fervent. But the notion that he was a "hot-headed" idealist whose zeal denied him significant employment is not true.[44] It is a hazard of Sidney interpretation to assume that he was directly responsible for his own political woes, but if endorsement of political Protestantism were reason for Elizabeth to deny someone a place, the power of Leicester and Walsingham is inexplicable. Surely Elizabeth ignored Sidney's ambition because—with all his wealth and power merely in expectation—she could afford to, and because the memory of his treasonous grandfather and the anger she felt at Leicester's marriage provided no incentive to trust another aspirant from the Dudley family.[45]

The *Letter* itself confutes the widely accepted view of Sidney as naive architect of his own ruin. Written in the deferential but direct manner of the Lady of May's speeches, it begins by noting that Sidney has "already delivered" to Elizabeth his opinion of the match (*LE* 46); what remains—he says—is to confirm his objections to it and refute claims of its value. The *confirmatio* avoids the overheated attacks on Alençon's person that marked other written protests,[46] evoking instead the acts of treachery and rebellion by Catholics abroad and at home: the massacre in Paris, the killings at La Charite and Issoire (in which Alençon had a part), the 1569 insurrection in the north of England. Any alliance with Catholic France would risk England's current stability and her role as haven for "the free exercise of the eternal truth" (*LE* 47). The *refutatio* suggests that Elizabeth would do better to stand alone than with Monsieur, who seems as willing to lie down with the Spaniards as with the English, and that she will win love (instead of contempt) if she continues her excellent care and trust of her loyal people: so will she be "the most excellent fruit of all your progenitors, and the perfect mirror to your posterity" (*LE* 57).

"Posterity" implies wittily that the Queen will eventually bear children, but in fact Sidney assumed the reverse. In 1575 Sidney told his friend Count Hanau that the Queen was "advanced in years," and though until then "vigorous," a "frail . . . thread" and "a Meleager's brand."[47] Sidney could not of course know with certainty whether or not the Queen would wed Monsieur, but he knew her well enough to see that if the great majority of the Privy Council could not force her to cease negotiation,[48] his voice would not tip the balance. In other words, Sidney had no real fear that a union with Alençon—or anyone else—would yield a dangerous heir to the throne, and he had no cause to believe that his arguments about the match would change Elizabeth's mind.

Sidney tells the Queen that he hopes the *Letter* "shall only come to your merciful eyes" (*LE* 46), but this is only polite feigning. Katherine Duncan-Jones tells us that many manuscripts of the *Letter* circulated and that it continued to interest readers long after Sidney's death. We cannot be sure of Sidney's motives, but it seems apparent that he used the *Letter* not only "as propaganda for the Leicester-Walsingham party,"[49] but also as a way to make known to foreign and domestic friends his understanding of foreign policy and his loyalty to the Protestant cause—even though he had for two years been without a place of power. In this the *Letter* succeeded: Languet himself, though he had cautioned Sidney about being too bold in counsel, expressed pleasure that it "has come to the knowledge of so many persons."[50]

By 1579 Philip Sidney was long accustomed to sponsors who sought to use him to advance their policies—not Sir Henry and Leicester alone, but also Herbert Languet, Sidney's father in international Protestant diplomacy. A Hugenot scholar and statesman who served the Elector of Saxony, Languet met Sidney in Paris in 1572 and saw in him a youth of sufficient rank and gifts to lead Languet's cherished project of a Protestant League.[51] Languet made himself manager of Sidney's introduction to European intellectuals and princes during the three-year tour, and his moral epistles followed Philip from city to city: "press on towards your destiny and, be it happy or sad, temper it with virtue"; "think of your position in life"; and—in warning him to escape iniquitous Rome— "God has bestowed mental powers on you which I do not believe have fallen to anyone else I know, and he has done so not for you to abuse them in exploring vanities at great risk."[52] After Sidney returned to England, Languet's anxiety for Sidney's development became increasingly confused with the elder's need for his protege's friendship. A break in Sidney's letters to Languet prompted rebuke:

> This neglect arouses the fear that your exceptionally brilliant mind will be encrusted in rust if you fail to exercise it. Never allow yourself to think that God gave you so fine a mind merely for you to let it decay from misuse. Instead, know that He demands more from you than from others to whom He has been less bountiful.[53]

Sidney admired Languet, acknowledged his political debt to his mentor, and praised him in the *Old Arcadia's* fable on government as "the best shepherd swift Ister ever knew" (*OA* 255).[54] But he did not accept uncritically Languet's plan for his career. Sidney established his independence by limiting his own letters and—typically—by feigning. In

March, 1578, Sidney replies to Languet's habitual accusations of neglect in a manner that also marks his fiction:

> The use of the pen, as you may perceive, has plainly fallen from me; and my mind itself, if it ever was active in any thing, is now beginning, by reason of my indolent ease, imperceptibly to lose its strength, and to relax without any reluctance. For to what purpose should our thoughts be directed to various kinds of knowledge, unless room be afforded for putting it into practice, so that public advantage may be the result, which in a corrupt age we cannot hope for? . . . But the mind itself, you will say, that particle of the divine mind, is cultivated in this manner. This indeed, if we allow it to be the case, is a very great advantage: but let us see whether we are not giving a beautiful but false appearance to our splendid errors. For while the mind is thus . . . drawn out of itself, it cannot turn its powers inward for thorough self-examination; to which employment no labour that men can undertake, is any way to be compared. Do you not see that I am cleverly playing the stoic? yea and I shall be a cynic too, unless you reclaim me. Wherefore, if you please, prepare yourself to attack me. I have now pointed out the field of battle, and I openly declare war against you.[55]

Languet writes back in aggrieved self-importance: "I do not so much wonder that you are remiss in writing, as that you venture to charge me with remissness; *me*, who for one letter of yours sometimes pay you five or six of my own. Is it not an insult, or at least a mockery of me, that . . . [you] complain that it is too much leisure that makes you neglectful?"[56]

Sidney *tells* his advisor that he is feigning (cleverly playing the stoic), and invites Languet to join him in reply. Sidney's ploy fails to alter the relentless highmindedness of his scolding master, but it does reveal the way Sidney's mind worked in the years when he had conceived but not yet completed the *Old Arcadia*.[57] Neil Rudenstine says that writing this work was for Sidney "an imaginative means of illuminating, exploring, and distancing problems which engrossed him."[58] The letter operates in like fashion. Under cover of "playing," Sidney indicates that experience—his experience—does not conform to the pattern Languet and others have defined for him and asks a genuine question: What should he do with his mind if he finds the established outlet for it (political service) closed to him? He hints at an answer—not mere intellectual cultivation, but Montaigne's way of "thorough self-examination." This is the way of self-knowledge through the making and the reading of feigned poesy that Sidney would later endorse explicitly in his *Defence*.

Languet's plan for Sidney failed, and as biographers since Greville have written, Sidney never gained a place at court worthy of his talents. His complaints that "the vnnoble institution of our tyme, doth keep vs from fitter imployments"[59] reveal that he saw the power his political fathers had promised eluding him. But what remains consistent is Sidney's assurance of the validity of human action within the greater action of God. To his father-in-law, Francis Walsingham, he writes in 1586 about Elizabeth's failure to provide essential money and supplies to the soldiers under Leicester's command in the Netherlands:

> If her Majesty wear the fowntain [of this effort] I woold fear considring what I daily fynd that we shold wax dry, but she is but a means whom God useth and I know not whether I am deceaved but I am faithfully persuaded that if she shold withdraw her self other springes woold ryse to help this action. For me thinkes I see the great work indeed in hand, against the abusers of the world, wherein it is no greater fault to have confidence in mans power, then it is to[o] hastily to despair of Gods work.[60]

Sidney suffered the failure of his great expectations, but he maintained the legitimacy of human striving and linked it with his faith in the active Providence of God. That conviction also marks his defense of poetry.

II

Sidney's most significant re-formation of the traditional active life projected for him by Sir Henry and Languet was his embrace of poetry, his "unelected vocation" (*DP* 73).[61] Sidney believed poetry to be a heroic human action: heroic because it demands virtuous effort, human because it is the labor of our wit rather than external inspiration, an action because the poetic faculty lies not in the text produced but in the inventing that the text represents. In the *Defence* he distinguishes "right poets" from those inspired by divinity and from those who simply versify information. Right poets "merely make to imitate, and imitate both to delight and teach; and delight, to move men to take that goodness in hand, which without delight they would fly as from a stranger" (*DP* 80 – 81). What they imitate is the shaping activity of nature, and more distantly, the creative invention of God. Through such mimesis the poet can fashion a striking verbal picture that approaches the validity and power of a Platonic ideal but that is reached by pushing the limits of human understanding rather than by the visitation of divine rapture.[62]

Sidney takes care to define mimesis as something the poet *does*:

> *Poesie* therefore, is an Art of *Imitation*: for so Aristotle termeth it in the word μίμησις, that is to say, a representing, counterfeiting, or figuring forth to speak Metaphorically. A speaking *Picture*, with this end to teach and delight.[63]

He stresses that the word *poet* means "maker" (*DP* 77) and that poetry consists not in versifying but in making images able to generate reader response. This sets him apart from neoplatonic theorists like Cristoforo Landino, who believes that

> just as God arranges his creation . . . according to number, measure, and weight [terms from the *Timaeus*] . . . , so the poet constructs his poem with number of metrical feet, with measure of short and long syllables, and with weight of sententious sayings and of passions.[64]

Sidney counters that "it is that feigning notable images of virtues, vices, or what else, with that delightful teaching, which must be the right describing note to know a poet by" (*DP* 81–82). At issue is not only whether poetry can be written in prose, but whether it is active or passive. To Landino, the harmonies found in verse come upon the poet in an ecstasy that carries him beyond human striving: "the divine frenzy . . . from which poesy . . . derives is more noble than the human excellence from which the other arts have their origin."[65] But Sidney explicitly rejects the claim of "a divine force, far above man's wit" as the source of poetry's superiority to the other arts (*DP* 109).

Unlike all other human actors, the poet is equal to nature, not subservient to her. Rather than finding the object of his effort in what nature has done—as with philosophers, rhetoricians, and historians—the poet does what she does:

> lifted up with the vigour of his own invention, [the poet] doth grow in effect another nature, in making things either better than nature bringeth forth, or, quite anew . . . : so as he goeth hand in hand with nature, not enclosed within the narrow warrant of her gifts, but freely ranging only within the zodiac of his own wit. (*DP* 78)

"Wit" means human reason of course, although it includes the cleverness associated with feigning. But Sidney quickly adds that the fruits of poetry are not less true than those of nature, even though the former are

> in imitation or fiction; for any understanding knoweth the skill of each artificer standeth in that *idea* or fore-conceit of the work, and not in the work itself. And that the poet hath that *idea* is manifest, by delivering them forth in such excellency as he had imagined them. (*DP* 79)

The combined "Aristotelian" stress on poetry as the work of human wit and "Platonic" reference to ideas as the *skill* of the poet can now be understood: the "fore-conceit" is the conceiving, the inventing—not an inspiration bestowed from beyond and clothed in language. It is the human act of inventing, in other words, that *makes poetry true*, even though the Cyruses and Aeneases it delivers are not to be found in nature. And that delivering itself is "not wholly imaginative . . . ; but so far substantially it worketh, not only to make a Cyrus, which had been but a particular excellency as nature might have done, but to bestow a Cyrus upon the world to make many Cyruses" (*DP* 79). Poetry is an inventing delivered in such a way as to occasion yet another inventing in its readers.

It is poetry's provocative power that makes it superior to the disciplines of philosophy and history. Poetry teaches more effectively than either because the poet "coupleth the general notion with the particular example" (*DP* 85), but Sidney makes *praxis* the foundation of his defense: "to be moved to do that which we know, or to be moved with desire to know, *hoc opus, hic labor est*" (*DP* 91). Poetry's *energeia* emanates from the delight it engenders; in feigning only to please, it moves to goodness by indirection:

> even those hard-hearted evil men who think virtue a school name . . . and therefore despise the austere admonitions of the philosopher . . . , yet will be content to be delighted—which is all the good-fellow poet seemeth to promise—and so steal to see the form of goodness (which seen they cannot but love) ere themselves be aware, as if they took a medicine of cherries. (*DP* 93)

This does not exclude a later discovery of "how and why the maker made" (*DP* 79), but it does make plain that for Sidney feigning is valid in part because its delightful images make knowledge "heart-ravishing" (*DP* 76). Poetry appeals first to that emotional territory of the soul that Plato found suspect, even as it eventually engages the full capacity of the reasoning mind Plato thought definitive of our humanity.[66]

If Sidney takes his stand on poetry's power to move, that power to generate well-doing radiates most actively from the "absolute heroical poem" (*DP* 81). After all other "parts" of poetry have been defended,

> There rests the Heroical—whose very name (I think) should daunt all backbiters: . . . who doth not only teach and move to a truth, but teacheth and moveth to the most high and excellent truth; who maketh magnanimity and justice shine through all misty fearfulness and foggy desires; who, if the saying of Plato and Tully be true, that who could see virtue would be wonderfully ravished with the love of her beauty—this man sets her out to make her more lovely in her holiday apparel, to the eye of any that will deign not disdain until they understand. But if anything be already said in the defence of sweet poetry, all concurreth to the maintaining the heroical, which is not only a kind, but the best and most accomplished kind of poetry. For as the image of each action stirreth and instructeth the mind, so the lofty image

of such worthies [as Xenophon's Cyrus and Virgil's Aeneas] most inflameth
the mind with desire to be worthy, and informs with counsel how to be worthy. (*DP* 97–98)

The passage recapitulates Sidney's defense of poetry as a whole, his
argument that the poet's images "ravish" us with knowledge so that we
cannot but act. But it also returns us to the dilemma of poetry's validity, for Sidney's praise of heroic poetry—the sort he endeavored to write
in revising the *Arcadia*—depends on his claim that what the poet feigns
is "the most high and excellent truth."

The Aristotelian understanding of imitation adapted by Sidney was
a response to Plato's charge that poetry can never be true.[67] Aristotle's
teacher banned poetry from his republic not only because it can corrupt
the young, but because it "estranges us from the truly real."[68] Imitating only the natural or manmade shadows of ideal form, it fails to work
substantially: hence the silliness for Socrates of Ion's claim to
grandeur—as a rhapsode he merely parrots what is already an echo as
thin as air. Aristotle counters that the poet imitates "men in action"—
or rather, what they would do "according to probability and necessity."[69] Through a process of observation and selection, the poet fashions a universal that is concrete but not bound by the accidents of
history. This is the source of Sidney's claim that through his human wit
the poet delivers a "golden world"—not a world innocent of the fall but
one in which the heights and depths of experience are focused so
sharply that they move us to love or loathing. The "universal" image
of men in action, fashioned in the poet's mind, therefore comes close to
the validity of Plato's ideas.

But there's the rub. How can what is feigned within the zodiac of
human wit be true? The matter is complicated further by Sidney's insistence on our "infected will," which "keepeth us from reaching" the perfection lost in Eden (*DP* 79). Sidney establishes poetry as an activity
begetting a corresponding activity in readers. But Sidney is not
Goethe's Faust, whose works are redeemed because he *immer strebend
sich bemuht*.[70] If the act of inventing that constitutes the poet's fore-conceit fails to participate in the design of God's providence—in transcendent truth—then poetry is vanity, a striving after shadows.

Yet Sidney was heir to a Protestant humanist tradition endowing
humankind with limited but effective powers analogous to those of God.
At the culmination of his declaration of the liberty and validity of the
poet's invention Sidney dares a parallel with the work of the Creator:

Neither let it be deemed too saucy a comparison to balance the highest
point of man's wit with the efficacy of nature; but rather give right honour

to the heavenly Maker of that maker, who having made man to His own likeness, set him beyond and over all the works of that second nature: which
in nothing he showeth so much as in poetry, when with the force of a divine
breath he bringeth things forth surpassing her doings—with no small arguments to the incredulous of that first accursed fall of Adam, since our erected wit maketh us know what perfection is, and yet our infected will keepeth us from reaching unto it.[71] (*DP* 79)

That man was made in the image of God is a claim as old as Genesis;
that the central feature of that image lies in human reason is as orthodox as Augustine.[72] But Renaissance Protestant conceptions of human
and divine action gave it a particular urgency relevant to Sidney's
claim.

For Calvin, and for Luther before him, God's creation is an activity
worked out through the body of time and space. The incarnation is the
definitive but not the only historical act in a process that began with the
first *fiat* and continues until "creation" is no more. In the opening book
of his *Institutes of the Christian Religion* (1559), Calvin insists that if we
stop at God's first making of the World, "we do not properly grasp what
it means to say: 'God is Creator.'" Rejecting the view of God the Creator as first mover only, Calvin says we must go on to God's omnipo-
tent Providence, which is "watchful, effective, active . . . , engaged in
ceaseless activity." Calvin stresses that this divine work does not
absolve humankind from action, but rather engages us in it: "he who
set the limits to our life at the same time entrusted us to its care; he has
provided means and helps [for us] to preserve it."[73] And so for Calvin
God's "will extends . . . to history and to that which is central in history, man's forming activity."[74] As Francois Wendel writes, this vision
"of a continuous action of God in the midst of his Creation" was held
as well by Luther.[75]

By profession an Old Testament scholar, Luther believed that "the
God of the Bible controls every move of time."[76] In explaining the first
article of the Creed ("I believe in God, the Father almighty, maker of
heaven and earth"), Luther makes no reference to the Genesis accounts
of Creation. Instead he writes that "everything we possess, and everything in heaven and on earth besides, is daily given and sustained by
God."[77] The principal object of this active omnipotence is humankind,
with whom God is not yet finished. Theologian Robert Jenson notes
that "Medieval theology . . . thinks of God's creating of human beings
as done once-for-all at some past moment. . . . Reformation theology,
on the contrary, thinks of man as in the making by the Word of God."[78]
The struggles and suffering within the Church give testimony to this
divine activity: "Now we are only halfway pure and holy," Luther

writes. "The Holy Spirit must continue to work in us through the Word, daily granting forgiveness until we attain that life where there will be no more forgiveness."[79] By calling the poet a maker made in the image of the Heavenly Maker, Sidney indicates that human invention attains validity because it imitates (in the earthly kingdom) this godly action.

What Sidney means by "invention" now needs clarification. Following Cicero, Thomas Wilson defines invention as the first of the five skills the orator must possess:

> The fyndyng out of apte matter, called otherwise Invencion [Latin *invenio*, to find], is a searchyng out of thynges true, or thynges likely, the which maie reasonably sette furth a matter, and make it appere probable. The places of Logique, geve godd occasion to finde out pleniful matter.[80]

Analogous to the research practice of "surveying the material" to learn past approaches, searching the places or topics enables the rhetorician to "discover hidden reasons lying behind a given proposition, and thus bring to light previously unseen connections that make discrete perceptions rationally comprehensible."[81] Though the foundation of any rhetorical effort, Wilson's invention remains a mechanical skill—the sort of work a computer does well. This is no doubt why Quintillian agrees with Cicero that invention is "within the reach of any man of good sense, [while] eloquence belongs to the orator alone," and why Francis Bacon "stresses the . . . distinction between the investigation of the unknown by way of his new logic, and [topical] 'invention,' that is, the selection of received assumptions about the natural world as premises for argument or display."[82] For Bacon true invention is not the finding of past arguments but the discovery of fundamental principles through a rational process of observing nature and making comparative judgments.

Sidney's *invention* resembles Bacon's new method in being the work of human observation and wit but differs in claiming freedom to exceed nature's bounds. Having noted that from his dependence on nature the "natural philosopher thereon hath his name," Sidney declares the poet's liberty: among practitioners of the arts "the poet only bringeth his own stuff, and doth not learn a conceit out of a matter, but maketh matter for a conceit" (*DP* 99). Murray Wright Bundy has noted that beginning with Stephen Hawes's *The Pastime of Pleasure* (1509) and continuing through Puttenham and Sidney, *invention* is used by English theorists to mean the poet's ability to make fiction rather than simply to find existing approaches or arguments.[83] Readers of Astrophil's first sonnet remember that this latter, traditional method fails him. He has studied others' "inventions fine,"

> But words came halting forth, wanting Invention's stay,
> Invention, Nature's child, fled step-dame Studie's blowes,
> And others' feete still seem'd but strangers in my way. (*AS* 1.6, 9–11)

The inventions Astrophil studies may be the topics, or they may be, as his "turning others' leaves" (line 7) implies, the approaches or the works of other poets. But the *Invention* of lines 9–10, Nature's child as opposed to stepdame Study's, cannot refer to this ineffectual, mechanical process; rather it must be Astrophil's ability to feign—to show his love in poetry. This invention is Nature's child in two interdependent ways. It "depends primarily on the genius of the writer," for it comes not from study but from Astrophil's "heart" (line 14), where Stella's image and his own poetic faculty lie.[84] And it is Nature's child in the sense of "he's his father's son": the child does what the parent does, in this case to make fictions.[85]

In this sonnet Sidney outlines the process central to his method in verse and prose fiction alike: established "inventions fine" are tested and found inadequate to the present dilemma; the poet is then driven to rely on his own invention, engaged in a making akin to nature's and, ultimately, to God's. The poet does not translate abstract "ideas" into material substance. Like nature and the Heavenly Maker of that nature, he continually invents, figuring forth his work in the body of the phenomenal world, until creation is done. In other words, for Sidney the making of fictions is valid because it is the most "natural" and "godlike" thing human beings can do. God's making and the poet's are not of course the same—the human maker cannot make himself free of sin, for instance—but they are analogous. That Sidney credits such analogical arguments can be seen when he defends poetic feigning by pointing to the parables of the Old and New Testaments even as he insists that "right poets" cannot match "heavenly discourse" (*DP* 87, also 93-94, 99). To steal a neoplatonic term, it is not the things in a finished poem which are "inspired"; what is inspired is the action of making things new, of imitating not "what is, hath been, or shall be," but ranging "into the divine consideration of what may be and should be" (*DP* 81). For Sidney, poetry is the incarnation of the human word.

III

But this argument may be—borrowing Sidney's phrase—understood by few and by fewer granted (*DP* 79). A decade ago Andrew Weiner rightly insisted that we cannot understand Sidney unless we see him as a Protestant poet.[86] Yet the Protestant thought so central to Sidney's poetics has been misinterpreted by many of his modern readers in a way that makes the analogy between human and divine invention outlined above incredible. Perhaps because they have read Calvin and Luther through the lens of seventeenth-century Puritanism (itself often misrepresented), they inform us that the defining feature of Renaissance Protestant experience is an overwhelming, even neurotic obsession with sin. This assumption yields a Sidney trapped (once more) between humanist ambition and "the self-doubt of sinful man."[87] Sidney's God becomes yet another well-meaning but domineering father he cannot finally reject. But such arguments turn the Reformation on its head. The radical experience that enkindled the imagination and will of Luther and Calvin was one of liberation: liberation from a destructive obsession with sin and liberation to do good work in this world. Part of Sidney's revolutionary achievement was to declare poetry a form of this good work.

"A Christian has no need of any work or law in order to be saved since through faith he is free from every law and does everything out of pure liberty and freely." Therefore, Luther declares in *The Freedom of a Christian*, "he should be guided in all his works by this thought and contemplate this one thing alone, that he may serve and benefit others in all that he does, considering nothing but the need and advantage of his neighbor."[88] He will then do good works as Adam and Eve did them before the Fall and as Christ did them on Earth—not to appease God, but to please Him and to serve humankind.[89] It is precisely because God in his mercy saves us that we are freed to act without self-interest for the good of others, as Christ did. And it is because salvation is something we receive rather than achieve that in Luther's *Treatise on Good Works* works become a broad realm of legitimate human activity limited only by each person's conviction that this work is consistent with faith in God.[90] It is "a good work when a man works at his trade, walks, stands, eats, drinks, sleeps, and does all kinds of things for the nourishment of his body or for the common welfare."[91]

Calvin licenses a similar freedom to act for good in matters not concerning justification, as Weiner has noted.[92] Both reformers believed themselves freed from the terror of the law's judgment by the good news of God's unshakable love. It should not be forgotten that Calvin saw even the doctrine of election, which he calls the "covenant of life," as a sign of *assurance*.[93] Thus liberated, Luther and Calvin practiced as they preached: their careers were devoted not only to declaring the gospel but also to asserting the value of humanist education and good government. And arguably their primary good works, as with Sidney's, were those they wrote.

Sidney places the work of poetry precisely in this common Reformation tradition. Right poets cannot do the salvific work of God, but they can work—better than any other—to teach and move us to "knowledge of a man's self, in the ethic and politic consideration, with the end of well-doing and not well-knowing only" (*DP* 83). Poetry can be defended because it serves and benefits others, to borrow Luther's phrase; writing poetry is a heroic work because it promotes "the ending end of all *earthly* learning," which is "virtuous action" (*DP* 83, emphasis added). To claim that right poetry is the inspired word of heaven would be impious: it is the work of human wit, of reason, to which both Luther and Calvin gave a valid place in enacting what Philipp Melanchthon called "civil righteousness."[94]

Sidney's comparison of the poet-maker to God is no neoplatonic flight but an orthodox expression of a vital Reformation paradox: only when we see that we cannot act like God in effecting our salvation can we act like God for the sake of others. Calvin writes that the justified, freed from the "perpetual dread" of the Law, are freed to do God's will with generous and hopeful hearts. They act no longer as servants but as sons, who trust "that their obedience and readiness of mind will be accepted by their fathers, even though they have not quite achieved what their fathers intended."[95] Sidney's poet, enabled by an "erected wit" though still beset by an "infected will" (*DP* 79), is just such a liberated son. In contrast to the sometimes reductive agendas of Sidney's humanist fathers, this Father God offers a pattern the poet can imitate rather than resist. Trusting in God's grace, he can turn to the good work of making to delight, to teach, and to move. In the act of inventing a speaking picture that prompts virtuous action, the poet is making the highest possible use of the freedom granted him by the mercy of God. As with other legitimate human work, so with poesy: the product counts for nothing before God's judgment; but in God's mercy the activity—the inventing in this case—attests to our being made in the image of Maker.[96]

Sidney's understanding of the poet's and the hero's work is one and the same: the courageous activity of invention in imitation of the work of nature and nature's God. This invention will not save us before God's law; only God's love will do that. But such imitation, conducted within the confines of our sin-burdened hearts, is the only thing we *can* do, as Luther advised Melanchthon when he told him to "sin boldly."[97] Invention so understood is the necessary condition of what Montaigne would call our "probationary" nature.[98] And it takes its validity from the invention and love of God, as Luther had in mind when in defining good works he cites Paul's advice to "have this mind among yourselves, which you have in Christ Jesus."[99] To conclude, in the act of invention the poet achieves his fullest and best humanity: the truest poetry is the most feigning. Because the poet feigns he writes with more *energeia* than the philosopher; because he feigns the poet is freed from the "bare *Was*" of history (*DP* 89) to range within the zodiac of his own wit and shape a golden world. His invention is the limited but real privilege afforded to the children of transforming nature and of the Maker God.

Poetry can move its readers to heroic action because poetry itself is such an action, not in the deeds of its characters only but also in its very work of "representing, counterfeiting, or figuring forth to speak metaphorically." That is why readers must "learn how and why the maker made" his poetry, and that is how readers must "use the narration but as an imaginative ground-plot of a profitable invention" of their own (*DP* 79, 103). Nowhere is this clearer than in the *New Arcadia*, whose characters' experience and whose narrative method call traditional "inventions fine" into question—most obviously the humanist invention of "the heroic personality . . . as a static embodiment of ethical universals."[100] In the revised *Arcadia* Sidney tests his culture's inventions fine by feigning. As the next two chapters reveal, he figures forth the fullest, most heroic representations of such constructs, expanding them throughout the narrative until they collapse under the weight of their own excessive claims.

2
The Invention of Justice

> But the fair thing is, first of all, to be a good man yourself.
> It is among such men that this stability of friendship . . .
> may be made secure; and when united by ties of goodwill,
> they will first of all subdue the passions to which other men
> are slaves.
>
> —Cicero, *De Amicitia*

In the first letter he wrote to his eldest son, Sir Henry Sidney sent this advice:

> Let your first action be the lifting up of your mind to Almighty God by hearty prayer. . . . And use this as an ordinary act, and at an ordinary hour; whereby the time itself shall put you in remembrance to do that you are accustomed to do in that time.
>
> Apply your study to such hours as your discreet master doth assign you, earnestly. . . . And mark the sense and the matter of that you do read, as well as the words; so shall you both enrich your tongue with words and your wit with matter, and judgment will grow as years grow in you. . . .
>
> Study and endeavor yourself to be virtuously occupied. So shall you make such a habit of well-doing in you as you shall not know how to do evil, though you would.

Readers should not be surprised by the father's formality, which is typical of personal letters between men of the age. Sir Henry dearly loved his son, and he knew the limits of boyhood: "Well, my little Philip," he concludes, "this is enough for me, and too much, I fear, for you."[1] But the manner as well as the matter of the letter—the series of imperatives, the movement from God to study to virtuous action—is a compliment to his son, an initiation of the twelve-year-old Philip into the humanist code of justice that defines the lives of all men who would

25

subdue those passions to which other men are slaves. Justice is the virtue of putting things in right order, of knowing what to subjugate to what. It is the virtue that makes philosophers kings. Sidney's life and fiction give every sign that he loved this human invention well, and every sign that he found it inadequate to human experience.

Son to an earnest and loyal Tudor governor, nephew to Leicester, and protege of Hubert Languet, Philip Sidney inherited a humanism that promised virtue and power to the man who consciously fashions himself in the image of its code. A humanism Platonic and Ciceronian in origin, it canonizes the ability to order one's soul according to an essential hierarchy of being and the consequent right to order one's society in similar fashion. This Tudor humanism follows the *Republic* and *De Officiis* in asserting the centrality of personal and public justice and stresses the value of education because it nurtures the self-control that gives one the authority to control others.

Like all forms of power, such humanism succeeds by recognizing the paradoxes in political human nature. If a man is to extend his control, he must set limits on the warring factions within himself: base desire must be subordinate to courageous will, and both to the commanding reason. The just man's power to act and to provoke change depends on his achievement of an inner stasis, making him impervious to threats both of fortune and of irrational longing.[2] In the revised *Arcadia* Sidney displays this invention in all its shining self-sufficiency in the stories Pyrocles and Musidorus tell after they fall in love. But into this glorious history he intrudes the private and public tragedy of Amphialus, in whom the vulnerability of even the just to desire and to ruin becomes ever more clear. By giving the invention of justice its fullest, most heroic representation and then revealing how Amphialus's efforts at "just" domination make him subject to the very forces this virtue promises to control, Sidney's fiction forces its readers to reconsider a code of conduct dear to Sidney's teachers and to his own generation of aspiring courtiers.

I

In Plato's construction of the tripartite human soul, the desires are a many-headed beast, the high spirits a lion, the intellect a man.[3] They exist in aristocratic, inverse proportion—the generative desires being the largest, the noble spirits smaller, and the definitive, properly ruling intellect the least in size. Not surprisingly, Socrates makes wisdom first among the cardinal virtues in Plato's *Republic*. Wisdom directs man to set "his gaze upon the things of the eternal and unchanging order," whose harmony will prompt him "to imitate them and, as far as may be, to fashion himself in their likeness and assimilate himself to them."[4]

But that fashioning itself is the work of the virtue called justice, which is "the doing of one's own business . . . with regard to that which is within and in the true sense concerns one's self," so that each of the three divisions of the soul performs its proper part.[5] This inner justice must precede public action: "having first attained to self-mastery and beautiful order within himself, . . . and having made of himself a unit, one man instead of many, self-controlled and in unison, he should then and only then turn to practice."[6] The *Republic* was written as a model for this just soul: its three classes of citizens (lovers of wisdom, victory, and gain) are the inner man, lion, and beast writ large in Socrates' proof that the just man is the most happy. In fact, if inner justice fails, one loses more than happiness: "to starve the man [the intellect] and so enfeeble him that he can be pulled whithersoever either of the others [lion and beast] drag him" is to lose "that which is human in us, or rather, . . . that which is divine."[7] The unjust man is not a man at all.

In *De Officiis* Cicero insists that "the whole glory of virtue is in activity" and that justice is "the crowning glory of the virtues."[8] Wisdom again defines human nature, since "the search for truth and its eager pursuit are peculiar to man,"[9] but on justice depend the remaining virtues and the heroic life. Courage rests on a regard for "moral rectitude as the only good," and temperance is a moral propriety enabling the subjection of passion to reason.[10] Without justice the "indifference to outward circumstances" that courage imparts is impossible; without justice the self-control given by temperance is lost. "For when appetites overstep their bounds . . . they clearly overlap all bound and measure."[11] Cicero makes the very writing of *De Officiis* an act of justice, his book a phoenix risen out of the ashes of his lost, beloved Republic: "amid all the present most awful calamities I yet flatter myself that I have won this good out of evil—that I may commit to written form matters not at all familiar to our countrymen but very much worth their knowing."[12] To the generation schooled in the risks of public service during the reigns of Henry VIII, Edward VI, and Mary—the generation of Sidney's father—Cicero's dual claim to independent moral assurance and to heroic action would have been particularly compelling. They would have seen Cicero as one of their own not royal but patrician class.

Justice bestows power because it makes one independent of those passions that subdue the weaker majority. Socrates believes that the good man "is most of all men self-sufficient unto himself for a good life and is distinguished from other men in having least need of anybody else."[13] In this the just man imitates the cosmos itself, constructed to be "One single Whole, compounded of all wholes, perfect and ageless and unailing."[14] Cicero makes this self-sufficiency the precondition of friendship, as does Seneca in his ninth epistle when he explains that wise men prefer to have companions but do not need them: "The Supreme Good . . . is developed at home, and arises entirely within itself. If good asks any portion of itself from without, it begins to be subject to the play of Fortune."[15] It is this invulnerability that establishes the just man as rightful governor. In effect, the classical tradition makes justice a self-justifying and exclusive virtue: even as the intellect is the smallest and highest division of the soul, so are the just among human society.[16] A city, says Socrates, can only be wise "by virtue of its smallest class and minutest part of itself," the philosopher-guardians.[17] Cicero represents the just not merely as guardians, but as the very makers of human society: "as the masses in their helplessness were oppressed by the strong, they appealed for protection to some man who was conspicuous for his virtue; and as he shielded the weaker classes from wrong, he managed by establishing equitable conditions to hold the higher and lower classes in an equality of right."[18]

That Cicero bills himself in *De Officiis* as such a man would only have heightened the admiration of Philip Sidney's humanist mentors. It is noteworthy that the great Republican was lionized as a moral and political champion in an age of consolidating monarchies. The praise for his ethics and rhetorical skills must be understood in light of the class that advanced it: gentlemen and scholars born to privilege but not to sovereignty. To such men the habit of justice makes both a refuge from uncertainty of royal favor and a foundation for action not dependent on it. This would have been particularly true for young Philip Sidney, who, as A. C. Hamilton says, "was not born great enough."[19] We should not forget that reading and writing courtesy books were acts of self-validation by the class that, like Cicero, had to invent and maintain its place in the structure of national power. Institutes like Erasmus's *Education of a Christian Prince* were written more for the educators than for their royal pupils.

The achievement of justice as the rightful means to personal and political control dominates the English and Continental courtesy books that informed Tudor humanism. Erasmus's *Education* warns that "you cannot be a king unless reason completely controls you. You cannot rule over others, until you yourself have obeyed the course of honor."[20] More precise parallels to the ancients appear in two works written for the English and French courts: Elyot's *Gouernour* (1531), dedicated to Henry VIII, and Pierre de la Primaudaye's *l'Academie francaise* (1577), dedicated to Henri III. Elyot adopts Plato's concept of the tripartite soul and cites Aristotle's *De Anima* to explain that the intellect is "diuyne, impassible [not subject to the passions], and incorruptible."[21] Justice is achieved by the man who "woulde not willingly abandone the excellencie of his propre nature," and it makes the just man the rallying point for social order.[22] Primaudaye, writing with Hugenot fervor, insists that the Bible must be the first source of knowledge, but he continues to be typically Protestant in his interest in sources for the guidance of earthly conduct (he of course is writing such a work of guidance himself). The classical understanding of justice governs his definition of virtue:

> a disposition and power of the reasonable parte of the soule, which bringeth into order and decencie the vnreasonable part, ... whereby the soule abideth in a comely and decent habit, executing that which ought to be done, according to reason.[23]

Primaudaye follows Plato in calling justice "an equall distribution" and Aristotle in naming it the sum of all virtue.[24] But he turns to the Romans to demonstrate the role of justice in fashioning political harmony: "Iustice (saith Cicero) is the mistresse of all the other virtues, and as it were their Queene. . . . She putteth a difference between the good and the bad, which being taken away (saith Seneca) nothing followeth but confusion."[25]

That Sidney knew this tradition requires little demonstration: his letters, his *Defence*, and his poetry testify to the educational and political order it established in Tudor England.[26] What does need mention is that the invention of justice works by subordinating—in many instances by excluding—central elements that motivate action in Sidney's poetry: sensual desire and women. The counsel of Plato, Aristotle, Cicero, and Seneca usually imposes "justice" on these elements in the simplest and most complete way: it ignores them. Tudor writers often follow suit, but they sometimes betray a more acute sense that the palace of justice is under siege. In *The Scholemaster* (1570), Roger Ascham declares, "*Erasmus* the honor of learning of all oure time, saide wiselie that experience is the common scholehouse of foles, and ill men: Men of witte and honestie be otherwise instructed."[27] Experience is opposed by Ascham to proper training, which makes one impervious to it, and plainly it does not mean the practical learning imparted by life at court. Experience is the Charybdis of eros and the Scylla of fortune, threatening to cast gentlemen out of the ship of justice—with its all-male order and clear course—into alien seas and onto foreign shores of the mind and heart. There they may lose not only their power but their cherished, just selves. To return to Ascham's metaphor, experience threatens to enroll them all in the schoolhouse of fools.

II

By birth and nurture the Pyrocles and Musidorus of the revised *Arcadia* are enrolled in the school of justice. In their lineage, education, friendship, and actions in Asia Minor Sidney presents them as models of heroic manhood as envisioned by his courtly contemporaries.[28] The Arcadian Amphialus has parallel credentials, but his use of them—as we will later see—shakes the foundation of virtue and power that justice makes.

The powers of perception and will Pyrocles and Musidorus display win them not only mutual admiration but alliance with the just and control over their enemies. When he finds Pyrocles stricken in Arcadia with melancholy idleness, Musidorus rehearses the nature of these powers in what sounds like the just man's creed:

> A mind well trained and long exercised in virtue, my sweet and worthy cousin, doth not easily change any course it once undertakes but upon well-grounded and well-weighed causes, for being witness to itself of his own inward good, it finds nothing without it of so high a price for which it should be altered. Even the very countenance and behaviour of such a man doth show forth images of the same constancy by maintaining a right harmony betwixt it and the inward good in yielding itself suitable to the virtuous resolutions of the mind. (*NA* 49)

His lecture does no good, for the elder cousin soon finds Pyrocles transformed into an Amazon. Musidorus reasons that this shameful metamorphosis logically follows Pyrocles' abandonment to passion, since even as the love of virtue makes one virtuous, "this effeminate love of a woman doth so womanize a man that, if you yield to it, it will not only make you an Amazon, but a launder, a distaff-spinner, or whatsoever other vile occupation their idle heads can imagine and their weak hands perform" (*NA* 72).

Musidorus's speech exalts the self-sufficiency and male dominance adapted from Plato and Cicero in the courtesy books. A man's face itself reveals the just calibration of his soul to the eternal order of truth; and the physical transformation of Pyrocles is an outward and visible sign that the Socratean pyramid of his psyche has been inverted. To yield to base desire is to be unjust to oneself; being womanized is a predictable outcome and sign of it. For Musidorus, Pyrocles' folly betrays "this name of friendship . . . which cannot be, where virtue is abolished" (*NA* 76). Implicit in the lover's first romantic lethargy is a fall from his participation in the "familiarity of excellent men in learning and soldiery" (*NA* 49). He has broken the (male) humanist code of justice written on the tables of their memory by the acts and guidance of Pyrocles' own father, King Euarchus: "And is it possible that this is Pyrocles, the only young Prince in the world formed by nature and framed by education to the true exercise of virtue?" (*NA* 70).

Euarchus, whose name means "good ruler," is the very type of justice. Spenser writes that "gentle bloud will gentle manners breed,"[29] and as Musidorus tells the tale, Euarchus's actions as king, as friend to Dorialus, and as joint guardian of both princes with his sister (mother of Musidorus) form the paradigm by which his son and nephew will live.[30] Musidorus represents him as a compendium of the cardinal virtues:

> he was most wise to see what was best, and most just in the performing what he saw, and temperate in abstaining from anything anyway contrary, so [that] . . . no thought can imagine a greater heart to see and contemn danger, where danger would offer to make any wrongful threatening upon him. (*NA* 159)

Significantly, Euarchus does not inherit power at his father's death. Orphaned, he comes to his majority to confront "the worst kind of oligarchy" (*NA* 159) and must by judicious use of capital punishment reinstate the Platonic hierarchy of king, counsellors, and commons. Only after he has been "the reducer of them into order" can his paternal care be effective: "then shined forth, indeed all love, among them, when an awful fear engendered by justice did make that love most lovely" (*NA* 160). Not need, but virtuous self-assurance and just action win him the alliance of King Dorialus. Euarchus weds his ally's sister and bestows his own in marriage on Dorialus "not so much to make a friendship as to confirm the friendship betwixt their posterity, which between them, by the likeness of virtue, had been long before made" (*NA* 161). When Dorialus dies, this Sidnean Cyrus directs the education of their sons, who are expected to imitate their fathers' friendship and the just power on which it was founded.

When Xenophon's Cyrus readies himself for his first military adventure, his father asks if he remembers that "those only who had made themselves what they ought to be had a right to ask for corresponding blessings from the gods." "Yes, by Zeus," answers the dutiful Cyrus; "I do indeed."[31] Likewise the princes must through education make the justice that is their birthright proof against treacherous experience. Musidorus now recalls that training with nostalgic pride:

> they were so brought up that all the sparks of virtue which nature had kindled in them were so blown to give forth their uttermost heat that, justly it may be affirmed, they inflamed the affections of all that knew them; for almost before they could perfectly speak they began to receive conceits not

unworthy of the best speakers; excellent devices being used to make even their sports profitable, images of battles and fortifications being then delivered to their memory, which, after, their stronger judgements might dispense; the delight of tales being converted to the knowledge of all the stories of worthy princes, both to move them to do nobly, and teach them how to do nobly, the beauty of virtue still being set before their eyes, and that taught them with far more diligent care than grammatical rules; their bodies exercised in all abilities both of doing and suffering, and their minds acquainted by degrees with dangers; and in sum, all bent to the making up of princely minds, no servile fear used towards them, nor any other violent restraint, but still as to princes, so that a habit of commanding was naturalized in them, and therefore the farther from tyranny, nature having done so much for them in nothing as that it made them lords of truth, whereon all the other goods were builded. (NA 163–64)

The curriculum moves from sight to memory to the proper ordering of images by rational judgment.[32] Pyrocles and Musidorus can command others because their just "dispensing" of virtue has taught them to command themselves. They embody Aristotle's idea of the proper self-lover: he who "takes for himself the things that are noblest and most truly good" by following his intellect, the "dominant part of himself."[33] Rightly knowing and loving themselves, they act with magnanimity, which *The Gouernour* calls "an excellence of mynde concernynge things of great importaunce or education, doing all thynge that is vertuous for the achieuynge of honour," a trait anglicized as "good courage." Elyot explains that "Aristotle saith, That man semeth to be of noble courage that is worthy, and also iugeth him selfe worthy to haue thinges that be great."[34] This is the conviction of self-worth that prompts Sidney's much praised Cyrus to say that as boy and man he always took what was best and that "there is nothing that I ever attempted or desired and yet failed to secure."[35]

Pyrocles and Musidorus triumph over weak, fearful kings because they believe their souls and actions reflect the justice that orders the cosmos itself. In the *Republic* Socrates defines the tyrant as one overwhelmed by the "anarchy and lawlessness" of his base desires; the tyrant is "unjust to the last degree" because he has not subjugated the passions within: "unable to control himself [he] attempts to rule over others."[36] The tyrant kings of Asia Minor fail because they do not practice that self-love whose essence is justice: they fail to place the self's "dominant part" on the psyche's throne. Governed by the base desires, they cannot see what is right. The literally blind Paphlagonian king, model for Shakespeare's Lear and Gloucester, is a tragic emblem of such disabled tyranny. Each tyrant becomes dependent on a self-seeking schemer to make his judgments for him: Phrygia on "accusing sycophants" (NA 196), Pontus on a greedy counselor, Iberia on his whoring queen, Paphlagonia on his bastard son. Most pathetic among the tyrants the princes meet is Antiphilus, whose name may refer to failure in self-love as well as in devotion to his doting bride, Erona. Suddenly elevated above his "mean parentage" to royal power, Antiphilus reverses the policy of justice practiced by Euarchus:

> But imagining no so true property of sovereignty as to do what he listed, ... he quickly made his kingdom a tennis-court where his subjects should be the balls . . . , presuming so far upon himself that what he did was liked of everybody . . . and all because he was a king; for, in nature not able to conceive the bonds of great matters, . . . he was swayed withal (he knew not how) as every wind of passions puffed him. (*NA* 299)

The totality of Antiphilus's failure in just self-love is evident in the figure on whom he becomes dependent: Artaxia, sister to his slain rival and now Queen of Armenia. Antiphilus is "so incredibly blinded with the over-bright shining of his royalty" (*NA* 300) that he angles to win the love of Artaxia and the crown of her dead brother. She detests Antiphilus and, at a meeting arranged to discuss their prospective union, imprisons both him and his hapless wife. Still the ironic dependency continues: learning of a plot to free both himself and Erona, he reveals it to gain Artaxia's favor (*NA* 303). Instead, she hands him over to the women of the city, who force him to leap to his death from a high monument. It is because Antiphilus stands "upon no true ground inwardly" that he is "ready to fall faster than calamity could thrust him" into ruin (*NA* 300–301). Within the scheme of humanist justice, his imprisonment and death at the hands of women follow predictably on failure to subjugate the blind, passionate desires of his soul to the manly sovereignty of intellect. Such "womanish" injustice is the very threat Prince Musidorus warns his friend Pyrocles against in the first love debate: to be subject to women is the outward sign and consequence of an inward breakdown.

The exemplary friendship displayed by Pyrocles and Musidorus throughout their pre-Arcadian travels is antithetical to the pattern of weak dependency in the tyrants they meet. The link between self-sufficient virtue and friendship is most explicit in Cicero's *De Amicitia*,[37] in which Laelius tells his young companions that "friendship springs rather from nature than from need" and illustrates by recalling his own friendship with Scipio Africanus Minor:

> to the extent that a man relies upon himself and is so fortified by virtue and wisdom that he is dependent on no one and considers all his possessions to be within himself, in that degree is he most conspicuous for seeking and cherishing friendships. Now what need did Africanus have of me? By Hercules! none at all.[38]

Hence Cicero dismisses with derision the claim that the desire for friendship is greatest among "helpless women" and "the poor," who presumably lack the "lamp of uprightness and virtue" that makes Scipio the complete friend.[39]

For the just, a friend may if need be a teacher and a preserver of one's life and virtue. Sidney's princes play each of these parts, but for them the friend is essentially what he is for the ancients: an image that reflects and reinforces one's own identity. A man cannot see and love virtue in another unless he first sees and loves it in himself, both actions being exercises in what Plato would call justice—putting first things first. So Laelius can say that "virtue is the parent and preserver of friendship and without virtue friendship cannot exist at all."[40]

Musidorus tells Pamela that friendship is the "child, and not the father, of virtue" (NA 184). This awareness unites the princes in the course of their boyhood training and inspires the loyalty and self-sacrifice displayed in their travels. Each acts out of love for the almost impersonal *tertium quid* of justice he sees in the other. Elyot writes that friendship among virtuous men will be intensified "if similitude of studie or lerninge be ioyned vnto the said vertues."[41] Musidorus tells Pamela that the princes' mutual education has made them lords of truth and that on truth's foundation was built "the memorable friendship that grew betwixt the two princes (such as made them more like than the likeness of all other virtues, and made them more near one to the other than the nearness of their blood could aspire unto)" (NA 164). That "nearness," as Pyrocles tells Philoclea, develops from their perception of virtue in one another, making each the other's instructor: Musidorus "taught me by word, and best by example, giving me in him so lively an image of virtue as ignorance could not cast such mist over mine eyes as not to see and to love it" (NA 235). Between them then is established a stable bond that serves each well in all encounters, however outwardly chaotic. Before setting out for Asia Minor they have achieved what Aristotle calls "a fixed disposition" not dependent on emotion: what Primaudaye terms "a communion of perpetuall will, the end whereof is fellowship of life."[42]

It is for the sake of the virtue they love in one another that these friends are willing to sacrifice their lives. Paradoxically, in the dispensation of justice, life itself must be subordinated to that which is not subject to base desire or fortune or time.[43] So it is that Musidorus offers himself as a substitute for Pyrocles when the younger is condemned to die by the Phrygian king—an exchange that recalls Cicero's account of Damon and Phintias (by others called Pythias) in De Officiis.[44] Yet what Musidorus stresses to Pamela is not his own heroism but the beautiful virtue displayed in Pyrocles, who returns in disguise to rescue his friend: "he, even he, . . . of the greatest blood that any prince might be, submitted himself to be servant to the executioner that should put to death Musidorus: a far notabler proof of his friendship, considering the height of his mind, than any death could be" (*NA* 172). Their ensuing triumph proceeds from a renewal of that communion of perpetual will instilled by education and sealed in friendship. Releasing his cousin, Pyrocles "was able to lead Musidorus to courage" so that with "just rage and desperate virtue" they prevail (*NA* 173). It is not "easy to find men who will go down to calamity's depths for a friend," says Cicero. "Whoever . . . has shown himself staunch, immovable, and firm in friendship ought to be considered to belong to that class of men which is exceedingly rare—aye, almost divine."[45]

Because "it is the just who are most pained at injustice," the true friend will "strive with all his might to arouse his friend's prostrate soul" if it becomes disordered.[46] And so Musidorus reminds his melancholy cousin in the first love debate of who he is in an effort to rekindle Pyrocles' shattered self-sufficiency, and so Musidorus stages a rhetorical retreat when it looks as if Pyrocles is (temporarily) too weak to respond to Ciceronian principles. Sidney invents a contrast to clarify this devotion not only to a friend's welfare but to his just soul. Each prince tells of the brothers Tydeus and Telenor, who serve the scheming Plexirtus. Their failure to love justice more than political loyalty involves them in an annihilation of the virtue that as friends they should preserve. In effect, they choose the wrong friend—not one another, but the seeming friendly villain. Musidorus recalls that the brothers are "disposed to goodness and justice," but because they were "brought up from their infancy with Plexirtus" they are by that chance corrupted to his service, choosing "rather to be good friends [to Plexirtus] than good men" (*NA* 184). They are fully implicated in the plot of Plexirtus against his father; but for their pains a suspicious Plexirtus later arranges for them to fight one another—each disguised so that he does not know the other until striking a mortal blow. Pyrocles tells Philoclea that in their final words, the brothers lament "their folly in having believed he could faithfully love, who did not love faithfulness; wishing us to take heed how we placed our good will upon any other ground than proof of virtue" (*NA* 264).[47]

Pyrocles and Musidorus' private practice of justice both impels and enables them to construct in Asia Minor a public communion of perpetual will analogous to their personal friendship. By the insight that is wisdom and the act of subjugation and exaltation that is justice, they forge a system of public alliance whose center is their own fixed disposition as lords of truth. Because "they would needs fall to the practice of those virtues which they before learned" (*NA* 164), the princes set out from Thessalia for adventures that will effectively recapitulate Euarchus's establishment of order in chaotic Macedon before their birth. A quick rehearsal of the foreign tour in which they "turn their learning to publick vse"[48] will recall the scope of their achievement.

Setting out to aid Euarchus in the siege of Byzantium, the princes are shipwrecked and washed ashore, Pyrocles in Phrygia, Musidorus in Pontus; after their mutual self-sacrifice described above, they re-establish justice in Phrygia and then in Pontus; next they aid Leonatus against Plexirtus's murderous companions and see the good brother crowned in his father's stead in Paphlagonia; from there the princes come to the rescue of Erona and defeat the forces of Tiridates in Lycia, where Antiphilus now becomes king; Pyrocles then has his private adventure with Dido, Pamphilus, and Anaxius, and is rescued from Artaxia's men by Musidorus and soldiers from Iberia; once in the Iberian court the princes are wooed and then imprisoned by the lecherous queen; escaping with the help of Palladius and Zelmane, they go on to end civil strife in Bythinia; after Zelmane's death they separate again, Pyrocles to rescue Plexirtus, Musidorus to aid the new king in Pontus; finally they set sail together for Arcadia, but a second shipwreck parts them once more.

In Phrygia and Pontus the princes institute social order because they employ the justice that Elyot says "is so necessary and expedient for the gouernour of a public weale, that without it none other vertue may be commendable."[49] What strikes readers so forcefully here is that the act of establishing justice demands in this case not merely subordination but elimination of that which disturbs its design. Like Euarchus before them, the princes do not shrink from using bloody justice in suppressing the tyrants who rule there: the Phrygian king "was slain by Musidorus, after he had seen his only son . . . slain by the hand of Pyrocles" (*NA* 174); in Pontus, where the king has murdered two faithful servants of the princes, the monarch is executed by Musidorus's command on the servants' tomb. This swift and severe suppression of chaotic powers conforms to classical injunction and to Tudor political practice. In *De Officiis* Cicero makes it clear that the social order owes a tyrant nothing but "the bitterest feud; . . . all that pestilent and abominable race should be exterminated from human society."[50] Sidney was himself a veteran of his father's campaigns against the Earl of Clanicard's rebellion in 1576, and he showed no hesitation in the *Discourse on Irish Affairs* about advocating force as a proper solution.[51]

The two princes' killing of monarchs does more than revisit the execution of justice by Queen Elizabeth and her predecessors. This becomes clear in what Pyrocles and Musidorus do next. Like Thomas More's Utopians, who free countries from tyranny but do not stay to rule, the princes refuse offers of monarchy and appoint native countrymen to sovereignty. The Phrygians offer the crown to Musidorus, "But he, thinking it a greater greatness to give a kingdom than get a kingdom" establishes in power "an aged gentleman of approved goodness" who is in fact "next to the succession" (*NA* 175). Pyrocles rejects a like offer in Pontus and marries the tyrant's daughter to a generous nobleman who becomes the new king. In both instances the social hierarchy is preserved and the moral hierarchy that must be its true foundation restored. But both acts—the killing of tyrants and the crowning of just kings—are accomplished by Pyrocles and Musidorus far from the security and power of their native lands. The sheer *energeia* of their virtue, product of their birth and learning, is their only authority. The invention of justice glorified in them here is not so much the work of kings and queens as it is the dream of Philip Sidney's own class, by which it was envisioned as a stay against royal caprice. That Sidney could put this cherished invention to so full and finally damaging a scrutiny as he eventually does in the *New Arcadia* reveals an exceptional measure of poetic independence.

Cicero declares that though great friendships are rare, the goodness that is their source must be directed "to the generality of men. For virtue is not unfeeling, unwilling to serve, or proudly exclusive, but it is her wont to protect even whole nations and to plan the best measures for their welfare."[52] The same justice that begets the princes' friendship engenders a growing public order as they travel. It is in Phrygia, "a kingdom wholly at their commandment by the love of the people and gratefulness of the king," that Pyrocles and Musidorus gather an army to execute justice on the tyrant in Pontus (*NA* 177), and it is the new-made king of Pontus, having dreamed that "those two princes whom he most dearly loved" are in danger, who rescues the princes as well as Leonatus and his father from Plexirtus's conspirators (*NA* 183). In his turn, Leonatus, now King of Galatia, comes to aid the princes when he learns that "two so good friends" are engaged in repelling an attack in Pontus (*NA* 271). This danger passed, they go to Pontus, where their new allies "would needs accept, as from us, their crowns, and acknowledge to hold them of us" (*NA* 271).[53]

A generation before, the virtue of the princes' fathers made a friendship and political alliance which led to the princes' birth; their birth and education fix within them that justice which orders the soul according to invincible truth; that inner justice creates in them the self-sufficient virtue that leads to their abiding friendship; that friendship creates—once again—a social order of reasonable, virtuous men.[54]

Even the second shipwreck does not instantly confound the just souls of Sidney's princes. As if to make the cataclysm of love as shocking as possible, Sidney presents one final, grand display of justice immediately before passion transforms the princes once and for all. The part that Musidorus and Pyrocles play in settling the war between the Laconian helots and the Lacedaemonian gentlemen provides a triumphant last example of the humanist heroism that characterizes their lives in Asia Minor. They begin the encounter in different places (Musidorus at Kalander's Arcadian house, Pyrocles in the helots' stronghold) and on opposite sides (Musidorus seeking to undo, Pyrocles to support the rebels), neither knowing the identity of the other until the end. Yet by their individual just actions they simultaneously renew their friendship and forge in its image a larger political alliance. In the stories of Book Two, Musidorus generally deals with what Sidney calls the politic or public consideration, Pyrocles with the ethic or private.[55] In this recapitulation these are, neatly, reversed, as if to heighten our awareness of the princes as mirrors of virtue.

Musidorus begins his part out of the private devotion of friendship. After the shipwreck that parts him from Pyrocles, he is nursed back to health by the Arcadian gentleman Kalander. In return, Musidorus determines to rescue Clitophon, Kalander's son, who has been captured by the rebels. Gratitude to his host motivates Musidorus, but that is not all. In Clitophon's plight he sees "the image of his dearest friend Daiphantus [Pyrocles], whom he judged to suffer either a like or a worse fortune" (*NA* 26 –27). Yet though sentiment prompts him, Musidorus acts with the insight and justice that first engendered that friendly sentiment between the two princes, using with striking skill the limited resources available to him in this "private cause" (*NA* 26).

Kalander's likable but incompetent king, Basilius, fails to see "that his office is not to make men, but to use men as men are" (*NA* 19). By contrast Musidorus understands, as Erasmus says the prince must, that even the least subjects can aid a prince if he knows how to manage them.[56] Musidorus learns that the ragtag rebels have grown disciplined and bold but that his volunteers are "like men disused with a long peace, more determinate to do, than skilful how to do" (*NA* 34). And so as Plato sets the commanding intellect over courage and turbulent desire, Musidorus sets his reason and military knowledge over this eager but confused band. He orders them to enter the helots' town with the least able men leading the most experienced in prisoners' chains and appoints an orator to claim that they are Arcadian rebels come to seek the aid of their fellow revolutionaries. Once this appeal to the helots' vanity gets the troop through the gates, Musidorus gives the signal to drop their chains and attack.

The Arcadians would have seized control had not the helots' captain, Pyrocles himself, returned to fire their dying spirit. Pyrocles' role differs in this episode from Musidorus's in being part of a public cause (the civil war) and in fashioning honor from expediency. Pirates take him into their ship after the princes' burns, and they enlist him in battle against a Lacedaemonian naval patrol. Pyrocles' party is overwhelmed and sent to prison but freed when the helots stage a surprise attack; Pyrocles wins through his fighting prowess their admiration and then their captaincy. The need to survive makes Pyrocles adopt the helots' cause, though Sidney has already taken care to show that it is defensible as a response to an unjust imposition of "not only tribute but bondage" (*NA* 34). As commander of these rebels Pyrocles immediately begins the dispensation of Platonic justice, for he "had brought up their ignorance and brought down their fury to such a mean of good government" that they triumph in several "great conflicts" (*NA* 34). In this battle he and his friend Musidorus will establish order between them and their oppressors.

Once Pyrocles enters the conflict with Musidorus's party his own assurance of worth evokes admiration and confidence in his frightened men.

> He made them turn face, and with banners displayed, his trumpet gave the loudest testimony he could of his return; which once heard, the rest of the helots which were otherwise scattered bent thitherward with a new life of resolution—as if their captain had been a root out of which, as into branches, their courage had sprung. (*NA* 37)

Likewise Musidorus has been rousing his men, "blaming those that were slow, heartening them that were forward, but especially with his own ensample leading them" (*NA* 36). Musidorus fights with such distinction "that the captain of the helots (whose eyes soon judged of that wherewith themselves were governed) saw that he alone was worth all the rest of the Arcadians" (*NA* 37). Just as Cicero says that friends are drawn together by the very virtues that make them self-sufficient, so are the princes drawn to one another by mutual recognition of each other's courage and might. The encounter ends when the princes encounter each other; Pyrocles, striking a blow that sends the helmet from his cousin's head, recognizes Musidorus.

With their reunion and the onset of night the fighting is over, yet for peace to follow, Pyrocles must exercise another function of the just man—that of orator. Pyrocles' speech to the helots is a brilliant piece of deliberative rhetoric fashioned to persuade them to accept the terms offered by the Lacedaemonians (see *NA* 40 – 41).[57] The prince's address reveals an inner justice that the orator must have so he can make judgments that will determine the content, structure, and style of his speech.

Aristotle, whose *Art of Rhetoric* Sidney in part translated, writes that orators must choose the type of persuasion demanded by circumstance: deliberative, forensic, or epideictic.[58] Pyrocles' situation requires the deliberative, whose end is to dissuade or exhort the audience about future events and whose subjects are "ways and means, war and peace."[59] Every orator has available to him three means of persuasion: the logical, employing deductive reasoning and examples; the emotional, appealing to the joys and sorrows, loves and hates of his listeners; and the ethical, relying on the moral character of the speaker himself.[60] Sources of the logical proof in deliberative oratory include the causes of happiness, the best expedient, and the forms of government.[61]

The art of Pyrocles' speech lies in the skillful simplicity with which he has used these proofs. Arguing logically, he notes that the helots' present happy condition rests on two fortunate events: the goodwill of the gods and Pyrocles' own recognition of the leader among the invaders. The clear moral is that next time they may not be so lucky. Pyrocles then announces that they have achieved the expedient they sought of freedom and franchise, and so there is no reason to continue the battle. To this he immediately adds an emotional appeal—flattering the rebels with their enemies' willingness not only to settle but to make the helots one with them, even in the raising of their children. Finally, Pyrocles makes a convincing ethical appeal by declaring that he has agreed to step down as their leader, sacrificing his own power for their liberty and peace.

Pyrocles chooses a structure and style suited to his audience of common freemen. Setting aside the elaborate seven-part organization recommended by the Roman writers,[62] he adopts the simpler format suggested by Aristotle: "the statement of the case and proof," with an exordium and epilogue if necessary.[63] Here there is little introduction: Pyrocles directly states their present condition and then shows the wisdom of accepting the Lacedaemonians' offer. He makes good use of an epilogue, however, adding the clinching detail that he will return and lead them again if the gentlemen break the treaty (*NA* 47). Recognizing the Aristotelian maxim that an orator's style constitutes a kind of ethical proof of the speaker's character,[64] Pyrocles employs the simple schemes of balance, antithesis, and parenthesis—the latter used chiefly for reminders of how fortunate the helots are. During the speech he introduces only one metaphor, one that dramatizes their escape "out of this gulf of danger, wherein we were alredie swallowed." The terms are accepted, and not incidentally, the life of Clitophon is saved.

The princes act with different motives and in initially opposing causes, but their conduct together forms a last and best revelation of the wisdom and inner command that have made them fast friends and the forgers of a wider alliance. No better instance than the outcome of this battle could be found to demonstrate Aristotle's claim that "friendship appears to be the bond of the state."[65] No better illustration of Cicero's assurance that friends "will first of all subdue the passions to which other men are slaves; and, next, they will delight in what is equitable and accords with law."[66]

In their adventures before meeting Basilius's daughters, Pyrocles and Musidorus are introduced to danger, to corruption in its manifold forms, and to loss. But in that uncertain world they act with a vigorous personal and public justice that figures forth the aspirations and "inventions fine" of Sidney's own humanist class. Sidney allows the princes to describe that invention from the inside, with the confident fervor of his teachers in virtue and with the same "just" exclusions: no emotion other than male loyalty to friend and ally survives, nor does any woman (Dido or Andromana) who poses an erotic threat to that communion. The one exception may be Pyrocles' lingering affection for Zelmane, the daughter of Plexirtus who languishes and dies in Pyrocles' service. And that affection will soon help engender a passionate disordering of his just soul that he cannot make right again. It is in the chapter following the princes' glorious settlement of the helots' rebellion that Pyrocles first hints that he has fallen from justice by falling in love.

III

The rehearsal of the princes' triumphant tour is staged in Sidney's revised *Arcadia* between the private and public collapse of their Arcadian counterpart in justice, Prince Amphialus. He enters the narrative, secondhand, in Queen Helen's story of her love for him, told to Musidorus in the two chapters between the first and second love debates with Pyrocles in Book One. Amphialus first appears in the present as a humiliated spy caught watching as the princesses bathe in the River Ladon, an episode that takes place in Book Two between Musidorus's recollection of his past and Pyrocles'. When those recollections come to an end, his captivity of the princesses in Book Three overtakes all the narrative. By casting this character new to his *Arcadia* in the mold of his magnanimous, just princes, and by exposing Amphialus in love to radical fragmentation of both his private psyche and political self, Sidney reveals the invention of justice (so gloriously displayed in the resolution of the helots' rebellion) to be inadequate to the demands of experience and of the heroic life.

The parallels between this Arcadian paragon and the princes, especially Musidorus, are extensive, but all the more ominous for the manner by which Sidney introduces them. As with Musidorus, Amphialus's father (brother to King Basilius) is dead. Like Musidorus he is raised together with the son of that dead father's ally, through whose care he receives "as good education as any prince's son in the world could have" (*NA* 61); like Musidorus he is bound in friendship to that foster-father's son (Philoxenus). Compared by Kalander's servant to the noble Argalus, Amphialus enjoys a commanding popularity among Basilius's subjects that confirms Queen Helen's summation of her beloved:

> Who follows deeds of arms, but every where finds monuments of Amphialus? Who is courteous, noble, liberal, but he that hath the example before his eyes of Amphialus? Where are all heroical parts, but in Amphialus? (*NA* 61)

Amphialus's picture is literally held before Musidorus by Helen as one "whose mind can be painted by nothing but by the true shape of virtue" (*NA* 61).

Because Amphialus's place as heir to Basilius has been lost at the birth of the king's daughters, his identity depends even more essentially on his role as the image of just character and action. Lose that, lose all. And yet Musidorus first encounters this prince not in Helen's portrait of justice but in the scattered pieces of Amphialus's armor, abandoned after the fatal fight with his friend Philoxenus. Their friendship broken when Helen chooses to love Amphialus, the prince flees only to be pursued by his angry friend and goaded into a combat that leaves Philoxenus dead and Amphialus in despair. As if to reverse the way in which the adventures of Pyrocles and Musidorus confirm the personal and public alliance that bound their fathers, the tragic death of Amphialus's friend destroys that parental foundation. In search of Philoxenus, his father finds him just as the youth dies at Amphialus's hand:

> sorrow of his son, and . . . unkindness of Amphialus, so devoured his vital spirits that, able to say no more but, "Amphialus! Amphialus! Have I—," he sank to the earth and presently died. (*NA* 65)

The paradigm for Amphialus's experience is the dream of Mira, which may be the dream he refers to at the Ladon, when he explains that he had fallen asleep by the riverside "till a dream waked him, and made him see that whereof he had dreamed" (*NA* 198).[67] In the dream, Amphialus is told by the aged, bickering Venus and Diana to award sovereignty to one of them; but he shocks and angers the goddesses by choosing instead to honor their silent youthful attendant, Mira. The goddesses accept his judgment but enact their revenge:

"Yet thou shalt not go free!" quoth Venus. "Such a fire
Her beauty kindle shall within thy foolish mind
That thou full oft shalt wish thy judging eyes were blind."
"Nay! Then," Diana said, "the chastness I will give,
In ashes of despair, though burnt, shall make thee live."
"Nay! Thou," said both, "shalt see such beames shine in her face
That thou shalt never dare seek help of wretched case." (*NA* 351)

The dream was given in the *Old Arcadia* to Sidney's namesake, Philisides, who sings it in the Fourth Eclogues to "impart the sorrow" the
shepherds see in him. When Philisides wakes from the dream, he falls
in love with Mira herself, but exiles himself to Arcadia when he is
"refused all comfort."[68] Perhaps this narrative poem became the genesis of Amphialus's character, since it typifies the patterns of his life:
the discovery that his part in the world has changed radically without
his conscious control; the division of his psyche by conflicting choices and desires; and the dependence of his fate on women—Helen,
Philoclea, Zelmane (at the Ladon), Cecropia, and, in his last scene,
Helen again. The poem begins in the evening with the earth and the
dreamer in a calm repose that reflects Amphialus's just nature:

Free all my powers were from those captiving snares
Which heav'nly purest gifts defile in muddy cares;
Ne could my soul itself accuse of such a fault
As tender conscience might with furious pangs assault. (*NA* 347)

In the first part of the ensuing vision, the dreamer's soul is lifted in an
ecstasy out of "fleshly bondage" to a pastoral country where with a "single [i.e., whole] mind" he ponders the everlasting stability of the heav-
ens and the immortal soul, "the depths of things to find" (*NA* 347–48).

But the depths he finds are not those he anticipates. I quote the opening of the second vision, which shatters the first:

When lo! with hugest noise (such noise a tower makes
When it blown down with wind a fall of ruin takes,
Or such a noise it was as highest thunders send,
Or cannons thunder-like all shot together lend)
The moon asunder rent, whereout with sudden fall
More swift than falcon's stoop to feeding falconer's call
There came a chariot fair, by doves and sparrows guided,
Whose storm-like course stayed not, till hard by me it bided.
I, wretch, astonished was, and thought the deathful doom
Of heav'n, of earth, of hell, of time and place was come.
But straight there issued forth two ladies (ladies sure
They seemed to me) on whom did wait a virgin pure. (*NA* 348)

Amphialus's dream serves as a myth of erotic wonder (hence Mira's name) and captivity (through the unexpected power of the aged goddesses), like the Judgment of Paris (see "Paris' doom," *NA* 350). Awakened but overwhelmed by "deadly fear," the dreamer concludes in shock and indignation: "O coward Cupid, thus doost thou thy honour keep, / Unarmed, alas, unwarned, to take a man asleep?" (*NA* 351–52). Throughout the *Arcadia* the sudden advent of eros compels the fearful recognition that the self-sufficiency that has sustained both Amphialus and the two princes is a fiction—useful, even predominant in some forms of experience, but wholly inadequate in others.

Like God's law in Renaissance Protestant experience, eros shatters the seemingly ordered psyche and makes it acutely aware not only of its need for some Other but also of its vulnerability to unknown, unpredictable powers—ultimately, to death. Waking from his vision and falling in love with Philoclea, Prince Amphialus faces this very disorientation and vulnerability. Rising from his dream at the Ladon, he is confronted by the furious Zelmane, who wounds him in the thigh; but he cannot flee to his adoring Venus, Queen Helen, for she too signifies his loss of control. In effect, Amphialus never escapes his dream, even when later he prepares his followers for the defense of his castle. In the midst of a command, "his inward guest [Love] did so entertain him, that he would break it off" and fall "to talk with his own thoughts" (*NA* 328). Immersion in military business offers no respite, for his mind is directed without relief toward his need for the beloved and the intimation of mortality with which it haunts him:

> O sweet Philoclea! . . . Thy heavenly face is my astronomy! thy sweet virtue, my sweet philosophy! Let me profit therein—and farewell, all other cogitations. But, alas, my mind misgives me, for your planets bear a contrary aspect unto me. Woe, woe is me! They threaten my destruction. . . . And by what means will they destroy? But by loving them. (*NA* 328–29)[69]

Sidney's Amphialus is an image, arresting in its extremity, of the just soul in panic, unable to discern any pattern but that of ruin. *Amphialus* means "between two seas." It could be said that with the princesses' imprisonment he is divided between duty to Basilius and love for Philoclea, but that conflict is only symptomatic. Indeed the very closeness of the claimants in that opposition (king versus king's daughter) suggests an internal division as well. Amphialus is between two *selves*: the just self whose virtue and power lie in rational division and subjection, and a prerational, volatile self whose defense against tyranny and neglect is to draw a man into an experience like death, "crowned with the panic fear of demoralization."[70] Amphialus's dream of Mira occurs the night *before* he falls in love with Philoclea and represents an inward event as well as a "divining" of his future passion for the princess (*NA* 346).

The dream can then be read as a speaking picture of the failure of justice when confronted by neglected, vengeful desire. With the sound of a tower blown down and with the sight of the moon rent asunder the second vision in Amphialus's dream begins. The image of the tower figures the just security and intellectual reflection of the first vision. The moon is the dreamer's psyche, broken by powers ignored in the serenity and self-proclaimed innocence of the initial vision. The singleness of mind declared there is a falsehood, a deceptive fiction achieved by an act of "just" exclusion. His uplifted soul still finds itself in desire's labyrinth.

From out of the sundered moon issues a chariot guided not by Plato's charioteer of the soul but in a "storm-like course" by the sparrows and doves associated with its passengers, an enfeebled huntress and an aged wanton, "on whom did wait a virgin pure" (*NA* 348). The dream may well employ the Renaissance topos of "the decay of belief in the planetary deities,"[71] but if so Sidney puts it to ironic use. Caught up in wonder at the beauty that literally attends the old, quarrelsome goddesses of love and chastity, Amphialus naively misjudges their power over him, assuming he can enjoy the pleasures of eros without its accompanying disorientation and acute sense of vulnerability. But the dreamer errs in thinking that Venus and Diana will not attend their attendant.

Sidney leaves no doubt about the source of this error. Diana proposes that in deciding whether she or Venus should reign they yield to the dreamer's "wit" (*NA* 350), that is, to his commanding reason. The dreamer, having being appointed a judge by these warring powers and having "waxed proud that I such sway must bear," binds them to "all what I decreed" and then proclaims his "verdict" (*NA* 351). But once he chooses to crown Mira, Venus and Diana instantly reject him as an "ungodly rebel" (*NA* 351) and impose *their* sentence on him: the heartravishing beauty and heartbreaking chastity of the maid, which together will make him despair. Significantly, they cannot overturn the choice of his "judging eyes" (*NA* 351), but they exact a devastating vengeance for his presumptuous failure to acknowledge the forces they command.

Amphialus finds himself betrayed by the very consciousness, the very just and rational soul that until now has defined and sustained his life. "Was it a dream?" he asks on waking. "O dream, how hast thou wrought in me / That I things erst unseen should first in dreaming see?" (*NA* 351). The "things erst unseen" are surely an anticipatory allusion to his experience with Philoclea, but they are also a reference to those powers within his own soul whose existence he has failed to perceive until they make his choice a hell. The agony of Amphialus's confusion is deepened because there is no figure in the scheme of male justice for him to turn to: his father, his friend, and his stepfather are dead; his uncle (Basilius) is a self-exiled fool and, later, Amphialus's opponent in the rebellion.

The breakdown and division of Amphialus's rationally directed self reveals the limitations of the heroic life formed by justice. In the *New Arcadia* Sidney constructs a vocabulary for this experience, a way of "speaking metaphorically" about his inner division: the pattern of subjugation to women. Throughout the account of Amphialus's love and suffering this narrative language functions as a visible sign of the inward defeat and "demoralization" of his just self by the unsuspected force of eros. The episode with Helen and his friend Philoxenus serves as a prelude: Amphialus is stunned by her irrational preference for him and through it is compelled to kill the friend whose identity has hitherto confirmed his own. Following the dream of Mira—whether immediately or not is impossible to tell—he is wounded by the wildly jealous Zelmane when he attempts to possess even a token part of Philoclea (her glove).

During the captivity in Book Three the pattern reaches its paradoxical, ruinous climax. Cecropia has the princesses kidnapped without his knowledge, and he is "as much amazed [by her act] as if he had seen the sun fall to the earth" (*NA* 317). But in his divided condition Amphialus cannot undo her deed: "I would not for my life constrain presence—but rather would I die than consent to absence!" "Pretty, intricate follies!" replies Cecropia, who has no use for such nice distinctions (*NA* 320). From now on Amphialus is hopelessly trapped and marked for the attempted self-destruction that ends his actions in the unfinished *Arcadia*. As long as he tries to imprison Philoclea, he will be imprisoned by the ruthless machinations of Cecropia, and he will be beyond the restorative aid of Queen Helen. Sidney is not writing allegory, but he has mastered a kind of imagery that in its recurrence and poetic force gives substance to the inner life of the revised *Arcadia*'s most important new character.

From his journey to Helen's kingdom until the moment on the battlements when his wrath sends his mother falling to her death and leaves him to attempt suicide, Amphialus is challenged and undone by women. If his division is between a king and the king's daughter, as suggested earlier, then we may take the king to be his just self and the daughter to be the myriad forms of the feminine that confront him at every turn in the maze of erotic and political desire. Ironically, the defeat of the Knight of the Tomb also conforms to this inescapable pattern: when victory reveals that he has killed Parthenia, Amphialus breaks his sword and falls into melancholy rehearsal of all his vain actions. Even his attempted suicide—a final effort at conscious self-control—brings him into the arms of Helen. In every effort at domination he finds himself dominated: to assert power over the beautiful and passive Philoclea is to discover himself overpowered by a scheming and ruthless Cecropia; to overthrow Cecropia (however unintentionally) is to be borne off by the woman whose passion began his agony. By the end the point is undeniable. Amphialus cannot escape the confrontation with women because they are aspects of something that is there, for ill or for good, at the core of his soul.

Each apparent subjugation only strengthens the hand of that which will not be subjugated, but must be acknowledged as a primary power. For Amphialus, that acknowledgment cannot come before every pillar of his just, heroic life has fallen. In depicting Queen Helen as "a Diana apparelled in the garments of Venus" (*NA* 254), Sidney may well have been preparing for a re-integration through her of the enraged elements first apparent in Amphialus's dream. But the unfinished revision cannot offer us this resolution. That Queen Helen in her union of Venus and Diana recalls the idealized image of Sidney's queen suggests an analogy between Amphialus's frustration at the hands of women and Sidney's own at the court of Elizabeth. This political parallel does not diminish the insight of Sidney's meditation on the limits of male-dominated justice; in fact it may have provoked a more acute, less orthodox awareness of womanly virtue and power.

It would be false to see in Amphialus a quiescent sufferer: his fragmentation increases with each effort to exert his customary control. Amphialus's self-division is not just in the eye of the reader: he continually betrays his own consciousness of it, as when he thinks that he has conducted himself with Philoclea "as one that could neither conquer nor yield, being of the one side a slave, and of the other a jailer" (*NA* 401). This sense of inner warfare engages Amphialus in a deceptive fiction-making intended to restore some measure of lost assurance. In confrontations with his beloved, with her father, with his other foes, and with himself, he seeks to impose the old "just" order of domination and submission, even as a dishonest poet might force order on a story he has yet to comprehend. The result is to reveal the prince's designs as all the more false, and all the more ruinous.

Amphialus portrays his relation to Philoclea as one that requires him to dominate her mind and body. When the princess exposes the hypocrisy of his initial call for pity by replying, "You call for pity—and use cruelty," he insists that he is only an actor in a tragedy of another's devising: "I find myself most willing to obey you; . . . but alas! that tyrant love, which now possesseth the hold of all my life and reason, will no way suffer it" (*NA* 322–23). But Amphialus has made *tyrant* just another name for Philoclea:

> It is you yourself that imprison yourself! It is your beauty which makes these castle walls embrace you! It is your own eyes which reflect upon themselves this injury! Then is there no other remedy but that you some way vouchsafe to satisfy this love's vehemency, which, since it grew in yourself, without question you shall find it—far more than I—tractable. (*NA* 323)

In Amphialus's divided psyche, the only solution to Philoclea's "possession" of him is a reversal of the matter, by which love's vehemence will be satisfied. Her terror at this speech, which leaves her pale and shaking, should not be dismissed as the hysterics of an innocent. The prince is shocked by his mother's eventual counsel to take "by authority" from Philoclea what she will not yield him by petition (*NA* 451). But that suggestion of rape—in fact all of Cecropia's perverse means of persuasion—is nothing but the conclusion of Amphialus's own violence in trying to make Philoclea choose his own self-proclaimed position as victim. Indeed Philoclea need only look on the battlefield to see that mother and son employ the same tactic—she offering violence to Amphialus's prisoners, he to those who would set them free.

As leader of the rebellion against Basilius, Amphialus constructs an illusion of public service—the restoration of justice—to win adherents to his treason. In fact, he commissions an actual text and causes it to be published. This written justification declares that

> the weal-public was more to be regarded than any person or magistrate that thereunto was ordained; the feeling consideration whereof had moved him, though as near of kin to Basilius as could be, yet to set principally before his eyes the good estate of so many thousands over whom Basilius reigned rather than so to hoodwink himself with affection as to suffer the realm to run to manifest ruin. (*NA* 325)

This general proclamation of patriotism is followed in Amphialus's text by the announcement of his right and duty to assume the control that Basilius has abandoned to the regent Philanax and to exercise that control by protecting the princesses within his castle. In contrast to his private fictions before Philoclea, this attempt at public domination through deceptive invention is thoroughly cynical: Amphialus employs it "because he knew . . . how few there be that can discern between truth and truthlikeness, between shows and substance" (*NA* 325). And soon the prince is compelled by his original lie to make his fiction appear true, for when Philanax is captured, Amphialus "was inclined (to colour the better his action, and the more to imbrue the hands of his accomplices by making them guilty of such a trespass) . . . to cause him to be executed" (*NA* 352). Only Philoclea's intervention saves the innocent man. Comparison with Pyrocles and Musidorus's just settlement of the helots' rebellion shows that the love-divided Amphialus operates in a radically different world than did the triumphant friends. The very courage and rhetorical skills the two princes use to execute justice are used here to execute the just.

The false construction of Amphialus's rebellion reaches absurdity when he allows himself to shift from commanding general to chivalric performer. The disastrous series of encounters from the first meeting with the Black Knight (Musidorus) to the last is fashioned as a theatrical escape from the private and public burdens of his rebellion, but it proves a bloody and finally self-destructive show. This has been interpreted as Sidney's illustration of the limits of male chivalry,[72] and it may well be. But if so this demonstration takes place within a much larger indictment of the invention of justice for which Amphialus has been so grand an emblem. In the courtesy books, chivalry (that is, the management of horses in battle and in the lists) is taught as a means to gaining control over other men. Elyot recommends it because it "importeth a maistrie and drede to inferiour persons" and because in battle a "hardy horse doth some tyme more domage under his master than he with al his waipon."[73] The masterful rider enacts the part of Plato's inward charioteer.[74]

Amphialus falls into the chivalric encounters not only because they allow him to return to familiar ground but also because they take place on the safer ground of regulated combat between men. Victory belongs, predictably, to the one who justly manages his mount and the inner beast of his emotions. The first meeting with the Black Knight begins accidentally within the public battle, but is "worthy to have had more large lists, and more quiet beholders," as in a staged performance (*NA* 345). Until an old advisor calls Amphialus back to his responsibilities as general, the prince and his rival conduct a violent but decorous show as they "guided the horses' obedient courage—all done in such order that it might seem the mind was a right prince indeed, who sent wise and diligent lieutenants into each of those well-governed parts" (*NA* 345).

The formal meeting with Phalantus is still more illustrative. Amphialus responds to the written challenge by accepting and by wishing he could make of his opponent a friend (*NA* 365–66), and they engage in an even fight until Amphialus (to shield his identity) tells Phalantus that he is a novice. Enraged, Phalantus spends his strength in a vain "storm" of blows, and Amphialus then strikes him to the ground. The victor then gives his true name and says once more that it would "be honoured by the title of his friend" (*NA* 369–70). Such combat is demanding, but its rules are straightforward and unchanging, an extension of the Tudor humanist insistence that political and military control first depend on inward management and that alliance is the product of like-minded, self-sufficient men.

After Amphialus publishes a general challenge to the Basilians, his chivalric shows become increasingly unreal and, paradoxically, increasingly ruinous to others and to himself. Their setting—an island in sight of Amphialus's castle so that "the ladies may have the pleasure" of watching (*NA* 365)—and the increasingly abstract series of "causes" sent by the opponents mock the seriousness of the prince's treason and the scores of those who die in the military battles. Amphialus now kills some of his opponents in the lists, including Argalus and Parthenia (the Knight of the Tomb), both of whom are defeated through a fatal loss of emotional control—he by losing his temper, she by losing her will to live. But with Parthenia's death Amphialus is returned to the confusion and mental anguish of his dream. The rules change without warning, and he falls into a desperate melancholy, responding to Cecropia's scolding "with a broken, piecemeal speech, as if the tempest of passion unorderly blew out his words" (*NA* 400 – 401).

The performance is both renewed and ended when Amphialus again meets the Black (Forsaken) Knight, Musidorus. Amphialus rides to the island wearing newly chosen armor all of black, "as if he would turn his inside outward"; he discovers his opponent "attired in his own livery," and mounted, like himself, on a black horse (*NA* 404). This furniture suggests melancholy, but also the unruly passions in Plato's equestrian metaphor of the soul. For each combatant, the sight of a mirror image only intensifies his fury: in this last chivalric show both players lose their inner control, and neither emerges triumphant. Significantly, in the initial, confused exchange of accusations and insults, Amphialus abandons the decorum of fighting in the lists at all, for "never staying either judge, trumpet, or his own lance, [he] drew out his sword" and attacked (*NA* 405). Unintentionally, Amphialus kills the Black Knight's horse, and the rest of the long battle takes place on foot. In the end, each man, overcome with weakness and rage, must be dragged from the stage by his seconds and left to berate himself for failure. Amphialus, back in his castle and grievously wounded in soul as well as body, not only reproaches himself for cowardice but also threatens literally to tear himself apart. He matches his speeches "with such effects of rage (as sometimes offering to tear up his wounds . . .) that his perplexed mother was driven to make him by force to be tended" (*NA* 414). The order of domination and submission has been carried beyond its capacity to make sense of experience, carried to the point where the only act remaining is to subjugate—this time by elimination—oneself.

Amphialus's attempted suicide is his final, ironic effort to restore the just order of his soul. Weakened by the inconclusive battle with Musidorus and learning all at once the fullness of Cecropia's torture of the princesses, "he needed no judge to go upon him, for no man could ever think any other worthy of greater punishment than he thought himself" (*NA* 440). After Cecropia—thinking her son's drawn sword meant for herself—has fallen to her death, Amphialus fashions one final and possibly fatal drama of justice. Taking up Philoclea's knives, he kisses one and says,

> O dear knives! You are come in a good time to revenge the wrong I have done you all this while, in keeping you from her blessed side. . . . Ah Philoclea! . . . I would yet thou knewest how I love thee. Unworthy I am! Unhappy I am! False I am! But to thee, alas, I am not false. But what a traitor am I, any way to excuse him whom she condemneth! Since there is nothing left me wherein I may do her service, but in punishing him who hath so offended her, dear knife, then do your noble mistress's commandment! (*NA* 442)

The delusion of forcing experience into a pattern that no longer can define the complexity of Amphialus's soul drives the knife of his beloved into his heart, even as his proud mistaken judgment in the dream of Mira first rent it asunder.

It is not possible to regard Amphialus as a conventional lesson in the dangers of failing to maintain a just soul. He is not the bad exception that proves the rule but the "ornament of his age"[75] whose fall exposes the limitations of the age itself—here in its invention of justice. We need to remember that his inner just ordering and the friendship that seals and signifies it are overcome *before* Amphialus falls in love with Philoclea. The sincere but destructive passion of Queen Helen makes clear that it is not only Amphialus who changes in the narrative; it is the world in which he moves and has his being. Even while revealing all the prince's flaws, Sidney keeps us from rejecting him as wholly unworthy by stressing his loyalty to Philoxenus, his initial innocence in the plot to kidnap the princesses, and his courtesy in contrast to the braggart Anaxius, who tells him during the rebellion that "you do debase your self" to be captivated by the "peevish, paltry sex, not worthy to communicate with my virtues" (*NA* 391). But finally it is Pyrocles and Musidorus who convince us that Amphialus represents the power and the vulnerability of Tudor humanist justice, for their experience is often (as the last battle with the Black Knight illustrates) a mirror of his own.

Oddly enough, in Amphialus's strivings to fashion a fictional self lies the possibility of a recovery. His divided psyche compels an effort at invention that fails because it seeks to impose a discredited ethic on alien experience, to hold new wine in old skins. But this is a case of a man's wit abusing poetry, not of poetry itself playing the man false. Unlike Pyrocles and Musidorus, Amphialus has no leisure in which to invent alternative fictions, so relentless and so manifold are the assaults within his warring soul. But as the two princes who share his experience of love reveal, to counterfeit is not always to deceive.

3

The Invention of Eros

Thus gan he make a mirour of his mynde
In which he saugh al holly hire figure,
And that he wel koude in his herte fynde.
It was to hym a right good aventure
To love swich oon, and if he dede his cure
To serven hir, yet myghte he falle in grace,
Or ellis for oon of hire servantz pace.
                    —Chaucer, *Troilus and Criseyde*

Though it will exact great pain, Troilus's act of absolute devotion proves to be the heroic "aventure" envisioned by his love-struck imagination. The narrator has no doubt that Troilus becomes a greater man when he sets his beloved's image at the center of his heart: devoted love makes him "the frendlieste wight, / The gentilest, and ek the mooste fre"—the best possible knight.[1] The courtly, Petrarchan, and romance traditions that composed the discourse of love written and read by Philip Sidney's Tudor generation diverge in many particulars, but they share a faith in the nobility of radical abandonment of one's self to the image and interest of another. Like the Tudor humanist invention of justice, this "invention fine" of eros became a means by which to re-present and to manage difficult experience, a way to extend moral and imaginative control. In fact, this invention exists in a curious relation to the "just" virtue of achieving self-sufficient knowledge and power through inward and political domination. Where such justice fails, eros can succeed: surrender becomes victory when by yielding himself to the beloved, the suffering lover is reborn to *la vita nuova*.

This chapter examines Sidney's feigning of erotic virtue, with reference to *Astrophil and Stella* and the *Defence of Poetry*, but concentrating on the full "heroic" representation of eros in the *New Arcadia*. There, as with justice, Sidney tests eros by feigning a series of contrasting narratives. Against the foil of grasping, debilitating desire in Dido and Pamphilus, Andromana, and Gynecia, the selfless devotion of such figures as Palladius and Zelmane, Plangus, and Argalus and Parthenia shines bright in the *New Arcadia*. But as with justice, this heroic invention is extended beyond its power to make sense of human pain and aspiration. It is not merely self-aggrandizing desire that Sidney tests and finds wanting; it is the entire discourse of love that governed much of the best poetry of his age, including his own.

I

This discourse is too familiar to need a full rehearsal.[2] Readers will recognize its central sentiment in the closing lines of Sidney's *Certain Sonnet* 25:

> Thus may I not be from you:
> Thus be my senses on you:
> Thus what I thinke is of you:
> Thus what I seeke is in you:
> All what I am, it is you.[3]

Godlike eros in the courtly, Petrarchan, and romance traditions begins with the capture of the lover's senses but quickly overtakes the mind so that identification with the beloved is complete: I (the new I) am you. Love's victory enlarges the territory of the spirit. It makes Troilus "To honouren hem that hadde worthynesse, / And esen hem that weren in destresse" (3.1789–90) and grants Petrarch both the need and the poetic power to construct "*tutte le carte / ov'io fama l'acquisto.*"[4] But such liberation is won at the price of captivity to the person or image of the beloved, so that desperation always lies close to joy. When Criseyde falls apparently lifeless at the realization that she must leave both Troy and Troilus, her lover draws his sword to take his life; in the *Rime*, as David Kalstone writes, the stress changes continually from the renewal of poetic imagination to "the fearful exhaustion, the painful frustration of separation from Laura."[5] From this exhilarating but terrifying dependence there is no release except in the forsaking of all earthly desire: Troilus can laugh at human sorrow only when life is over and heaven is sure; Petrarch seeks escape from his poetic addiction to forever lost beauty only in his final appeal to the Blessed Virgin and his pledge to sing *her* glory.

The desperation of eros appears even more plainly in the three direct romance sources for Sidney's *Arcadia*: desperation is the engine that

drives their plots and their songs.   A. C. Hamilton writes that Sannazaro's *Arcadia* (1504) evokes "the happy memory of the Garden of
Eden but also the nostalgic awareness that man's life within it has been
irretrievably lost.   In its innocent life, it is man's true home;   but it is
also a forbidden place of death."[6]   Ralph Nash notes in his translation
of Sannazaro that this "genre devoted to the celebration of love may be
in some danger of becoming a celebration of sickness and death";   he
cites the illness and longing for dissolution in Sannazaro's lovers: Sin-
cero, Clonus, and Carion, this last being brought to the verge of suicide.[7]   In the opening sequence of Heliodorus's *Æthiopian History*
(translated 1569), Cariclea and Theagenes are eager to die when each
thinks the other lost or slain.   But it is in Montemayor's *Diana* (1559)
that the perils of erotic abandon strike most forcefully.   In a story close
to Pyrocles' account of young Zelmane's devotion to him, Montemay-
or's Felismena disguises herself as a page to serve her beloved Don
Felix.   But in this disguise she finds herself loved by another woman,
Celia, who cries out to her in despair: "I will have no other remedie for
the harme, which thou hast done me, but death it selfe, the which with
mine owne hands I will take in satisfaction of that which thou deser-
vest."[8]   Celia's death that very night fulfills this threat.

These late medieval and Renaissance representations of eros offered
to Sidney's aristocratic, humanist circle the means to shape the disruptive power of desire by making it the source of noble action, of poetry, of liberating wonder.   But in all cases there is no escape from the
terrible dependence on another, single soul.   Rarely in these traditions
does eros lead to the mundane business of ordinary marriage, with its
sometimes irksome but saving demands of children and domestic economy.   It is not until after Sidney's death that wedded love becomes a
central concern of English poetry in the work of Spenser, Shakespeare,
Donne, and others.   For Sidney's earlier generation there was another
possible means of achieving through eros a lasting liberation from sorrow and fear: the heady promises of Florentine neoplatonism.   But by
the time he revised *Arcadia* Sidney had lost whatever faith or substantial interest he had ever had in Plato's and Ficino's ladder of love.[9]

Marsilio Ficino and the most influential popularizer of his ideas,
Baldassare Castiglione, tell their readers that the light of beautiful
goodness in a particular man or woman leads one to consider the goodness shining through earthly beauty in general.   The lover is then
drawn by stages toward enjoyment of and union with God, beauty's
Source.   Love acts as a magnetic power carrying the soul away from
what Castiglione calls "bodies subject to corruption, that . . . be
nothinge elles but dreames and most thin shadowes of beauty."[10]   That
this runs counter to even the most paradigmatic patterns of love in the

revised *Arcadia* becomes evident in the story's first scene, which has sometimes been read as a paean to neoplatonic rapture.[11]

Placing the scene in the season when "the earth begins to put on her new apparel against the approach of her lover" (*NA* 3), Sidney evokes the fecund springtime reunion of earth with sun. Such wedded joy and promise of fruitfulness clash immediately with the sorrow of Strephon and Claius as they enact the rites of remembrance for their beloved, absent Urania. But the physicality of the opening sentences, the bond of love with earthly delight, remains:

> Yonder, my Claius, Urania lighted. The very horse, methought, bewailed to be so disburdened; and as for thee, poor Claius, when thou wentst to help her down, I saw reverence and desire so divide thee that thou didst at one instant both blush and quake, and instead of bearing her, wert ready to fall down thyself. There, she sate vouchsafing my cloak (then most gorgeous) under her. At yonder rising of the ground, she turned herself, looking back toward her wonted abode. . . . At that turning, she spake unto us all, opening the cherry of her lips—and Lord! how greedily mine ears did feed upon the sweet words she uttered! And here, she laid her hand over thine eyes when she saw the tears springing in them, as if she would conceal them from other, and yet herself feel some of thy sorrow. But (woe is me) yonder, yonder did she put her foot into the boat, at that instant, as it were, dividing her heavenly beauty between the earth and the sea. But when she was embarked did you not mark how the winds whistled and the seas danced for joy, how the sails did swell with pride, and all because they had Urania? (*NA* 4)

Like Stella's, the shepherdess's beauty may be heavenly, but in the shepherds' memory Urania appears charged with a radiant physical energy. The neoplatonist's passion is inspired by sight; in its higher forms it will not condescend to touch. Echoing Ficino, Castiglione's Pietro Bembo pleads that the lover "laye aside the blind judgemente of the sense" to avoid falling "into the most deepe erroures."[12] But though his desire remains chaste, Sidney's Strephon obeys no such strictures. For him, it is unthinkable "to leave those steps unkissed wherein Urania printed the farewell of all beauty" (*NA* 3), to forget the gorgeousness of the cloak beneath her, the parting of her lips, the pressure of her hands on her lover's weeping eyes. Even the joy of ship and sea in receiving her is palpable.

All this is now loss to the shepherds, but their "desire to seem worthy in her eyes" (*NA* 5) has engendered a liberating understanding. Has she not made us, says Claius, "to mark our selves? Hath not she thrown reason upon our desires, and, as it were, given eyes unto Cupid? Hath in any, but in her, love-fellowship maintained friendship between rivals, and beauty taught the beholders chastity?" (*NA* 5). The power of love to inspire virtue would be familiar to any reader of Chaucer's *Troilus* or Petrarch's *Rime*. What matters here is that the shepherds never turn away from their image of the woman herself—either from her "unspeakable virtues" or from the "best-builded fold" of her body (*NA* 5), recalled with the ardor of the Song of Songs.[13] Ficino's advice, paraphrased from Plato's Diotima, would be sacrilege to Sidney's lovers:

> You value little the beauty of each man . . . if you compare it with your Idea [of beauty distilled from many individuals]. You possess that, not thanks to the bodies, but thanks to your own soul. So love that image which your soul created and that soul itself, its creator, rather than that crippled and scattered exterior.[14]

Strephon and Claius cherish the image of Urania, but what they yearn for is *her*, her physical, living presence. To withdraw from her "crippled exterior" to contented contemplation of their own souls would be a betrayal. Urania may be called platonic in being a good and beautiful goal, delivering the soul from an idle and pedestrian consciousness, but she is neither abstract Good nor a mere shadow to be forgotten in the philosopher's quest for that Good. In the event, the shepherds' bittersweet Petrarchan rites are cut off by sight of a man (Musidorus) washed ashore, and it is in this moment that the opening scene functions as a pattern of love in the *New Arcadia*. Devotion to the beloved can ennoble, but it cannot forestall danger and disaster. The shepherds retain their love for Urania, but they must set its pains and satisfactions aside to act in response to the urgent demands of present experience.

When he came to revise his *Arcadia*, Sidney had already tested the neoplatonic way of love and love poetry and found it wanting.[15] Sidney would have rejected neoplatonism on both religious and poetic grounds. Charmed by Castiglione's Cardinal Bembo, we can easily forget that neoplatonism has little interest in what we call romantic love and none whatever in the messy business of daily conjugal life. Ficino's famous "Venus is two-fold" passage—allowing for the earthly Venus of generation as well as "that intelligence . . . in the Angelic mind" that prompts one to seek "the beauty of God"—is misleadingly cited if used to suggest any substantial interest in the "erotic" love between a man and woman.[16] Such love need not enter the matter at all, as I will note in a moment. In its Italian sources, neoplatonism is a mental and moral discipline designed to win for its initiates union with divine beauty, mind, and power.

Thomas Greene writes that in Pico della Mirandolla's *Oration on the Dignity of Man* the "really astonishing aspect . . . is the reliance Pico places on a pedagogical curriculum to elevate him to the Godhead."[17]

Although this curriculum varies from Ficino (Pico's teacher) to Pico to the monomaniacal claims of Giordano Bruno, it always depends on assigning to the human soul a place and power beyond the limits of physical nature and original sin. For Ficino, this soul, "greatest of all miracles in nature," "the center of all things, . . . the bond and juncture of the universe," enables those who cultivate it properly to attain divinity in the life that follows death.[18]

Pico attributes to man "a rank to be envied not only by brutes but even by the stars and by minds beyond this world."[19] Ficino's central location of the soul is too modest: Pico's Adam is wholly free to "fashion thyself in whatever shape thou shalt prefer."[20] Bruno, finding in Copernican heliocentrism the recovery of the divine light of truth, and embracing the magic of the *Hermetica,* declares that he himself "has thrown wide those doors of truth which it is within our power to open." Bruno's wisdom can now make of man a god, for "divinity dwells within through the reformed intellect and will."[21]

This act of self-reforming begins in intellectual vision and proceeds by divorce from all things bodily. In the *Commentary on Plato's Symposium* Ficino posits a hierarchy through which love descended from God to physical being: God himself exists beyond even the eternal world and is one; next is the Angelic Mind, the eternal realm of multiple Ideas created by God; then comes the World Soul, the middle element between Mind and Body, partly subject to time; and below the Soul is the World Body, the realm perceived by sense, moving only through the agency of Soul and entirely subject to time.[22] Only by retracing upward the descent of love's divine light can the devotee hope to enjoy the pleasure of divine beauty. This climb requires the rejection of the physical for the sake of higher understanding and control. In Plato's own work, Diotima accommodates those "pregnant" of body, who satisfy their desire for "engendering and begetting upon the beautiful" through fathering children, yet she elevates those pregnant of soul, whose love fathers virtue.[23]

Ficino acknowledges the necessity of the lesser Venus, but argues that loving men and adults carries one higher than loving women and children, since the former excel in that intellectual beauty "most essential to knowledge."[24] Later he says bluntly that those who seek a higher beauty must "subtract" all beneath it.[25] Castiglione's Bembo maintains that beauty increases in perfection the less "she is coopled with that vile subject," the body, and urges the male lover to control not only himself but "with lessons and good exhortations" to check the appetites of his lady.[26] Indeed, when a lover on the first step of devotion is enkindled by *universal* beauty, he "shall not passe upon the lesser, and burnynge in a more excellent flame, he shall little esteame it, that he sett great store by at the first."[27] Pico scorns not only the earthly but even the celestial as a stain on the divine within the human soul: "Who will touch the ladder of the Lord with either fouled foot or unclean hands?"[28] For such a mental traveler to confine himself to anything so inconsequential as an individual woman would be, paraphrasing Jaques, to shackle Jove in a thatched house.

"Augustine says that he found all things in the Platonic books except this one thing, that the Word was made flesh."[29] Martin Luther's declaration of the limits of philosophy can frame discussion of Sidney's response to neoplatonic thought. To one who lamented the "infected will" that keeps us from achieving perfection and who valued the "poetical part of Scripture" for bearing "the consolation of the never-leaving goodness" to those "in sorrowful pangs of their death-bringing sins" (*DP* 79, 80), the neoplatonic deification of the soul would have seemed false to doctrine and to experience. The incarnation of God in Christ reverses the neoplatonic way: God reaches down; humanity does not climb up. The Creator's grace frees his creatures to do good work (like writing poetry); but in all orthodox Protestant theology, popular and academic, no intellectual discipline can *achieve* that grace.

The divergence is as great in Christian ethics as in its understanding of salvation, for the force of Ficino's quest carries his disciples away from Christ's demand that his followers imitate him in loving the unlovely, humbling themselves even to a cross. The dramatic sixth speech of Ficino's *Commentary* begins by banishing the unclean, the impure: "go far from his heavenly feast, ye profane, go hence, I say, you who [are] covered with earthly stains."[30] At such a feast there is no place for the woman taken in adultery, for the prodigal son, nor for any person not enamored by "perpetual joy of mind."[31] How different the feast that concludes the "heavenly discourse of the lost child and the gracious father" praised by Sidney in the *Defence* (*DP* 87).

We can assume that the Protestant Sidney found neoplatonism false in part because the poet Sidney so plainly found it a distortion of experience. Arguing that "Sidney perceived and made important allowances for earthly experience," Dorothy Connell writes that in the *Defence* he

> suggests that well-doing is in fact tested as much by falling into a ditch [like the hapless astronomer] as by looking at the stars. When Sidney later wrote of Astrophil's love, he chose to describe the experience of his hero in terms of the same story. For love makes Astrophil
>
> > . . . fare like him that both
> > Lookes to the skies, and in a ditch doth fall.[32]

Astrophil's confrontation with the unreality of neoplatonic aspirations, his habit of moving "down the Platonic ladder,"[33] is familiar to all readers of the sequence. What is worth stressing here is that he continually associates the neoplatonic scheme for virtue with the intellectual static generated, almost mechanically, by conventional court discourse. This should not surprise us. Neoplatonic love—practiced by learned men to command those "passions to which other men are slaves"—is in fact the most intoxicating form of that humanist justice so dear to Elizabethan courtiers. As I argued above, Sidney both admired this justice and found false its claims to define and direct human nature. To travel inward and upward beyond the shadow of earthly existence would be to Sidney an extreme and distorting act of such justice, scorning all that is physical and subject to time. Despite Astrophil's many and obvious failings, addiction to this Faustian dream of superior knowledge and power is not one of them.

From the first sonnet on, Astrophil insists that his verse comes from the heart: poetry springs not from reductive convention but from looking directly at his experience of loving Stella. He practices an Aristotelian poetics—an imitation of what the poet observes in human life and transforms in the zodiac of his wit—rather than composition inspired by rapt contemplation of ideal virtue. To Astrophil, loving Stella becomes a discovery of the complexity and intractable quality of experience: he understands that earthly beauty "can be but a shade," yet "I must *Stella* love" (*AS* 5.10, 14); he writes "To ease / A burthned hart" but encounters "*Stella's* great powrs, that so confuse my mind" (*AS* 34.1–2, 14); like Petrarch he sees in his beloved "How Vertue may best lodg'd in beautie be," yet "Desire still cries, 'give me some food'" (*AS* 71.2, 14).

To represent such experience requires "a feeling skill" (*AS* 2.14) at odds with the courtier's conviction that by an act of virtuous will an educated and prudent man can bypass or appropriate for his own advancement the multiple claims of desire. Nowhere is that conviction clearer than in the advice offered in the twenty-first sonnet:

> Your words my friend (right healthfull caustiks) blame
> 　　My young mind marde, whom *Love* doth windlas so,
> 　　That mine owne writings like bad servants show
> My wits, quicke in vaine thoughts, in vertue lame:
> That *Plato* I read for nought, but if he tame
> 　　Such coltish gyres, that to my birth I owe
> Nobler desires, least else that friendly foe,
> Great expectation, weare a traine of shame.
> 　　For since mad March great promise made of me,
> If now the May of my yeares much decline,
> What can be hoped my harvest time will be?
> Sure you say well, your wisdome's golden mine
> 　　Dig deepe with learning's spade, now tell me this,
> 　　Hath this world ought so faire as *Stella* is?

The tone here recalls Sidney's replies to Hubert Languet's overwrought demands for exemplary conduct and vigilant ambition. Astrophil's friend has appealed to their shared rhetoric of self-control for the purpose of private virtue and public gain, citing both nature ("to my birth I owe / Nobler desires") and education ("*Plato* I read for nought") to shame the lover into right action. Not only in his loving but in his "owne writings" he betrays this definitive moral and political code, out of control on the chariot of his soul.[34] None of it avails: learning can find in "wisdome's golden mine" no answer to the beauty of Stella; her undeniable reality makes legitimate both what he feels and what he writes.

Sidney is not Astrophil, though the many biographical references invite us to see an analogy between them—the author finding value and legitimacy in his unelected vocation, his persona finding them in his response to Stella. Whatever else happens in *Astrophil and Stella*, Sidney paints with "feeling skill" his discovery that the courtly discourse of neoplatonic love can no longer represent the labyrinthine paths of human perception and human longing. Sidney's decision to revise the *Arcadia*, his decision to *elect* the vocation of a poetry immersed in the particulars of this "too much loved earth" (*DP* 78), was itself a rejection of the arts that promised pleasure and power to those who separated themselves from it.

II

Sidney inherited not only the courtly conventions of eros but also the convention of representing love pictorially for the sake of moral instruction. In manuscripts belonging to his family and friends, he would have been impressed by picture after picture of heroic and amatory import (Amazons, Hercules, Eros, St. George), offering what Rosemund Tuve calls "hosts of familiar but vivid pictured 'examples.'"[35] As a courtier Sidney enacted (and may have composed) a speaking picture designed to provoke a moral choice in love. The Four Foster Children of Desire was performed at the Whitsuntide tournament in 1581 and featured a plea by the Foster Children that the Queen "no longer exclude vertuous Desire from perfect Beautie." When Elizabeth refused to grant their request, one sonneteer urged before her the demands of desire that "no forces can withhold" and another the remorse that follows if desire has its way. Not surprisingly, Elizabeth favored the latter's suit, and the Foster Children vowed to be "slaves to this Fortresse for ever."[36] This tradition of pictorial exempla appears in the European sources for the *Arcadia* too, as in the painted scenes above the temple door in Sannazaro's work[37] and in the pictures on the obelisk at Felicia's court in the *Diana:* "histories and examples of chaste Ladies worthie to be eternized with immortal fame thorow the whole world."[38]

The convention of representing love through didactic pictures is pervasive enough to shape Pyrocles' conversation in the *New Arcadia*. As he recalls for Musidorus the scene in which he watched Philoclea as the equally smitten Basilius and Gynecia watched him, Pyrocles entitles it "a notable dumb show of Cupid's kingdom" (*NA* 88). In fact, Pyrocles can read the stories of other lovers as portraits of viciousness and virtue in love. He tells his beloved Philoclea about Andromana's perverse desire so that "by the foil thereof you may see the nobleness of my desire to you" (*NA* 250). He invokes for the princess the devotion of Queen Helen to Amphialus

> because you may see by her example . . . that neither folly is the cause of vehement love, nor reproach the effect; for never, I think, was there any woman that with more unremovable determination gave herself to the counsel of love (after she had once set before her mind the worthiness of your cousin Amphialus), and yet is neither her wisdom doubted of, nor honour blemished. (*NA* 254)

But Pyrocles *misreads* Helen's story—perhaps because he is using it to gain Philoclea's affection. The public Helen, Queen of Corinth, may well appear "a Diana apparelled in the garments of Venus," as Pyrocles calls her (*NA* 254), and we cannot doubt her absolute commitment to Amphialus or her charitable offices in restoring the disfigured Parthenia to beauty. Yet her sudden, passionate rejection of Philoxenus, the friend whose suit to Helen Amphialus has pleaded, proves ruinous. The scorned lover, convinced he has been betrayed, hunts down Amphialus and provokes a fight in which Philoxenus dies at Amphialus's hand. Folly may not be "the cause of vehement love," but it is clearly the effect. Indeed it is Helen's willingness to sacrifice everything on the altar of Eros—her beloved's friend and her abandoned country—that makes her inadequate as the example Pyrocles offers.

That Sidney can think of narrative pictorially is certain. His defense of the singular teaching and moving value of poetry depends on it:

> No doubt the philosopher with his learned definitions—be it of virtue, vices, matters of public policy or private government—replenisheth the memory with many infallible grounds of wisdom, which, notwithstanding, lie dark before the imaginative and judging power, if they be not illuminated or figured forth by the speaking picture of poesy. (*DP* 86)

For Sidney it is this "feigning notable images of virtues, vices, or what else, . . . which must be the right describing note to know a poet by"

(*DP* 81–82). Jon S. Lawry has written most fully on the practice of pictorial poetry in the *New Arcadia*, arguing that "Pictures tend to inform the action, on the one hand [those in Kalander's summerhouse and at Phalantus' tournament, for example], and narratives tend to recede into a collection of instructive tableaus on the other." Lawry analyzes "processionally" the pictorial narratives of the lovers whose stories weave in and out of the princes', discovering their "meaning as it accumulates."[39]

Yet I would stress the distinction between the "speaking picture" of love *within* the story—the picture the characters themselves "read"— and the speaking picture which *is* the story. The *New Arcadia*—what we read—functions as such a picture. But it is designed to question the invention of eros as Sidney found it in contemporary poetry, including its representation in such contrasting exemplary stories as Pyrocles invokes when trying to win Philoclea. Neither Andromana nor Helen— the prince's morally bad and good examples—doubts the validity of eros as the cause and end of human action, nor, in his passion, does Pyrocles. The "debate" of contrasting narratives witnessed by the *New Arcadia*'s four young lovers continually privileges what may be called the noble love of such figures as Helen or Argalus and Parthenia. The larger question of whether even well-intentioned passion matches the complexity of experience is outside its bounds. Yet though the narrative parade of contrasting lovers is "still . . . compassed within the circle of a question according to the proposed matter" (*DP* 78), the full story is not. It is the action of the *Arcadia* as a whole, not any of its variously admirable and flawed figures, that fashions the speaking picture we must read.

III

We encounter the procession of lovers in a sequence of opposing pairs that urges us to choose between two extremes of eros: the corrosive desire for mere possession of another and the self-denying ardor for absolute communion with another's life and interest. Pyrocles' appalled observation of the jaded Dido and Pamphilus is quickly countered in his experience with the innocent, self-sacrificial Zelmane and Palladius; accounts of the politically shrewd but sexually crazed Andromana are interwoven with the erotic *bildungsroman* of Prince Plangus, loyal to the imprisoned Erona; and as the princes discover the amorous folly of Basilius and the soul-destroying infatuation of his wife they hear the story and witness the marriage of mutually constant Argalus and Parthenia. Notably, this series of contrasts does *not* present an opposition of physical to "pure" love, nor of cringing fear to daring. Zelmane and Palladius seem presexual beings, but Plangus is fully experienced, and Argalus and Parthenia conclude their passion in marriage. On the other side of the tableau, with the exception of Pamphilus even the morally corrupt lovers may be termed "heroic" in the sense of risking everything to achieve their heart's desire. No one would call Gynecia timid.

Sidney's contrast of erotic extremes makes love as jailer and torturer the foil to love as liberator and healer. And in each case the former poisons family and civil bonds while the latter honors and defends them. For Dido and Pamphilus, Andromana, Gynecia, and to some extent Amphialus, the urgency of desire is such an affront to self-possession that it prompts them to seek satisfaction in ownership and abuse—verbal or physical—of the one they hold responsible. And so to Pyrocles, the wretched Gynecia cries, "I am forced to fly to thee for succour, whom I accuse of all my hurt; and make thee judge of my cause, who art the only author of my mischief" (*NA* 123). (Amphialus will later press almost identical charges against the captive Philoclea.) Though the remnants of conscience restrain Gynecia from violence, no such scruples trouble Dido and Pamphilus or Andromana, all of whom capture or imprison those they desire—Dido and Pamphilus each other, Andromana the two princes, whom she "with equal ardour . . . affected" (*NA* 249).

Andromana attempts to make "force . . . the school of love" (*NA* 251), but it is in Dido and Pamphilus that eros degenerates most terribly to ownership and intimacy to mutilation. In a dark, tree-enclosed landscape that would feel like the country of Freudian nightmare if it were not for a Sidnean hint of farce, Pyrocles finds a woman who admits that the appeal of a notorious philanderer to her is the thrill of mere possession:

> I must confess even in the greatest tempest of my judgement was I never driven to think him excellent, and yet so could set my mind both to get and keep him, as though therein had lain my felicity—like them I have seen play at the ball grow extremely earnest who should have the ball, and yet everyone knew it was but a ball. (*NA* 238)

The erotic fury displayed by Dido and the other jilted women who assail Pamphilus with bodkins is simply the end point of this perverse ambition—reversing the abuse he has enjoyed at their expense. And so the scene that parallels this one, in which the rescued Pamphilus whips a bound Dido and intends to murder her before her father's eyes, is pathetically predictable. Equally predictable in such possessive longing is the inner constriction and panic that drives Andromana, as well as Amphialus, to attempt suicide.

Sidney makes the contrast of these doomed figures with his self-sacrificial lovers as clear as possible, for the latter are as radical in service as the former in abuse. For them the beloved's interest is the defining imperative of life, as Plangus reveals in his response to the suggestion that he moderate his passion for the imprisoned Erona: "O soul, whose love in her is only spent, / Whate'er you see, think, touch, kiss, speak, or love, / Let all for her, and unto her, be bent" (*NA* 202). All these lovers are would-be liberators: Zelmane (with Palladius's help) of the princes from Andromana's dungeon; Plangus of Erona from Artaxia's castle; and one could add, with some allowances, Helen of Amphialus from his bondage to false love. The young, more or less asexual passions of Palladius and Zelmane—he for her, she for Pyrocles—offer the simplest version of the pattern common to all. Pyrocles remembers that she "felt with me what I felt of my captivity, and straight laboured to redress my pain (which was her pain)" (*NA* 252). Such capacity to project oneself into the mind of the beloved for his or her good divides Zelmane radically from Dido and Pamphilus, as does Palladius's willingness to aid her in rescuing Pyrocles despite his own desires.

The suicidal mechanisms that govern the likes of Andromana are countered in their opposites by a convergence of interest with the beloved's that enables them to resist hopelessness in unrequited passion. The Iberian Plangus, hated by his father and unloved by Erona, insists that he "must live some help for her to try / Though in despair, for love so forceth me. / Plangus doth live, and shall Erona die?" (*NA* 201). Even in Queen Helen, morally complex as she is, this identification with the beloved nurtures courage and charity. When in Book Three she learns of Amphialus's wounds in battle with the Black Knight, "full of loving care which she was content even to publish to the world, how ungratefully soever he dealt with her," she wins the king's permission to try to restore him (*NA* 443). On finding him apparently lifeless, she faints, but when urged by an old man that "it was fitter to show her love in carrying the body to her excellent surgeon, . . . than only show herself a woman-lover in fruitless lamentations," she sets off with her beloved to Corinth (*NA* 445). Indeed there is, with some adjustment for Renaissance decorum of gender, an equality of doing and suffering in all these figures that makes the counselor's slur of "woman-lover" unjust. Palladius endures silently his rejection and also fights out of love to free the princes; Zelmane accepts Pyrocles' inability to return her love and enlists in service as his page; and so on. Sidney does not in these secondary figures (or in any of the principals) reject active "male" virtue in favor of passive "female" patience. He gives both human goods the fullest possible honor.[40]

The sharp distinction between the two sets of lovers extends from the ethic to the politic consideration, for the corrupt figures destroy the familial and civic orders that their opposites uphold. Andromana, imagining "that the enamelling of a prince's name [Plangus's] might hide the spots of a broken wedlock" (NA 216), betrays her first husband. Once made Queen, she attempts to betray her new husband and to engineer the death of her former lover when he rejects her renewed advances. Amphialus's passion provokes civil war. Only the story of Gynecia equals that of Amphialus in its psychological intricacy and in its potential extrapersonal effects. In her Pyrocles discovers an inward violence that threatens ruin to more than the queen herself. He tells his cousin that

> all her countenances, words, and gestures are miserable portraitures of a desperate affection, whereby a man may learn that these avoidings of company [the royal family's retreat from public life] do but make the passions more violent when they meet with fit subjects. (NA 87–88)

Gynecia's downfall into eros is presented in the language of war, as when she leaves Pyrocles "with such a battle in her thoughts, and so deadly an overthrow given to her best resolutions, that even her body, where the field was fought, was oppressed withal" (NA 124).

This inner combat, heightened rather than tempered by her stricken conscience, leads Gynecia to self-directed violence when she "furiously tare off great part of her fair hair" as a "miserable sacrifice" to her "forgotten virtue" (NA 224). But it also is presented as spinning in wider and more destructive circles beyond her. This appears most clearly in her poisoned image of her rival for Pyrocles, Philoclea, towards whom now "nature gives place. The growing of my daughter [in his affection] seems the decay of my self; . . . the fair face of Philoclea appears more horrible in my sight than the image of death" (NA 279). And as Jon Lawry has emphasized, Sidney introduces the wild rabble who threaten the royal family just as Gynecia casts away loyalty to husband and daughter.[41] Turning to Pyrocles, the queen begins to reveal "the storehouse of her deadly desires," when she and the fearful prince are "overtaken by an unruly sort of clowns . . . which like a violent flood were carried, they themselves knew not whither" (NA 280). Associating her "deadly" longing with the rebels does not of course indicate that she *causes* their mutiny; it does however bring to a climax (before the narrative shift to Amphialus in Book Three) her moral degeneracy. She has fallen to their level of madness. In her Eros has become a tyrant deity, "deadly" first to her own virtue, but threatening now to pull all those around her—husband, daughter, even Pyrocles himself—into the vortex of her own furious heart.

Sidney's more noble lovers honor those familial and patriotic obligations cast aside by Andromana, Amphialus, and Gynecia. Zelmane honors her father, Plexirtus, despite his wickedness, and exacts from Pyrocles a promise to "pardon my father the displeasure you have justly conceived against him" and rescue him from "present danger of a cruel death" (*NA* 268, 266). Plangus, too, remains loyal to his father and king despite the loveblinded sovereign's efforts to destroy his son. Sidney's Argalus dutifully completes the Herculean labors assigned him by Parthenia's mother, who favors another suitor to her daughter; he tries to rescue his friend Clitophon from the helots; and he answers Basilius's call to arms against Amphialus, despite his new wife's pleas. Most memorable, however, is the fidelity Argalus and Parthenia display to one another. The only pair of lovers in the story to marry, they maintain before marriage a truth to their beloved's interest that comes as close as possible—in Sidney's pre-Christian setting—to honoring the church's institution of wedlock. The hideous disfigurement of Parthenia's face caused by Demogoras's poison shocks Argalus:

> But within a while, truth of love which still held the first face in his memory, a virtuous constancy and even a delight to be constant, faith given, and inward worthiness shining through the foulest mists, took so full hold of the noble Argalus [that he pressed] . . . to hasten the celebration of their marriage. (*NA* 30 –31)

For her part, Parthenia releases him from his vows and bids him seek one "fit both for your honour and satisfaction" (*NA* 32). When she returns, restored but claiming to be a Corinthian, Argalus refuses this image of his lost beloved, insisting that "it was Parthenia's self I loved, and love" (*NA* 44). She then reveals herself as his true Parthenia, and they are wed. From the beginning, then, their private devotion involves a public commitment—in spite of her mother's opposition, in spite of Demogoras's vengeance—that makes them Sidney's most complete image of eros: passionate, faithful, willing to live their devotion in a full public context. No wonder then that at their deaths, Basilius's subjects commend them to the earth as "blessed relics of faithful and virtuous love" and adorn their tomb with "marble images to represent them" (*NA* 399). The ethic of noble eros is epitomized in their epitaph.

His being was in her alone,
And he not being, she was none.
   They joyed one joy; one grief they grieved;
   One love they loved; one life they lived.
   The hand was one; one was the sword
   That did his death, her death, afford.
As all the rest, so now the stone
That tombs the two is justly one.
                Argalus and Parthenia (*NA* 399–400)

IV

Zelmane languishes for love of Pyrocles and dies. Plangus is helpless to aid Erona. Helen bears substantial blame for the death of a man who loved her and for the desperate misery of a man who does not. Argalus dies in a rage. Parthenia forces a combat to insure her own death. Is this simply the poem's image of the cruel chaos of the world, a sad but uncritical recognition of the risks of absolute devotion? Or is it the revelation of chaos overtaking the poem itself, undoing Sidney's speaking picture of heroic love as fast as he constructs it? Neither one: Sidney drives the Arcadian love debate to extremes so as to figure metaphorically the limits of its terms, just as he does in his speaking picture of justice, just as he did much earlier in the false choice imposed in *The Lady of May*. What Stephen Orgel writes of Sidney's masque applies precisely in this case: "Sidney . . . is redefining the convention behind his work, examining and judging the values it implies"; "the solutions [to his critical questions] . . . are arrived at only after all the traditional assumptions have been discarded."[42] In the *New Arcadia*, it is Sidney's purpose to show that the invention of noble eros cannot meet the full demands of experience.

Like the reason-versus-passion, action-versus-contemplation debates that will occupy Pyrocles and Musidorus, the antithesis between vicious and virtuous love seems to protest too much. As one contrast follows another, the narrative gradually encloses itself in such a way as to prompt us to step aside from it and consider the legitimacy of its terms. One sign of this invitation to judgment lies in another sort of contrast in love: that between the principals, especially Pyrocles and Musidorus, and the secondary figures I have been discussing. The former are far more humanly jumbled in love: silly, courageous, sexually ambitious, deceitful, self-denying, plagued by uncertainty of perception and resolution. The latter—excepting Amphialus and

Gynecia—suffer little doubt about what they want and how they will try to get it. In a certain kind of romance this "purity" of character might be used to clarify the ugliness of evil and the beauty of good. But this will not work in fiction like Sidney's, a narrative that continually makes us reflect on the complexity of morality and desire.

Another way of setting Sidney's method in relief is to compare it with Chaucer's in *Troilus and Criseyde,* a poem singled out for praise in the *Defence* (*DP* 112) and current in the literary culture of the English court.[43] As Mark Lambert has argued, in the first three books of the *Troilus* Chaucer writes so as "to make grand passion a hearthside phenomenon": the social ease of eating and gossiping, the "maternal" image of Chaucer's Helen as bedside comforter, and above all the comic, prosaic business of Pandarus all create a "domestication of heroic intensity" that makes fearful Criseyde feel secure.[44] That Sidney is capable of creating such a comfortable and ironic portrayal of love is plain from his use of the worldly, witty narrator in the *Old Arcadia*. But that moderating voice has been erased in the revised story, removing any obstacle to taking the representation of these secondary figures to extremes. The only domestic moment in the entire "procession of lovers" is the reading scene with Argalus and Parthenia, and that is quickly cut short by the call to battle. Every thought and action in the sequence of lovers veers instantly toward wretchedness or elation. Sidney chooses to push his "exemplary" lovers—bad and good—beyond moderation so he can extend their opposing images to the breaking point, their divergent paths each to its baffled end. The radical polarity he gives them has the odd result of linking them together in our imagination and making us doubt their claims to an all-inclusive vision of love.

That Sidney expects us to admire the courage and determination of lovers like Zelmane and Palladius, Plangus, Helen, and Argalus and Parthenia is certain: as with his exemplars of justice, he recognizes within the invention of heroic love a real strength. But that strength is limited. All of these figures are ineffectual in their efforts to control events; they seem to beat on the door of the present, central narrative unheard, unable to break in and create change. Zelmane and Palladius do aid the two princes in escaping Andromana, but they have neither the cunning nor the experience to survive their first encounter with evil or loss: Palladius is cut down in the melee by one of his mother's henchmen, and Zelmane wastes away in unrequited ardor for Pyrocles. Fragility is the price of their innocence.

Prince Plangus displays nothing if not endurance in his quest to rescue Erona. But his only accomplished "act" is the work of Petrarchan remembrance, as his repeated "Can I forget" to Basilius reveals. If I forget her, he vows,

> Then let me eke forget one hand from other;
>> Let me forget that Plangus I am called;
>> Let me forget I am son to my mother;
> But if my memory must thus be thralled
>> To that strange stroke which conquered all my senses,
>> Can thoughts still thinking so rest unappalled? (*NA* 204)

This is his dilemma: to remember is to know that he can do little or nothing to save Erona—always thinking, he is always "appalled." Bound by agreement to let Pyrocles and Musidorus fight to win Erona's release, he sets out to find them only to hear they have perished through the practice of Plexirtus; discovering that Artaxia has besieged the knight who holds his beloved, he cannot again fight for her himself since his allies in that country "were utterly overthrown" (*NA* 306). He cannot turn to his father, the Iberian king, for the old man has spurned any reconciliation after the death of Andromana and Palladius. Plangus leaves Arcadia (and the narrative) having told his plight to Basilius—who declines to help him—in an effort to enlist the aid of Euarchus. Richard McCoy describes Plangus as "fusing agonized pathos with a tense, defiant energy."[45] I do not follow McCoy in assigning Plangus's frustration to a hostile relation with paternal authority; much less do I implicate Sidney's story as a whole in such a pattern of inevitable frustration.[46] But his description of Plangus is on target: the prince is a speaking picture of eros at the limits of its power.

Because Argalus woos and weds Parthenia, he is enclosed in a life of mutual love that shields him from much of the isolation and doubt that torment Plangus in his unanswered passion. But an irony operates in the presentation of Argalus that bears notice: outside that enclosure of happy love he can act with only very limited success. Argalus is introduced in the narrative as a knight with credentials worthy of the two princes and Amphialus; gifted with "valour of mind and ability of body," though "somewhat given to musing," he has accomplished many "heroical acts" (*NA* 27). But unlike the princes and Amphialus, nowhere in the story, *except in his courtship,* does he win a clear victory. Seeking to avenge Parthenia's disfigurement on Demagoras, who now leads the helot rebels, Argalus enters their stronghold disguised and finds his enemy heavily guarded. But Argalus "could delay his fury no longer for a fitter time" (*NA* 32), and he attacks him immediately, giving Demagoras what becomes a mortal wound but at the price of being imprisoned himself and at the mercy of the helot's new captain. Fortunately this captain turns out to be Pyrocles, but this little story presages a later and far sadder one to come.

Argalus's decision to obey Basilius and challenge Amphialus has been read as vanity and weakness, a yielding to "the tyranny of honour" (*NA* 373) and tragic betrayal of heroic love.[47] But the story suggests that another, and more complicated, problem operates in the sequence of events that leads to his death. In parting from the wife who begs him to stay, Argalus is in character as the deliberate, "musing" man introduced in Book One. Reading Basilius's command, his "countenance figured some resolution between loathness and necessity"; having finished it, he hands it to Parthenia to read (*NA* 372). Nothing rash marks his departure—there is only sorrow for Parthenia's anxiety and his spoken assurance to her—and nothing rash marks his challenge to Amphialus, whom Argalus seeks "by all means . . . to dissuade . . . from his enterprise" (*NA* 373). In this sober context Sidney's description of Argalus leaving Parthenia "carried away by the tyranny of honour" simply means that honor feels tyrannical to this loving husband who must ignore his wife's protestations—not that Argalus loses his head. The fact that Basilius' motive in sending Argalus is impure—to avenge the defeat of Phalantus—makes no difference.[48] If Argalus were to refuse, he would not only flatly disobey his sovereign but also leave unchallenged a rebel who has imprisoned the royal family and published treason. Parthenia loves him for his allegiance to the good; is he to abandon it when put to the test?

Argalus' battle gear identifies him as an image and a defender of true and faithful love against destructive and rebellious passion. In white armor "gilded over with knots of woman's hair" and wearing a sleeve sewn by Parthenia, he bears a shield featuring "two palm trees near one another, with a word signifying, 'In that sort flourishing'" (*NA* 374)— what Maurice Evans calls "an emblem of married love."[49] As we know from his battle with Phalantus, Amphialus rides a horse decked in "the straw-coloured livery of ruin" and carries a shield featuring a "torpedo fish" (*NA* 367), which "paralyses the angler who catches it,"[50] as he claims to be paralyzed by the princess he has imprisoned. The combat represents the "war" between ignoble and virtuous love that has been building "processionally," to use Lawry's term, throughout the story. Why then does Argalus fail and die?

Though Sidney's *New Arcadia* makes plain that it is morally better to be Argalus than Amphialus, it never suggests that in a contingent, dangerous world noble love will always triumph, nor that "passive" resistance is stronger than active defense. The innocent and quietly devoted die as well as the experienced and aggressive. In Argalus's case, when he ventures outside the enclosure of noble eros, he faces difficulties for which that fortress is no defense. This happened before, in his awkward attack on Demagoras, when he "could no longer delay his fury." It happens, fatally, again. When Amphialus first gains the advantage, he chivalrously offers mercy, but humiliated, Argalus calls on the resources of "spite" to renew his attack (NA 376). When Parthenia then intervenes and successfully appeals to Amphialus as a lover to save her beloved, Argalus is further shamed. He prepares to attack again, "But the fire of that strife, blown with his inward rage," induces new bleeding and finally death (NA 377).

That Argalus makes a mistake here in not accepting his enemy's mercy is obvious, though we are told that Amphialus would have rejected the same offer, for "neither [of the two knights] affected to overlive a dishonour" (NA 377). But this is beside the point. Heroic love is good, but it is not a human invention sufficient to all the risks that sooner or later invade experience. Nor does the battle represent a victory for the ruinous passion Amphialus has come to represent. The death of Parthenia at his hands is the contingency that undoes him, even as frustrated pride undoes the better man and better lover who was Amphialus's opponent and victim. That Argalus fails and dies is harder to accept because we have been guided by the narrative of contrasting loves to esteem him and Parthenia as its highest representatives. But this is exactly the design of Sidney's fiction. He praises and extends the best inventions of his culture until we see their breaking point. That the invention *does* break down is not proof that Sidney's personal and political frustrations overwhelm his fiction, nor that his poetic power is out of control. It is the sign of highest art: looking steadily within the labyrinth of desire, honoring what is noble but refusing to reduce the mystery of human frailty and pain.

The happy scene in which Basilius's messenger finds Argalus and Parthenia before his message parts them is the highpoint of virtuous, mutual love in Sidney's poem. Argalus is

> sitting in a parlour with the fair Parthenia; he reading in a book the stories of Hercules, she by him, as to hear him read—but while his eyes looked on the book, she looked on his eyes, and sometimes staying him with some pretty question, not so much to be resolved of the doubt as to give him occasion to look upon her—a happy couple, he joying in her, she joying in herself (but in herself because she enjoyed him); both increasing their riches by giving to each other; each making one life double because they made a double life one. (NA 371–72)

In the pagan setting of Arcadia, this idyll comes very close to the joy of Christian marriage, as praised by such popular Sidnean contemporaries as Primaudaye:

If we could (saith Plato) with bodily eyes the beautie that honestie hath in hir, we would be farre in loue with her: but she is seen only with the eyes of the mind. And truely with the same eyes we may behold it in marriage, if we consider mannerly the honestie of the coupled life, when it is in every respect absolute, the holy bond whereof the earth hath nothing more beautiful or honest.[51]

In their absolute devotion to another, single human being, Argalus and Parthenia define the height and limit of the *Arcadia*'s speaking picture of love. As with Zelmane, love gives Parthenia her being, and the loss of her beloved takes it away. She finds no other recourse. Parthenia has no power to save Argalus's life; like Plangus she must seek the aid of others. Indeed she exercises her power only to continue their "double life" by taking her own. This too, like Argalus's failure, is predictable, since Parthenia warns him that "Parthenia shall be in the battle of your fight! Parthenia shall smart in your pain; and your blood must be bled by Parthenia!" (*NA* 373). The "word" on her shield as she enters combat as the King of the Tomb makes clear her purpose: "No way to be rid from death, but by death" (*NA* 396). Mortally wounded, she thanks Amphialus for his service to her and welcomes death as the passage to "sweet life." "I come, my Argalus! I come!" (*NA* 398).

This scene has the force of a kind of pagan sacrament, a sacrifice on Love's altar on which we hope the gods throw incense. But it also defines the terrible boundary encircling the invention of eros as Sidney perceived it. Made in the image of love, Parthenia cannot exist outside its embrace.

It is significant that of those "worthies" whose "image . . . most inflameth the mind with desire to be worthy, and informs with counsel how to be worthy" (*DP* 98), Sidney praises Aeneas most often and most highly.[52] An "excellent man every way" (*DP* 79), Virgil's hero is extolled as a "virtuous man in all fortunes" (*DP* 98) and commended for preserving his father and for obeying God's commandment to leave Dido, "though not only all passionate kindness, but even the human consideration of virtuous gratefulness, would have craved other of him" (*DP* 98). Sidney reads Aeneas as a complex character who maintains his identity and purpose—not without great struggle—to a truth and an imperative beyond that of eros.

Eros is not evil; it is just not enough. The contrast between Aeneas's choice and the tragic decisions of Argalus and Parthenia underscores that they have no third thing outside the enclosure of their "double life" to which they can look for definition and courage. Beyond that enclosure, Argalus experiences frustration and confusion at his weakness;

Parthenia finds there to be nothing outside it all but the invitation to death. In her dying voice, Parthenia asks for divine pardon, but her chief prayer is for the restoration of her lost world of mutual devotion, that "we may love each other eternally" (NA 398).

Unlike Spenser and Shakespeare, Sidney is not a poet of married love. He may honor it, but he does not make either the daily comedy or the Christian institution of marriage his subject. Perhaps he felt bound by careful notions of the province of "right poetry" to remain within the confines of his pre-Christian setting; perhaps, having married only the year before he began his *Arcadian* revisions, he was not ready to write on the subject. We can only speculate. What is sure is that by avoiding the mundane humor and the many decidedly nonerotic demands of wedded life, he keeps even the noblest of those lovers who have been the topic of this chapter "compassed within the circle" of Petrarchan and romance convention. There is none among them who could say to the beloved, as Rosalind does to her Orlando, that "men have died from time to time, and worms have eaten them, but not for love."[53] Nor do any of the *Arcadia*'s characters, for all their obsession with desire, enter the labyrinth of adult sexuality in the way of Spenser's Amoret. In this sense Sidney's is an oddly chaste book.

Protestant encomia of marriage rest on the conviction that in choosing and sustaining wedded life the couple commit themselves to that which transcends their mutual affection: the will of God. Calvin writes that "Christ deems marriage worthy of such honor that he wills it to be an image of his sacred union with the church," and Luther stresses that marriage is an "estate . . . [that] does not sit well with the devil, because it is God's good will and work."[54] Luther goes on to argue that even the drudgery attendant on caring for children and supporting the domestic economy are sanctified, for Christian faith "looks upon all these insignificant, distasteful, and despised duties in the Spirit, and is aware that they are all adorned with divine approval."[55] All such tasks, preeminently the raising of children, are good work. And in his popular *Golden Boke of Christen Matrimonye* (translated by Coverdale in 1543), Heinrich Bullinger praises "the state of honorable wedlocke" in part because it "refusethe no kynd of payne and trouble, so that it maye bryng any profyt at all to the publique weale of Christendome."[56] It is in fact the *public* character of Christian wedded life—its role as earthly image of God's love, its outward-looking devotion to children and to the common weal—that helps clarify for us by contrast the profoundly private character of eros, good as well as evil, in Sidney's *Arcadia*. Zelmane, Plangus, Helen, Parthenia, and Argalus grandly cast themselves deep within the well of another soul. But in the larger world that glorious abandon proves of little avail.

One final limitation of heroic love as offered in these figures needs mention. Their very status as icons of eros keeps them at a distance from the princes and princesses and from us. The Aeneas so often offered to us in the *Defence* as worthy of our imitation is a complex heroic character who in an ever-shifting sea of circumstance must struggle with his "inward self" and "outward government" (*DP* 98). Not so Sidney's emblematic figures. In them the erotic transfer of self to another appears instantaneous and complete. Notwithstanding their suffering, none of them wrestles with the transformation of self by love or with love's public requirements in such a way as to fulfill Sidney's demand for heroic poetry, which "informs with counsel how to be worthy" (*DP* 98). With the possible exception of Zelmane, whose gentle service and sad death are commemorated in Pyrocles' adopted name, their radical adoration of the beloved does not move any of Sidney's main characters to change.

Sidney finds both Tudor humanist justice and the Renaissance glorification of heroic eros wanting. But in so doing he engages the reader as fully as possible in testing their worth. Through strategies of contrast he makes them shine as bright as their most fervent defenders could hope for. Yet by feigning in stories their best and most extensive claims to measure and define experience, he compels us to witness the inventions of self-sufficient justice and self-surrendering eros as they are borne beyond their capacity to serve as an image of life. Fulke Greville's memorable praise of the *Arcadia* as a poem enabling us "to set a good countenance upon all the discountenances of adversity, and a stay upon the exorbitant smilings of chance" is true only if qualified.[57] The *New Arcadia* represents a heroic response to suffering and contingency; the "pictures" within it contribute to that image, but they cannot be lifted out and made models for conduct. Like Pyrocles and Musidorus, who achieve only intermittent success, we must read and read again the conventions within the narrative to discover what portion of the truth they encompass and what they do not. If the heroic life lies in certainty, Sidney's fiction never finds it.

4

The Work of Invention

> Were my mind setled, I would not essay, but resolve my
> selfe. It is still a Prentise and a probationer.
> —Montaigne, *Of Repenting*

Hallet Smith writes that the choice of Hercules at the crossroads defines
the argument of Renaissance heroic poetry. Sidney would have known
the story from Cicero, who had it from Xenophon:

> When Hercules was just coming into youth's estate (the time which Nature
> has appointed unto every man for choosing the path of life on which he
> would enter), he went out into a desert place. And as he saw two paths, the
> path of Pleasure and the path of Virtue, he sat down and debated long and
> earnestly which one it were better for him to take.[1]

In Xenophon, Pleasure offers easy satisfaction, while Virtue warns that
"of all things good and fair, the gods give nothing to man without toil
and effort."[2] The popular pictures of Hercules at the crossroads often
draw Virtue's path as daunting but leading to a final pastoral rest, Pleasure's as promising fair but delivering foul.[3] The lesson, Smith says, is
that the hero must reject the illusion of effortless luxury and take the
harder road: the "desired state must be earned, must follow the
achievement of fame and glory through action."[4] For readers of the *New
Arcadia* this paradigm presents a problem.

When Musidorus finds Pyrocles dressed as an Amazon, the latter
wears a jewel engraved with "a Hercules made in little form, but set
with a distaff in his hand (as he once was by Omphale's commandment)
with a word in Greek, but thus to be interpreted: 'Never more valiant'"
(*NA* 69). Native to Hercules' Thessaly, Musidorus is shocked by this
transformation, though he will soon undergo his own, from confident
prince to lovelorn shepherd. In the *New Arcadia,* we meet Pyrocles and

76

Musidorus in the middle of things, a fact that makes the Herculean model very difficult to apply. By the time we first encounter them, the princes have *already* made the virtuous choice at the crossroads: as they are quick to tell Basilius's daughters, they have been framed by nature and nurture to be lords of truth, and they have imposed justice in the disordered kingdoms of their journey. But in Arcadia, unruly experience has doubled back on them. Love compels Pyrocles to defend his transformed self as the heroic equal of his past character, though he is by no means always sure of this claim, a claim which often involves him in self-pity and deceit. In Sidney's fiction the roads of choice keep on crossing. The princes must choose not between inglorious *otium* and heroic striving, but between conventional categories for managing experience and the unsettling reality of perpetual change. Sidney's revised story relentlessly implies that for them the work of invention is never complete.

It is the habit of all Sidney's poetry to provoke awareness of contingency through eros, whose convention-shattering force exposes human need and human vulnerability to chance and death. Love is strong enough to break down habitual modes of perceiving the self and the world. But romantic love in Sidney—this has been misunderstood—is a means, not an end. Love is his favored metaphor for the shifting, transforming power of experience at large; eros is not less, but not more than an "imaginative ground-plot for a profitable invention" (*DP* 103). This means that the common critical tactic of pitting love against the heroic life in his fiction and declaring that they are, finally, either reconciled or not, obscures the more significant debate between given Tudor formulations of experience and Sidney's uncompromising display of their insufficiency. If it does prove to be "heroic love" that Sidney finally champions, we will have to find a language for it other than pastoral lament or encomia to singular devotion. A good place to begin considering what this debate means to Sidney's image of the heroic life is with the debates of the princes themselves in Book One.

Musidorus takes the humanist high road in the exchanges of chapters 9 and 12, marshaling a formidable array of rhetoric to his cause.[5] But his speeches lack the engaging cleverness and emotional force of Pyrocles' replies. The debates are about perception: Musidorus insists that Pyrocles has fallen victim to self-delusion, Pyrocles that he has escaped it. Platonic justice and the demands it makes on friendship govern Musidorus's efforts: Loving Pyrocles' virtuous self, he is, as Plato's Diotima advises, "resourceful in discoursing of virtue and of what should be the good man's character and what his pursuits."[6] As I pointed out in chapter 2, the just man who serves as Musidorus' ideal recognizes the true structure of value masked by appearances and fashions his own soul in the image of that structure. He is then self-sufficient against the confusion of experience and thereby privileged to construct political order after the calibrations of his own soul. Musidorus's appeal in the first debate is to that paradigm of justice, which has bound Pyrocles to him as friend: Pyrocles' virtuous mind, "being witness to itself of his own inward good," must give itself "to the knowledge of those things which might better your mind," not the least of which is "the familiarity of excellent men in learning and soldiery" (*NA* 49)—men like Musidorus himself.

At the second debate, Pyrocles' transformation into an Amazon provokes a sterner rebuke, a rhetorical slap in the face:

> And is it possible that this is Pyrocles, the only young prince in the world formed by nature and framed by education to the true exercise of virtue? Or is it indeed some Amazon that hath counterfeited the face of my friend, in this sort to vex me. . . . Remember, for I know you know it, that if we will be men, the reasonable part of our soul is to have absolute commandment, against which if any sensual weakness arise, we are to yield all our sound forces to the overthrowing of so unnatural a rebellion. (*NA* 70)

For Musidorus, the old choice of Hercules remains the measure of experience. One travels up to virtuous and noble command, or down to base "lust and idleness" (*NA* 71). That Pyrocles has betrayed that choice is shamefully evident not only in his Amazon's costume but also in his submission to love something less than his own reasonable soul: a woman. Musidorus warns that "this effeminate love of a woman doth so womanize a man that, if you yield to it, it will not only make you an Amazon, but a launder, a distaff-spinner, or whatsoever other vile occupation their idle heads can imagine and their weak hands perform" (*NA* 72). The ironic note of hysteria here testifies to the fact that Pyrocles has broken the (male) code by which the two princes have so far, so effectively conducted their lives.

Musidorus has a fixed convention by which to interpret and manage experience; the most striking difference in Pyrocles throughout the debates is that he does not. He is alternately hesitant, embarrassed, and inspired by his sudden change of circumstance. If he is constant, it is in the humility of one who believes that he has seen more of the truth than he previously imagined and who simply wishes to attest to this newfound perception. "Look!" is the answer he gives his methodical friend. The Arcadian landscape itself has become a source of wonder:

> Do you not see how all things conspire together to make this country a heavenly dwelling? Do you not see the grass, how in colour they excel the emeralds, everyone striving to pass his fellow—and yet they are all kept of an equal height? And see you not the rest of these beautiful flowers, each of which would require a man's wit to know, and his life to express? (*NA* 51)

What impresses Pyrocles now is the sheer otherness and complexity of that which lies outside his past province of understanding. Hence his rejection of Musidorus's call to confine himself within the circle of excellent men:

> the mind itself must . . . sometimes be unbent, or else it will be either weakened or broken; and these knowledges [praised by Musidorus], as they are of good use, so are they not all the mind may stretch itself unto. Who knows whether I feed not my mind with higher thoughts? Truly, as I know not all particularities, so yet I see the bounds of all these knowledges. (NA 50)

In the second debate, Pyrocles answers Musidorus's charges against women and love with self-effacing wit, but the condition of his newfound understanding—the loss of his assured self—makes him waver. To Musidorus's denigration of women, he replies that he was born and nursed of woman, that women are endowed with the same minds as men to practice virtue, and that "this estate of Amazons, which I now for my greatest honour do seek to counterfeit, doth well witness that . . . they neither want valour of mind, nor yet doth their fairness take away their force" (NA 73). And Musidorus's "bitter objections [against love] . . . rather touch me, dear Musidorus, than love. But I am good witness of mine own imperfections, and therefore will not defend myself" (NA 74). But when Musidorus commands Pyrocles "to purge your self of this vile infection" or end their friendship (NA 75), the lover prostrates himself before his accuser and begs him to forget all his "vehement" defense of love (NA 76). Sudden insight, sudden doubt: Pyrocles can fall rapidly from liberating concentration on that which is beyond his past "knowledges" to desperate fear at any threat to his conventional self. If his claim that love must be "counted without measure . . . because the workings of it are without measure" (NA 75) is true, Pyrocles seems not at all resolved to enter that unsettled and unsettling condition.

For the princes, eros displaces their virtuous confidence and prompts them to reread and revise themselves, as when Pyrocles explains his change into Zelmane by saying that "love, the refiner of invention, had put in my head thus to disguise myself" (NA 80). But eros is not enough. Pyrocles and Musidorus continually confront the need to *think*, to use their wit—like a poet—in reconstructing their self-knowledge in the light of their Arcadian experience. This is one of the complexities that distinguish them from such exemplary but more limited figures as Plangus and Argalus. Love compels a difficult and not always welcome reappraisal.

Twice in the Book One debates this reconstruction is defined by a term that stresses self-conscious invention. Musidorus asks if "some Amazon hath *counterfeited* the face of my friend," and, as noted above,

Pyrocles insists that "I now for my greatest honour do seek to *counter-feit*" the "estate of Amazons" (*NA* 70, 73, emphasis added). Musidorus later uses the same term to describe his clever wooing of her— "I began to counterfeit the extremest love towards Mopsa" (*NA* 129)—as Pamela does in telling her sister of his ingenuity (*NA* 152).

Counterfeiting is a central term in the *Defence of Poetry*:

> *Poesie* therefore, is an Art of *Imitation*: for so Aristotle termeth it in the word μίμησις, that is say, a representing, counterfeiting, or figuring forth to speake Metaphorically.[7]

So used, the word has no necessarily pejorative intent; it came through French from the Latin *"contra-facere,* to make in opposition or contrast, hence in opposing imitation" (OED). Chaucer uses it so in the *Book of the Duchess,* when the man in black says of his lost beloved, "I kan not now wel counterfete / Hir wordes."[8] It means "To represent, portray, or reproduce in writing or by literary art," or "To represent by a picture, statue, or the like" (OED 9b and 9). The imitation is then "opposing" because it is in a different medium from the original: a stone image from a living body, a written narrative from actual life. The counterfeit is always an analogy, never a replica, of the original. Of course the term more commonly means to forge an image in order to deceive (OED 1– 6). In the *Defence*, Sidney recognizes that poetic counterfeiting can both reveal and mislead: poetry should be "εικαστικη, (which some learned have defined: figuring forth good things)," but may be "φαυαστκη (which doth, contrariwise, infect the fancy with unworthy objects)" (*DP* 104). But the two kinds of counterfeiting are separated by a much contested border, and both types of counterfeiting may in fact be practiced at once.

This is the case with Pyrocles and Musidorus. Their counterfeiting does not always imply a gain in self-understanding (love does not set them on some inevitably progressive course), yet neither does it always engage them in deceit. What Robert Stillman writes of the princes' performances in the *Old Arcadia* applies as well in the *New:* they display "poetry's capacity for constructing solipsistic worlds" but also illustrate how it strives after a more true and honest representation.[9] In Sidney's revised narrative, counterfeiting becomes deceptive (a case of man's wit abusing poetry) when the princes seek to confine themselves "within the circle of a question according to the proposed matter" (*DP* 78)—when it involves their effort to reclaim their old, lost self-definition and control. Their counterfeiting becomes heroic when it represents an active and honest response to the volatile, unfolding design of experience with which Arcadia confronts them.

In other words, false counterfeiting is an act of deliberate blindness to the inadequacy of their much cherished, virtuous souls; true counterfeiting begins with sight, with a recognition of the reality of that which they cannot, at least quickly, understand or categorize. Pyrocles recognizes both the glory and the difficulty of such a true effort when he says that each Arcadian flower would "require a man's wit to know, and his life to express" (NA 51).

Two difficulties now arise. First, what can the princes make themselves an "opposing imitation" of? If I am correct in arguing that Sidney finds the imitation of humanist justice and the imitation of a single beloved insufficient, what would be? This I will try to answer after analysis of Pyrocles and Musidorus's poetic performances in the New Arcadia. Second, where would Sidney have found any legitimate basis for such an act of imitation? How can the poet seek to "counterfeit" what is beyond full understanding and control? This question has been addressed in part in chapter 1. But I now return to the affinities between Sidney's fiction and the vision of human work found in Reformation and skeptical humanist thought, focusing this time on the nature and need of counterfeiting. If nothing else, this should make it clear that if such human work is to be valid, it must always be re-forming.

I

Reformers like Luther and Calvin, as well as latter-day humanists like Montaigne, believed that our unstable human condition necessitates continual transformation. Protestants insisted that the great transformation that justifies us is the work of God alone, but equally that in lesser matters—everything else—the labor must be ours, undertaken in thankful obedience and imitation of God's creating and redeeming acts. What I have been calling counterfeiting is for them not only a legitimate act: it is the *only* valid human work. In the Protestant activists Sidney would have found a view of human beings as historical, time-burdened creatures and an impatience with abstract schemes for wisdom and virtue. These attitudes underlie Sidney's argument for the validity of poetry and for its affective superiority to philosophy: by forming a "speaking picture" of active goodness, poetry reforms its humanly flawed readers, drawing them "to as high a perfection as our degenerate souls, made worse by their clayey lodgings, can be capable of" (DP 86, 82).

"Now since the being and nature of man cannot exist for an instant unless it is doing or not doing something," writes Luther in *The Treatise on Good Works*, "well then, let him who wants to be holy and full of good works exercise himself at all times in this faith in all his life and works."[10] Freed from the burden of the law through grace, such a person can act without a spiritual ax to grind, imitating Christ (and Adam and Eve before the fall) to work for the good of others.[11] Indeed being human he has no choice but to "exercise himself" for better or worse. Calvin shares Luther's stress on the necessity of life-long transformation. Our "restoration does not take place in one moment or one day or one year: but through continual and sometimes even slow advances God wipes out in his elect the corruptions of the flesh."[12] God works out our nature over time; we, as justified souls, have the privilege of imitating this act. This is how we are, in Calvin's terminology, no longer servants but sons of God.[13]

So that we can learn to counterfeit this godly work, God—acting like Sidney's right poet—has given us in the Bible a speaking picture to teach and move us. Calvin writes that Cicero and Seneca,

> while they wish particularly to exhort us to virtue, announce merely that we should live in accordance with nature. But Scripture draws its exhortation from the true fountain. It not only enjoins us to refer our life to God ...; but ... it also adds that Christ, through whom we return to favor with God, has been set before us as an example, whose pattern we ought to express in our life.... For we have been adopted as sons by the Lord with this one condition: that our life express Christ, the bond of our adoption.[14]

Our bodily, historical nature makes transformation inevitable; it also makes the appeal to "historical" images the best way of motivating that change. So in Exodus, the inspired author Moses shows God to his readers "not as he is in himself, but as he is toward us: so that this recognition of him consists more in living experience, than in vain and high-flown speculation."[15] No doubt these convictions also helped prompt the reformers to adopt the humanist insistence on reading scripture in its historical and linguistic context, distrusting the "high-flown speculation" of the allegorical method.[16]

For Luther and Calvin alike, the liberating gospel is that our eternal worth—our justification—lies in the unshakable and sovereign love of God. This merciful love bestows freedom on humankind: freedom from the dread of Hell and freedom for (godlike) action for others' good. Luther was inclined to stress the human discovery of this God-given grace and the release it bestowed from anxious introspection, Calvin the absolute sovereignty of God in granting it. In either case Christian life must be *eccentric*[17]—not a matter of ruthless self-examination but rather its opposite: seeing not only oneself but also all of creation in light of God as Maker, Redeemer, and Sustainer of life. Should we be inclined to forget that our worth lies in what is bestowed from without, the law reminds us of the inadequacy of our unaided efforts, always driving us to the liberty that comes (in the familiar paradox) in seeing that only God can restore us.

For Luther, this discovery enables "the freest service, cheerfully and lovingly done."[18] Christ having "put on" the sin of his bride, the church, and made her spotless by his righteousness, the Christian then "should 'put on' his neighbor, and so conduct himself toward him as if he himself were in the other's place."[19] Calvin allows the regenerate soul a freedom to work out the implications of God's saving act, but this freedom is always triggered by divine grace and always remains the freedom to do God's will.[20] He stresses that we "read" this saving God in the text of scripture, for "the Word itself . . . is like a mirror in which faith may contemplate God."[21] Having received this freedom and this example, the Christian is enabled to use whatever gifts God has given for working out God's purposes on earth.[22] Hence the enormous zeal in Calvin himself for a *thorough* reform—educational and civic as well as religious—of human society.[23] For Luther and Calvin, salvation is eccentric, and so is the work it liberates the justified soul to do.

The call of both reformers is to a new perception. "Look!" is their argument, as it is the love-inspired Pyrocles'. Look at the saving grace that lies outside fruitless inner struggle and empty observance, and made free by that sight, look at the world and labor for good. Luther and Calvin shared with Sidney a dissatisfaction with given modes of reading experience and of defining human worth and work. All three faced a crisis in the great expectations of their fathers and teachers, though it is probably accurate to say that Sidney's and Calvin's reassessments were forced less by a Lutherlike inner anguish than by the reality of political circumstance: Sidney's by Elizabeth's failure to advance him as he thought fit and Calvin's by his association with Rector Nicholas Cop, whose reformist address of 1533 necessitated Calvin's flight from Paris and led him at the point of decision in 1534 to reject Catholic ordination.[24] In any case, all three could and did claim as a consequence of this crisis an "unelected vocation" that they felt enabled to define and defend.

Sidney's *counterfeiting* provides a key to and image of ethical human action as Protestant thinkers understood it. Freed by grace from the threat of spiritual ruin, the sons of God look to what is Other—to the saving acts of God as they appear in scripture—and make an "opposing imitation" of it in their own human work. Counterfashioning is the only possible human action, since all is initiated by the Heavenly Maker. One faces the irreducible fact of God's law and God's grace and acts in response—neither cowering in needless fear nor passively resting on the gift of justification, but working in imitation, however limited, of God's recreative love. This is why Calvin could declare that the chief Christian virtue is humility[25] and yet establish Geneva with such reformist fervor. As for Luther, he never forgets that though the "inner man" is justified by faith and "needs neither laws nor good works," the "outer man," the physical being who must live between Christ's resurrection and the general resurrection of the dead, must like Christ be "the servant of all."[26]

Finally, I note once more that perhaps the most substantial work accomplished by these *sola gratia* reformers is their *written* work. For Luther and Calvin, as for Philip Sidney, writing was a means of teaching, and in particular of teaching the failure of conventional formulae for granting legitimacy to human life and labor. Calvin considered himself as one who filled the role of teacher, intending his *Institutes* as a guide for theology candidates.[27] Luther was already a teacher when he publicly declared his opposition to Bishop Albrecht's indulgences in 1517, and in his later career he was not above poetic feigning to expose the inadequacy of what he considered Roman abuses. His anonymous 1542 pamphlet advertised the indulgence granted for viewing Albrecht's collection of relics, which included such rarities as flames from the burning bush, a piece of the shout that toppled Jericho's walls, and "Two feathers and an egg from the Holy Spirit." Only after the pamphlet was well known did Luther reveal the spoof.[28]

It is pleasant to learn that Luther had a sense of humor. But the central point must be that both his written works and Calvin's were acts of counterfeiting. Believing themselves freed by the saving work of God as revealed in his incarnate and written Word, they labored to foster new and faithful understanding in the incarnation of the human word. And that is Sidney's vision of poetry, whose earthly maker honors the heavenly creator in the act of "opposing imitation."

We should remember with A. G. Dickens that "the initial impulses underlying the new Protestantism in England sprang predominantly from Luther"; that those theology students who met at "Little Germany" (the White Horse Tavern) in Cambridge—Coverdale, Cranmer, Latimer, and Parker—were principal framers of the new English scripture and creed; and that Cranmer had agreed with Lutheran clergy on many articles of Melanchthon's *Augsburg Confession* and had them in mind when under Edward VI he drafted the original forty-two articles of the English Church.[29]

Yet Dickens was right to declare that following the Marian persecutions, "Calvinism became the weightiest of the many foreign influences brought to bear upon the English Reformation."[30] Some caution needs to be observed here. To embrace Genevan theology in England was to renounce neither episcopacy nor Cranmer's *Prayer Book.* Calvin himself accepted English church polity and was not pleased by the polemical excesses of Christopher Goodman and John Knox. Indeed Calvin wrote to William Cecil, Elizabeth's principal minister, to make clear that he had nothing to do with Knox's *First Blast* (1558), which so offended Elizabeth, and Cecil sent a very cordial reply.[31]

Equally significant is the fact that those who embraced the doctrine and zeal of Geneva remained within the Anglican fold, though they disagreed about how it should be purified of Roman practice. The very designation *reformed,* applied chiefly to non-Lutheran Protestants in the seventeenth century, was used throughout the sixteenth to refer to the followers of Luther, Zwingli, and Calvin alike. When she wrote in 1577 to the Palatinate prince about the meeting that led to the Form of Concord, Elizabeth indicated that she took "this assembly of theologians most seriously because, while as a result of it many persons will be experiencing difficulties, no one will be acquiring any benefit therefrom except the common Papist enemies of reformed religion, who consider Lutherans and Zwinglians one and the same."[32] Though presumably more enlightened than the Papist enemies, the queen places all Protestants under the "reformed" banner.

Sidney's acquaintance with Calvinist thought is well known. His father-in-law Walsingham had been an exile in Basel and was afterward not only the most ardent of the "godly" among Elizabeth's advisors but also a patron of the English congregation in Antwerp, to which he appointed Thomas Cartwright as minister.[33] Sidney's uncles Leicester and Warwick favored more aggressive church reform and more aggressive military policies against Catholic Spain. Sidney himself apparently translated some part of his Hugenot friend Duplessis Mornay's *De la verite de la religion Christienne.*[34] For Sidney's awareness of Lutheran ideas we can point to his association with the "German nation" at the the University of Padua, his friendship with many German scholars and politicians, and his sojourn in Germany after the St. Bartholomew's Day Massacre.[35] His European mentor, Languet, converted to the reformed faith after reading the *Loci Communes Theologiae* and traveling to Wittenberg to meet its author, Melanchthon. Languet later advised his protege to learn to read German, because the German "influence and power in Christendom are now preeminent and will doubtless increase still further."[36]

Andrew Weiner has been right to stress the Protestant character of Sidney's poetics, and also right to stress the difficulty in determining Sidney's precise place in Protestantism.[37] The difficulty is in itself significant: if Sidney wanted to eliminate bishops and the Anglican form of worship, he wrote and said nothing known to us about these matters.

Sidney's acceptance of income from clerical benefices and his sympathy for the suffering of certain recusants imply a less doctrinaire habit of mind. As Sidney's biographer Malcolm Wallace notes, Sidney profited from the fining of some Catholics, "but his condemnation was reserved for their treason, not for their religion."[38] Katherine Duncan-Jones suggests that his 1577 conversations with the Jesuit Edmund Campion in Prague may well have stemmed from genuine seeking on Sidney's part.[39] When Sidney invoked the doctrines and intentions of Reformation thought, it was to defend his poetics and his politics, not to engage in close doctrinal dispute.

In politics Sidney plainly inclined to the Calvinist vanguard because he saw in it the opportunity to unite Protestant Europe against the Catholic empire ruled by Spain. A. G. Dickens' general account of Elizabethan Protestant response to the danger of Romanism can be applied properly to Sidney: "The greatest dangers ... did not ... lie in recusancy but in the assassination-plots directed against the Queen and in the threat of a foreign invasion which would tempt English Catholics to desert their national allegiance."[40] Hence Sidney's enthusiasm for a Protestant League and his preference for a direct attack against Spanish territories.[41] Fine points of dogma that divided the German and Genevan Protestants seemed not to interest him unless they had obvious diplomatic implications. When Sidney wrote to Walsingham during his 1577 embassy about the danger in the Elector Ludwig's shift from Calvinism to Lutheranism, it was as part of his assessment of support for the Protestant League, about which the Lutherans appear to have shown little interest. Sidney expresses the hope that the Elector's brother, Sidney's Calvinist friend Count Casimir, can win Ludwig back to Genevan ways since "Prince Lodovick is of a soft nature, ledde to these things *only through conscience*."[42]

My argument has been that Sidney's poetry draws on the central inheritance of Protestant thought, on what Luther's and Calvin's vision of human nature and human work have in common. With them Sidney operates from the conviction that God's saving grace frees—in effect empowers—the justified to act for the individual and public (ethic and politic) good of others. This activity is undertaken as an imitation or "counterfeiting" of the creative and reforming activity of God. Our historical, unfinished nature and our new role as "sons" of the Heavenly Maker both require and legitimize it. In this light, one last point about Sidney's Protestantism must be made: Sidney's writing offers no signs that he was paralyzed by a sense of sin or that an oppressive conviction of depravity warred with his general humanist faith in the value of the written word—a faith he shared with the reformers. Whatever morbid self-analyses may appear in later Puritan diaries, whatever scorn for the value of earthly experience and for earthly beauty that may have infected others among the godly, Sidney did not anticipate them. Nor did such debilitating habits of mind govern Luther and Calvin. What drew Sidney to reformed thought, and what no doubt particularly appealed to him in Calvin, was the conviction that "God's grace" set free "man's powers,"[43] that to accept the sovereignty and grace of God was to find one's full and most creative humanity.

Sidney's sympathy with Reformation thought is profound but not exclusive. The breadth of his humanist knowledge and convictions appears everywhere evident in his writing, poetical and otherwise. Strikingly apparent is his affinity with that particular late and skeptical development of humanism exemplified most impressively in Montaigne. This parallel will clarify Sidney's perception of human nature and heroic work and help us interpret the counterfeiting of the princes in his *New Arcadia*. The differences between a young English Protestant impatient for public service and international acclaim and an aging French Catholic wanting nothing more than to be left with his own thoughts and a few friends only heighten the parallels in their vision of experience. In fact, both were products of a classical education that begot in them an exceptional, sometimes painful self-awareness; both wrote in the context of significant personal or professional losses that confirmed their skeptical regard of the Platonic and Ciceronian path to virtue and power. In both we discover a stress on the self as a text for reading and revision, a text we can neither "settle" nor escape, a text that experience continually compels us to reform.

"I had rather understand my selfe well in my selfe then in Cicero," writes Montaigne in *Of Experience*. "Out of the experience I have of my selfe I finde sufficient ground to make my selfe wise were I but a good proficient scholler."[44] For Montaigne the self must be the central text because it represents to him most plainly that multiformity and change that define earthly life:

> Others fashion man, I repeat him; and represent a particular one, but ill made; and whom were I to forme a new, he should be far other than he is. . . . The world runnes all on wheeles. All things therein moove without intermission; yea, the earth, the rockes of Caucasus, and the Pyramides of Aegypt, both with the publike [general planetary movement] and their own motion.[45]

The constancy of change exposes the inadequacy of cherished constructs and drives home the need to make the self over in light of more mysterious but nonetheless valuable models. So Montaigne counsels that "When reason failes us, we employ experience. . . . Which is a

meane by much more weake and vile. But truth is of so great consequence that wee ought not disdaine any induction that may bring us unto
it."[46] There is a cyclical pattern operating in the *Essayes*: the introspective quest is invaded by some unpredictable revolution—sudden
passion, physical danger, illness, political change—that breaks down
the old self and requires a revised self-knowledge. In other words, our
contingent nature makes counterfeiting the one legitimate heroic act.
"Were my mind setled, I would not essay, but resolve my selfe. It is still
[ever] a Prentise and a probationer."[47]

The perception of contingency makes the essayist disdainful and
weary of proliferating legal and moral logic chopping. Whether his
topic is the strictures of law or diet, Montaigne finds our life not
amenable to rules, for they must be endlessly refined to meet the particulars of any real human occasion. "Of one subject we make a thou-
sand," he complains; "in multiplying and subdividing we fal againe
into the infinity of Epicurus his Atomes." With a deconstructionist eye
he sees in the very unquestioned assumptions of human interpretation
sources of instability:

> I commonly find something to doubt-of, where the commentary happily
> never deigned to touch, as deeming it so plaine. I stumble sometimes as
> much in an even smooth path, as some horses that I know who oftner trip
> in a faire plaine way than in a rough and stony. Who would not say that
> glosses increase doubts and ignorance, since no booke is to be seene,
> whether divine or profane, commonly read of all men, whose interpretation
> dimmes or tarnisheth not the difficulty?[48]

For Montaigne, even more radically than for Sidney, no human science
can be contained "within the circle of a question according to the proposed matter" (*DP* 78). The questions continually change because the
matter changes, including our vision of it.

Montaigne's skepticism coexists with his devotion to the persistence
of truth and of design. It is exactly because "truth is of so great consequence" that we ought not reject "any induction unto it," even the
"weak and vile" induction of experience. The effort to represent one
continually re-forming subject (himself) is difficult, but not fruitless:
"the lines of my picture change and vary, yet loose [sic] they not themselves."[49] This returns us to Sidney, who shares Montaigne's interest
in self-knowledge and his conviction that experience offers for us a pattern worth attention and application. Poetry surpasses philosophy and
history because it is best framed to "the highest end of the mistress-
knowledge, by the Greeks called ἀρχιτεκτονική, which stands (as I
think) in the knowledge of a man's self, in the ethic and politic consideration" (*DP* 82-83).

The *New Arcadia*'s story of Pyrocles and Musidorus implies throughout that such self-knowledge comes neither by resisting the incursions of personal and public turmoil nor by passively enduring them. What is required is a new perception and a re-creation of the self in that light. The stoical self-sufficiency Musidorus urges on Pyrocles in the early debates represents a failure in self-knowledge, a blindness to the complexity of his own life, as he later and unhappily admits: "I find indeed that all is but lip-wisdom which wants experience" (*NA* 106).

Their recognition of the truth of inconstancy and of ways in which it necessitates heroic counterfeiting is probably what led both Montaigne and Sidney to write in flexible forms and nondogmatic contexts. Making himself the text, Montaigne is free to imitate the developing, sometimes slow, sometimes sudden, nature of human experience that is his argument. The notorious wandering of his essays in, around, and away from their announced topics forms only the most elementary instance of a central conviction governing his composition. Here too we can find an explanation for the much noted mingling of genres in the revised *Arcadia*.[50] The shifting from pastoral to heroic has received considerable study, though I would argue that by the time one reaches the break in Book Three the form of the *New Arcadia* appears to be *sui generis*—an intentional effort to imitate the experience of its characters and to create a like experience in its readers.

II

In the *Old Arcadia*, Pyrocles and Musidorus's adventures begin when they set out from Thessalia to visit Pyrocles' triumphant father in Byzantium. A storm drives them ashore in Asia Minor, through which they travel for a year, journeying at last to Egypt. They determine there to return to their native Greece, planning "to exercise their virtues and increase their experience." So it is that, "taking Arcadia in their way, for the fame of the country, they came thither newly after that this strange solitariness had possessed Basilius" (*OA* 11). All this is told in less than twenty lines. In the *New Arcadia*, the princes' story begins with a shipwreck—Musidorus washed unconscious onto the Laconian shore and Pyrocles taken up by pirates.

The revision is a telling one. This time the two travelers will take many chapters (in Book Two) to recall their Asian achievements, trying to convince the Arcadian princesses and themselves that they retain the just assurance of men who subdue those passions to which others are slaves, that their privileged place in the aristocracy of virtue remains secure. But this is delusion, for the shipwreck is inward too.

From now on they will never be allowed to forget that, like ordinary men and women, they are subject to the revolutions of chance, not only from external threats but also from those within. They make many attempts to escape the pained awareness that their world runs all on a wheel; they also sometimes appear to seek ways to accept such an ever re-forming experience and to frame a heroic life within it. And so all their Arcadian performances can be called counterfeits: efforts to deceive; efforts to make of themselves an imitation of truth as they now know it.

"Arcadia, Arcadia was the place prepared to be the stage of his endless overthrow. Arcadia was . . . the charmed circle where all his spirits for ever should be enchanted" (*NA* 136). So Musidorus describes himself to Pamela, speaking better than he understands. Together with Pyrocles, he has practiced that Aristotelian self-love by which the dominant intellect bestows confidence and power. Even now, as he speaks to Pamela, he sounds as much like one who has *lost* his beloved as found her. The account of his birth and education in which this outcry appears is of course a way of declaring his princely identity to Pamela, but it is equally an effort to deny the "endless overthrow" that is now his lot. He seeks to impress on the volatile present his just past, apparently thinking that he can bring the current revolution within that old, self-affirming hierarchy. It has been suggested that the princes' Asian heroism "is made the explicit guide to inward virtue in the present,"[51] but in fact the princes' perplexity arises because they cannot apply old justice to their present dilemma. Having made the choice of Hercules, they find themselves on the wrong road. This explains Musidorus's embarrassed recollection of those lost days and shame at his unjust submission to eros: "I must say for him . . . that well doing was at that time his scope, from which no faint pleasures could withhold him" (*NA* 135). We are left to wonder how Pamela, the "faint pleasure" in question, receives this line.

Throughout the revised story's first two books, these princely lovers are never far from self-indulgent nostalgia and comic disorientation. Only the sudden peril of the captivity in Book Three breaks this pattern. However much they defend the imperatives of love, Sidney leaves no doubt that the princes often feel ridiculous—debased—in their disguises as Amazon and shepherd. Musidorus's continuous subtext in his talks with Pamela is *This abject figure is not Musidorus*—a variation of Astrophil's "I am not I, pitie the tale of me" (*AS* 45.14). Pyrocles argues well for the virtues of womankind in the second debate, but he concludes by weeping and fainting. His jewel may be inscribed "never more valiant," but he sings of defeat:

Transformed in show, but more transformed in mind,
I cease to strive, with double conquest foiled;
For (woe is me) my powers all I find
With outward force and inward treason spoiled.

For from without came to mine eyes the blow,
Whereto mine inward thoughts did faintly yield;
Both these conspired poor reason's overthrow;
False in myself, thus have I lost the field. (*NA* 69)

This first lyric is like Amphialus's "Dream of Mira": a lament for
the just and victorious self. Pyrocles neither complains of his mistress's
cruelty nor eulogizes her perfections. It is a still dearer beloved he
mourns:

> I take to witness the eternal spring of virtue [he tells his cousin] that I have
> never read, heard, nor seen anything; I had never any taste of philosophy,
> nor inward feeling in myself which, for a while, I did not call for my suc-
> cour. But alas, what resistance was there when ere long my very reason
> was . . . conquered. (*NA* 79)

This *after* he has fallen in love with Philoclea, disguised himself to woo
her, and defended his choice to his friend. Pyrocles uses the language
of justice even though his very acts discredit it; as with Amphialus, he
can only picture himself here in defeat. Like Heliodorus's Theagenes,
he confesses his love, "in token that by force, and against his will, he
was subdued by the maide."[52] The pervasive conceit in his complaint
is military; as readers will soon learn, it is a business in which he has
excelled until Arcadia. Subject now to something and to someone he
has been trained to regard as beneath his dominant and "virtuous"
mind, he no longer knows himself. So it is with an awkward union of
pride and despair that he at last tells Philoclea his true name:

> O only princess, attend here a miserable miracle of affection! Behold here
> . . . Pyrocles, prince of Macedon, whom you only have brought to this game
> of fortune, and unused metamorphosis; whom you only have made neglect
> his country, forget his father, and lastly, forsake to be Pyrocles. (*NA* 231)

The reference to his father Euarchus strikes home: the basis of his
judgment, the "good ruler," has been effaced. In love the princes feel
not only turned from their victorious Asian progress; they also feel
robbed of their ability to apprehend the good. No longer lords of truth,
they find their just identity wandering the present like a ghost.

Happily for us, Sidney cannot always take the princes as seriously
as they do themselves, a fact implying that their funerals for virtue may

not be in order. Comedy overtakes their old habits of domination, as well as their newfound subjection to the base, physical element at the bottom of Plato's human pyramid. When Pamela at last declares her love to Musidorus, the very assurance of his worth and power plays him false. In his passion, "never acquainted with mediocrity, [he] could not set bounds upon his happiness, nor be content to give desire a kingdom but that it must be an unlimited monarchy" (*NA* 308). But when this heroic magnanimity is answered with maidenly horror, he is banished from her presence. His bold play for dominance only deepens his subjection to woman and things "womanish."

Castiglione's Bembo counsels that the proper lover should "call backe again the coveting of the body to beawtye alone, and . . . beehoulde it in it self simple and pure, and frame it within in his imagination sundred from all matter."[53] Sidney's princes prove delightfully inept at heeding such advice. Even as readers admire Pyrocles' courage in saving Philoclea from Cecropia's lion, they cannot fail to notice that there is an ironic affinity between victorious man and beheaded beast. Having encountered the animal "with the swiftness of desire" and killed it, Zelmane/Pyrocles now chases the princess, lion's head in hand, even as a passion driven Gynecia chases him,

> so that it was a new sight fortune had prepared to those woods, to see these great personages thus run one after the other, each carried forward with an inward violence. (*NA* 112–13)

Soon after this episode, Musidorus pauses suddenly in his woeful account of Pamela's disdainful majesty to envy the liberties of Dametas' cattle: "Their minds grudge not their bodies' comfort, nor their senses are letted from enjoying their objects; we have the impediments of honour, and the torments of conscience" (*NA* 128). No stock pastoral rhetoric, no elegant lament, can spare Sidney's heroes from the comedy of desire.

In the Pyrocles and Musidorus of Sidney's *New Arcadia* A. C. Hamilton finds a final "triumph of love and virtue" that would render "the continuation of the story in the *Old Arcadia* [with its embarrassing capture of the princes and its morally awkward trial] inadequate, however much revised."[54] But in their endless overthrow Sidney does not excise the contradictions in their conduct: once the princes fall into Arcadia and into love, contradiction *is* their nature. That is why they, rather than a "purer" Argalus or Parthenia, are at the center of the narrative, drawn as complicated and contradictory figures so that their image may counsel likewise impure readers. In the *New Arcadia* love effects no inevitable gains in self-knowledge or well-doing: it is neither more nor less than

Sidney's means of casting the princes into the labyrinth of experience. Like poetry in the *Defence*, it becomes an occasion for use or abuse.

Once in love, the princes are alternately insightful and blind. Pyrocles and Musidorus sometimes stop grieving their lost self-image long enough to see the world outside them, to acknowledge its reality and worth with a becoming humility that echoes the honest devotion of Strephon and Claius. Readers have seen this already in Pyrocles' impassioned wonder at the Arcadian landscape and in his eloquent defense of the strength and virtue of women. Though Pyrocles is generally the more meditative of Sidney's pair, this humility born of new insight can be found in Musidorus as well. Repulsed by Pamela, he verges toward self-hatred, but "love only strave with the fury of his anguish, telling it that, if it destroyed Dorus, it should also destroy the image of her that lived in Dorus." Of course he remains worried about his suit, but in "loving in himself nothing but the love of her," he sees that something—someone—outside his own injured vanity must be taken into account (*NA* 309). A small gain, but a real one.

What is activated here is not just flickering inspiration, but an enhanced power to *think*—to recognize the real and act on it. This appears in more dramatic contexts too, as when Pyrocles saves Philoclea and the rest of the royal party from the rebellious mob by reading their muddled desires and persuading them to peace. More clearly still, it guides him when in Book Three he encourages the rigidly chaste princesses to temporize with Anaxius, urging them not to choose martyrdom until no other honorable course remains. They must *look* and use their *wit*, "for then would be the time to die nobly when you cannot live nobly" (*NA* 456).

Yet throughout the story as we have it, these same lovers also act with a foolish and sometimes dangerous arrogance born of blind self-regard. In contrast to the battle that drew them together and led to settlement of the helots' rebellion, the meeting of Musidorus and Pyrocles as the "ill-apparelled" and black knights at the tournament in Book One is merely chaotic. Unknown to one another, they fall to boyish bickering and launch a three-way fracas with the champion that is likened to "a matachin dance" (*NA* 102). Here there may be some Sidnean soldier's humor, but not in two episodes from Book Three. Musidorus has been favorably contrasted with the rebel Amphialus during the siege; Pyrocles' challenge of Anaxius has been read as signaling the clearing of his confused emotions during the captivity.[55] But in both cases the two mimic Amphialus, matching his vain efforts at domination and his inability to think his way clear.

In the battle of Musidorus with Amphialus, no knowledge is gained and no victory, personal or political, is achieved. After a choleric exchange of letters—much different from those passed earlier between Argalus and Amphialus—Musidorus meets the rebel to discover both are dressed in a melancholy black that betrays an "alliance of passions" (*NA* 405). Falsely suspecting a rival in one another, they fight with a mingling of anger and shame, Amphialus with "revenge in his heart" and Musidorus "guided by the storm of fury" (*NA* 409). Significantly, the battle ends in a draw. Musidorus appears close to a fatal advantage when Amphialus is rescued by his seconds. Nothing is resolved: Amphialus castigates himself as a coward, and Musidorus chafes to fight again before his wounds have healed. As for Pyrocles, he is overcome by possessive fury. Later in the siege, he gains a weapon to fight Anaxius and his brother. He overcomes Lycurgus—who yields—but when Pyrocles sees on his enemy a jewel he had given Philoclea, "remembrance, feeding upon wrath, trod down all conceits of mercy" and he made his "sword drink the blood of his heart" (*NA* 462). If this is an echo of Aeneas killing the defeated Turnus (wearing the dead Pallas's belt), it is not a flattering one.

This union of blindness and insight, self-deceit and heroic counterfeiting in Pyrocles and Musidorus appears most fully in those words and acts that are poetic performances. These in fact compose the majority of their Arcadian conduct: theatricals, songs, and epic narration. In most cases these "acts" comprise a counterfeiting in both senses of the term at once: deception as well as poetic invention. The counterfeiting begins when the princes assume new false names: Pyrocles-Daiphantus becomes the Amazon Zelmane, Musidorus-Palladius the shepherd Dorus. For both princes this occasions a double forgery, practiced against the Arcadians and themselves. It is first a means of courting Basilius's daughters, undertaken against his express decree. Initially this seems harmless enough, especially in light of Basilius's stubborn folly, but by persisting in their falsehood Pyrocles and Musidorus make violation of hospitality and even violence ever more likely. How else can they devise a union with the princesses when the oracles of Books Two and Three reveal that the king and queen would continue in their present resolves? What choices but lies and secret flight or open war?[56]

Adopting these false names also generates self-deception and hypocrisy. Pyrocles' playing the Amazon's part—fully armed and wearing the "never more valiant" broach—is an attempt to retain the control over disruptive experience he has so long enjoyed. But all his misadventures as a womanized Hercules mock this effort. Musidorus, having just counseled Pyrocles that a virtuous man's acts must "not only better himself but benefit others" (*NA* 52), violates his own principle in his transformation from prince to shepherd. He sends the shepherd Menalcus—who has been his host, kept his presence secret, and finally given him Menalcus's own clothes—to his house in Thessalia to deliver a letter. But Musidorus's letter orders the staff to lock the bearer up and not allow him to speak to anyone until further notice. We can only assume that poor Menalcus is still there.

Yet these transformations of name and nature also signify heroic invention: they are counterfeits that speak metaphorically a real change in perception and a newfound humility that does not preclude vigorous action. Musidorus's simplified name and shepherd's weeds figure his own genuine poverty before the wonder and goodness of those things "womanish" he has so recently mocked. Pyrocles' new name indicates a more dramatic change. In the *Old Arcadia* he takes the name Cleophilia (found in Book Nine of *Amadis of Gaul*), neither more nor less than a pun on Philoclea. But in becoming Zelmane, Pyrocles binds his love of Philoclea with the self-sacrificial devotion of the young woman who helped him escape from prison and who languished and died in his service. An element of self-pity may taint this act, yet taking this name acknowledges the value of outer-directed love even as it reveals Pyrocles' determination *not* to decline in silence like his namesake. We should recall that it is as Zelmane that the prince makes his defense of womanly virtue in response to Musidorus's jeers about mental and emotional infirmity.

Without distortion the entire conduct of Pyrocles and Musidorus in Arcadia can be called a performance, an act. Musidorus literally becomes an actor in his dressage, dancing, and dialogue staged before Pamela, the last of which features himself as Paris to a Priamus played by his doltish master, Dametas (*NA* 153–54). In discovering the breaking point of their Ciceronian self-assurance, the princes experience both the discomfort and the strange release of inventive power that marks those figures in Shakespeare who, in C. L. Barber's terms, pass from a life understood as ceremony to a life understood as history:

> The Renaissance . . . was a moment when educated men and women were modifying a ceremonial conception of human life to create a historical conception. The ceremonial view, which assumed that names and meanings are fixed and final, expressed experience as pageant and ritual—pageant where the right names could march in proper order, or ritual where names could be changed in the right, the proper way. The historical view expresses life as drama. People in drama are not identical with their names, for they gain and lose their names, their status and meaning—and not by settled ritual: the gaining and losing of names, of meaning, is beyond the control of any set ritual sequence.[57]

The disastrous resort to ritual identity appears most memorably in the *New Arcadia* when the rebel Amphialus tries to regain his lost personal and public control through the fatal charade of chivalric performances in Book Three. Amphialus's very name ("between two seas") displays his necessarily "dramatic" nature, but he drives himself toward ruin by refusing to acknowledge the need to counterfashion a new self. Yet I think Amphialus's struggle is emblematic of another shift in the perception of experience in Sidney's revised story: not from a "medieval" conception of life as ritual to a "Renaissance" one, but from the Tudor humanist ideal of inner stability (and its immunity to the treachery of experience) to a conception of life as "endless overthrow," requiring constant though by no means futile invention in response to what Raleigh called "this stage-play world."[58]

The generation of Sidney's father sought in its aristocracy of educated virtue a stable political and cultural identity not subject to royal favor and court intrigue. One of the remarkable feats of Sidney's writing is its insistence that such a stability cannot be maintained without ruin of the psyche and without denial of the designs of providence. To counterfeit—with all its attendant potential and danger—is the only response left in such a contingent world, if human wit is to play any part at all. The painful self-awareness and instability that accompany this "dramatic" effort continually inform the princes' conversation, as in Musidorus's lament to his friend over their schemes: "O heaven and earth! . . . To what a pass are our minds brought, that from the right line of virtue are wried to these crooked shifts!" (*NA* 109). Such simultaneous dis-ease and inventive force appear most fully in those songs and heroic narratives by which they strive to compose their "history."

Apart from verses in the eclogues, which have no authority in the *New Arcadia*,[59] the princes compose nine songs, most of them during the courtship in Book Two. Not one of these lyrics, all written first for the *Old Arcadia*, has the wit and motive force of the sonnets and songs of *Astrophil and Stella*. Studied in new critical purity, few repay our toil in the thicket of schemes, tropes, and metrical calisthenics that made them a useful school for Sidney's unelected vocation. But read dramatically, they form a picture of the princes' radical transformation, of the "endless overthrow" that forces on them the question of how they will define their lives. Like Montaigne, being of unsettled mind, the princes cannot resolve themselves, but must ever be making *essais*. These speech-acts are then counterfeits, imitations in words of the experiential patterns unfolding outside of them and within. As such, they display both deception and honest reformation.

The two songs in Book One use the moral vocabulary of the princes' old life to call their transformation weakness and defeat even as these lyrics acknowledge the reality of change and of the princes' desire to embrace it. Pyrocles' sonnet "Transformed in show" (*NA* 69), quoted above, and Musidorus's ten-line "Come shepherd's weeds" (*NA* 105) dwell on each poet's shock at the "outward force" (*NA* 69) that has overthrown the interior stability of his mind, making the Amazon-prince "False in myself" (*NA* 69) and the shepherd-prince one who "spoils himself of bliss" (*NA* 105). This provokes each song's awkward self-consciousness, whose verbal imitation lies in the reflexive syntax and puns: "Transformed in show, but more transformed in mind" and "What marvel, then, I take a woman's hue, / Since what I see, think, know, is all but you?" (*NA* 69).

Each song is in fact an extended play on the singer's altered dress, itself an "opposing imitation" of an interior metamorphosis. Musidorus's song actually addresses this new dress:

> Come, shepherd's weeds, become your master's mind:
> Yield outward show, what inward change he tries;
> Nor be abashed, since such a guest you find,
> Whose strongest hope in your weak comfort lies.
>
> Come, shepherd's weeds, attend my woeful cries:
> Disuse yourselves from sweet Menalcas' voice,
> For other be those tunes which sorrow ties
> From those clear notes which freely may rejoice.
>   Then pour out plaint, and in one word say this:
>   Helpless his plaint who spoils himself of bliss. (*NA* 105)

As with Pyrocles-Zelmane's "Transformed in show," this lament employs the princes' accustomed language of just command; each main verb is imperative: come, become, yield, attend, disuse, pour out. But each command now becomes an ironic acknowledgment of inward overthrow. Musidorus's borrowed clothes are of course a ruse to reach Pamela, but they also signify the inadequacy of his "just" self, for they are to "become" his mind—meaning both to befit and to stand for his experience of "inward chance." Though plainly dismayed, and though already plotting an inevitably dangerous deception of the exiled Arcadian court, the princes-become-lovers have already gained a new power to figure their altered lives. In C. L. Barber's terms, their lives have become dramatic, their acts a performance "beyond the control of any set ritual sequence."

The next two lyrics present alternate readings of yielding to love: one as an occasion for self-pity, the other as an ingenious defense of virtue in desire. Once more, in the first two chapters of Book Two, Pyrocles sings a sonnet and Musidorus a lyric shorter by one quatrain. As with "Transformed," Pyrocles' "In vain, mine eyes" (*NA* 121) is performed before an unseen audience, in this case the tormented Queen

Gynecia. This sonnet signifies more baffled resignation than the self-accusations of "Tranformed," a note of self-pity born of the frustrations created by the singer's womanish disguise. "In vain" moves from quatrain to quatrain to sestet arguing that because Philoclea's image governs Pyrocles' eyes and heart and head, he has no recourse but to "yield my life" to "this strange death" (*NA* 121). The intervention of Basilius's sonnet, "Let not old age disgrace my high desire"— comically accompanied by the old king's "fetching a little skip, as if he had said his strength had not yet forsaken him" (*NA* 123–24)—forms a bathetic counterpoint to Pyrocles' verse, calling the prince's desperation into question and preparing us for his cousin's more hopeful variation of the theme of "In vain."

Musidorus's "Since so mine eyes" is a double performance: not only sung before an audience but also staged to win Pamela through her loutish servant Mopsa, for whom "Dorus" counterfeits a passion.

> Since so mine eyes are subject to your sight,
> That in your sight they fixed have my brain;
> Since so my heart is filled with that light,
> That only light doth all my life maintain;
>
> Since in sweet you all goods so richly reign,
> That where you are no wished good can want;
> Since so your living image lives in me,
> That in myself yourself true love doth plant;
>> How can you him unworthy then decree,
>> In whose chief part your worths implanted be?
>
> (*NA* 129–30)

The opening quatrain presents the same triple subjugation of eyes, heart, and head ("brain") of Pyrocles' sonnet, but Musidorus uses it as the initial premise of a clever syllogism completed by the second quatrain and couplet: since you rule my sight, mind, and desire, and since you reign as monarch of "all goods," how can I do anything but imitate your virtues? Like Strephon and Claius, both princes think themselves to be new made in the image of the beloved, but Sidney structures the sequence of songs so that Pyrocles' sorrowful surrender becomes the prelude to his fellow lover's witty claim to value and virtue in love.

Yet even Musidorus's happier song involves self-deception, for like Pyrocles' it denies any measure of choice in love, implying an abandonment of every faculty to all-controlling eros. This tactic acts to protect the integrity of the princes' old and much cherished identity as lords of justice and truth. If love alone is to blame, then that Ciceronian self can be a pitiable prisoner rather than a failure. For that reason it is pleasant to turn to Pyrocles' next composition, filled with erotic wonder but free of "vain" self-consciousness. Anthologized and quoted by Sidney's contemporaries more than any of his other verses,[60] "What tongue can her perfections tell" is a long and rapturous effictio on Philoclea as seen by the lover who watches her bathing (*NA* 190 – 95). No analysis of the verse is needed, but a comparison of its context in the revised story with that in the original will help explain its significance.

In the *Old Arcadia*, the song appears in Book Three as the quarrel in Philoclea's bedroom has ended and Pyrocles has been revived from his faint by his beloved's embrace:

> So that, coming again to the use of his feet, and lifting the sweet burden of Philoclea in his arms, he laid her on her bed again, having so free scope of his serviceable sight that there came into his mind a song the shepherd Philisides had in his hearing sung of the beauties of his unkind mistress, which in Pyrocles' judgement was fully accomplished in Philoclea. (*OA* 237-38)

But in the *New Arcadia* the song is occasioned by Pyrocles' sight of Philoclea in "the transparent veil of Ladon":

> taking up the lute, her [Pyrocles-Zelmane's] wit began to be with a divine fury inspired, . . . while her body was the room where it [Philoclea's beauty] should be celebrated, her soul the queen which should be delighted. And so together went the utterance and the invention that one might judge it was Philoclea's beauty which did speedily write it in her eyes, or the sense thereof which did word by word indite it in her mind, whereto she, but as an organ, did only lend utterance. (*NA* 190)

There are two significant changes here. Most obvious is that Sidney now spares Pyrocles both the indiscretion of bedding Philoclea and the humiliation of being caught by Dametas, both of which happen after the song in the *Old Arcadia*. The song in the *New* does not link the experience of being "kindled with wonder" (*NA* 190) with the shame of bad judgment and defeat. This time it is Amphialus who is caught in shame and defeated by Pyrocles for spying on the bathing princesses. Equally important is that in the revised story it is Pyrocles himself who composes the poem, "utterance and invention" united in the fury of inspiration. I think the neoplatonic language is written tongue in cheek, since the singer so quickly falls from "divine fury" to furious jealousy of Amphialus. But the song itself remains an invention free of the wearisome laments Pyrocles customarily sings: to see and love with uncluttered pleasure that which is outside himself, to re-present that experience without self-pity and self-reference, is act of counterfeiting both poetic and honest.

The final poems, which appear in Book Two, display the princes in stalemate. Dramatically these lyrics represent an intensifying introspection leading not to clearer vision of self and world but to an impasse of blindness and self-pity. Here is an occasion, borrowing from Stillman's commentary on the *Old Arcadia*, "where song corrupts more than it cures," displaying the "distortions of the impassioned mind" governed by "self-love."[61] In the revised story these last songs form an emotional logjam that makes readers ready for the sudden plot break in Book Three.

I believe Sidney would have turned his story again toward a trial like that which forms the penultimate turn of events in the *Old Arcadia*; but in the middle of the revised narrative he wanted and found a way to release the princes' and the reader's frustration with their accelerating self-examination in love. The captivity episode carries the princes, especially the prisoner Zelmane-Pyrocles, further out of their past self-guided orbit, forcing new occasions for heroic action on them and giving them something undeniably real to worry about. As I noted above, their response is as mixed as ever in motive and insight, but the ploy works: readers and lovers alike cannot live indefinitely by thinking.

"Over these brooks, trusting to ease mine eyes" (*NA* 229), Pyrocles' last poem, is a counterfeit in the pejorative sense of the term, though it is himself the prince tries to deceive. Forgetting his first defense of love in the debates, Pyrocles falls into a narcissistic meditation, imagining that the water, air, and riverbank (into which he engraves his verses) exist merely to redouble his inward trauma. The prose prelude to his lyric reveals as much as the verses:

> "Fair streams," said she, "that do vouchsafe in your clearness to represent unto me my blubbered face, let the tribute-offer of my tears unto you procure your stay a while with me, that I may begin yet at last to find something that pities me, and that all things of comfort and pleasure do not fly away from me. But if the violence of your spring command you to haste away . . . , yet carry with you these few words, and let the uttermost ends of the world know them. A love more clear than yourselves, dedicated to a love (I fear) more cold than yourselves, with the clearness lays a night of sorrow upon me, and with the coldness inflames a world of fire within me." (*NA* 228–29)

If "clear" means free of deceit, then Pyrocles makes a false image of his own experience. Even in her confusion about his gender, Philoclea never regards him coldly: she shows him nothing but courtesy and flattering attention. In contrast to his original pity for Philoclea, prompted by the memory of Zelmane, Pyrocles now sees and pities himself alone. Each of the six-line stanzas of "Over these brooks" reproduces the image of the lover in love with his own sorrow: "trusting to ease" his sight, he finds that the "wat'ry glass" only reflects his woes; releasing oppressive thought into the air, he only hears it "with echo's force rebound"; seeking to "discharge my mind" in words on the sand, "my tales foretold I find, / And see therein how well the writer fares" (*NA* 229). The poem is a hall of mirrors, self-enclosed, lacking any reference to the beloved—even any sense of invasion from external force. Pyrocles' obsessive use of anadiplosis—"mine eyes, / (Mine eyes)," "my face, (my face)"; of polyptoton—"my tales foretolde," "In wat'ry glass my watered eyes I see"; and of other forms of repetition intensifies this exercise in debilitating pity.[62] This counterfeit exists merely to save its author from the burden of real sight and so, of real choice. Fortunately, Philoclea arrives to save him (and us) from further lament.

A similar evasion governs Musidorus's "Unto a caitif wretch whom long affliction holdeth" (*NA* 311–14), the verses sent to Pamela after his too ardent advances provoke her to dismiss him. This last of Musidorus's poems is long and tedious, not just because we take little pleasure in its quantitative verse, but because its speaker indulges in constant hyperbolic self-dramatization: the work is "the last monument of his anguish"; he cannot sue for pity, for "despair hath giv'n me my answer, / Despair, most tragical clause to a deadly request" (*NA* 311). Pleas for mercy yield to abject praise—"Oh, wretch! What do I say? Should that fair face be defaced? / Should my too much sight cause so true a sun to be lost?" (*NA* 313)—and at last to false resignation: "banished do I live . . . , / Since so she will, whose will is to me more than a law" (*NA* 314). And so he concludes, "If then a man in most ill case may give you a farewell, / Farewell, long farewell, all my woe, all my delight" (*NA* 314). This final sentence has more beauty and power than the rest of the lament. But with it Musidorus ends on a note of paradox and paralysis resembling the frustrated conclusion to Astrophil's invention, except that Astrophil's is the better poetry:

> So strangely (alas) thy works in me prevaile,
> That in my woes for thee thou art my joy,
> And in my joyes for thee my only annoy.
>
> (*AS* 108, 12-14)

In the *Old Arcadia* this "elegiac" (*OA* 310) is sung in the fourth eclogue by Philisides, who says that he sent it to Mira before exiling himself, having decided "by perpetual absence to choke mine own ill fortunes" (*OA* 341). In making Musidorus the author of it here, Sidney gives him the same blindness and petulant failure to take responsibility. In the revised story the poem concludes the first chapter of Book Three, right before Cecropia's confederates capture the disguised Pyrocles and the princesses. Sidney understood that if his counterfeiting princes were to be turned from self-deception, another catastrophe—something undeniably real against which to shape their "acts"—was in order.

The princes' most sustained effort at counterfeiting is the narration of their own past to the princesses. Pyrocles and Musidorus's pre-Arcadian adventures include battle, shipwreck, and confusion abounding, but they leave the princes' cherished inner structure of virtue not only unshaken but also confirmed by the cousins' power to withstand temptation and make order of political chaos. The heroic fiction they make of this past authenticates their courtly credentials for the princesses, whom they hope will love them for the dangers they have passed. But this fiction also attempts to fashion a reassuring image of themselves, and like the composition of their songs, involves both honest imitation and deceit. Evoking a glorious progress in their lives before Arcadia allows the two to recall and to present themselves as capable of virtuous choice and action. I see no reason to question the essential truth of their accounts; in fact, taking stock of their past selves is needed if they are to choose what they must now become—what is pastoral leisure for if not for such a retrospective? Their stories make little or no accommodation to their present experience, no effort to question the code of conduct whose limits have been in Arcadia so forcefully brought home. This is a fiction that canonizes a lost life of inner command, which is the very price love exacts of them.

In this way, the tales *are* unreliable—forgeries designed to fool the tellers into believing that they retain the self-possession and powers of manipulation of which love has robbed them. Even the urgency of youthful desire rarely draws them far enough from old assumptions to regard them as ripe for reassessment. So they call the present a stage of overthrow and ruin, construing the past as a rising action before the catastrophe of Arcadian experience. That Arcadian breakdown engenders a sometime capacity to counterfeit a new self, more fully heroic in self-knowledge because more fully directed outside the self-sufficient soul of their past. But in Sidney's unfinished story this is a capacity the princes perceive only in part and act on only occasionally. Because they try desperately to keep unchanged that Ciceronian soul that has been their sure defense, they appear only in moments of acute distress to consider the risk and the value of that "eccentric" counterfashioning that must from now on define the heroic life.

III

I remarked at the start of this chapter that Sidney's poetry habitually employs the force of eros to expose our vulnerability to contingency, to the work of chance and death by which conventional management of experience is undone. This may seem to be an end in itself. Certainly such a view appears to be the conclusion of Shakespeare's Jaques and Macbeth, for whom all human performance ends in mere oblivion, signifying nothing. I do not think this is Sidney's conclusion. But I believe that such a possibility provokes a troubling question for readers of the *New Arcadia*: does Sidney reveal a human inventive power arising from the breakdown of convention only to show that such a power reveals the vanity of all human striving? If the conventional modes of justice and radical romantic devotion do not provide adequate models for "opposing imitation" in the lives of Sidney's princes, what does? Are they merely to spin tales out of themselves in a fashion "wholly imaginative, as . . . by them that build castles in the air" (*DP* 79)? Certainly the answer to this last question is no: as the princes' songs become more exclusively introspective and overwrought, they lose aesthetic as well as moral force. Sidney's own story exposes this practice as a poetic narcissism that can bear no fruit but passivity and self-pity. The disaster of Book Three rescues Pyrocles and Musidorus from infatuation with their own weakness and provides them with something both precious and "other" to worry about—the welfare of the beloved. But if my reading in Chapter Three is correct, then the beloved alone cannot serve as a complete object of imitation. As the story of Argalus and Parthenia implies, if the beloved is all, then bright things will quickly come to confusion. What then must serve?

A Shakespearean analogy may offer some guidance. When Hamlet returns from his abortive voyage to England, he gives up his career as scourge and minister and stops the manipulative plotting that has until then made him more and more like those of the court whom he detests. Events on the ocean crossing have led him to believe that

> Our indiscretion sometime serves us well
> When our deep plots do pall, and that should learn us
> There's a divinity that shapes our ends,
> Rough-hew them how we will.[63]

His conviction that there is a "heaven ordinant" in his experience, that "There is a special providence in the fall of a sparrow"[64] could be read as terminal megalomania. But his graveyard humor, his deliberate rejection of further melancholy introspection, his pardon of Laertes, and his prevention of Horatio's suicide all suggest otherwise. On what basis does he find a way to act? What he must and apparently does embrace is the mystery of providential design, revealed oddly enough in the work of chance and death—in the undoing of Claudius's plan to murder him and in the silent witness of Yorick's skull. By seeing what *is*, Hamlet can counterfeit an active and effective life within the moral and physical vulnerability that defines his human nature. He will no longer plot, but rather wittily follow the plot of events unfolding before him, always "ready." Interestingly, in classic Lutheran fashion Hamlet is enabled to act for the "civic" good by the recognition that the final good is not his to produce.[65]

Sidney believed that the apparently accidental moves within the design of the heavenly maker; but within the labyrinth of desire his princes (like Prince Hamlet) seldom enjoy such a consoling perspective. What they must imitate—or love, since Musidorus is right to say that the love transforms "the lover into the thing loved" (*NA* 72)—is the continually shifting and unfolding pattern of experience, even as it shatters the life and the self they have so long prized.

Martin Luther, Eric Gritsch says, saw "sin as the sphere of God's merciful action" as well as the cause of all our woe. Luther stressed the need to define each human being as *simul iustus et peccator*, the *totus homo* whose full nature is engaged by the Maker's saving design.[66] Montaigne warns of the danger of a reductive grasp of experience and of the need for the Sidnean virtues of doing and suffering in facing its contingencies:

> A man must learne to endure that patiently which he cannot avoyde conveniently. Our life is composed, as is the harmony of the World, of contrary things; so of divers tunes, some pleasant, some harsh. . . . What would that Musition say that should love but some one of them? He ought to know how to use them severally and how to entermingle them. So should we both of goods and evils which are consubstantiall to our life. Our being cannot subsist without this commixture, whereto one side is no lesse necessary than the other.[67]

With Luther and Montaigne, Philip Sidney shares a habitual doubt of traditional humanist claims to completeness in their formulation of the virtuous life; for him the citadel of humanist justice all too often shuts out the sphere of action in which heroic transformation takes place. Nor is he content to substitute the opposing but also limited claims of romantic devotion. Either would deny the reality of that fiction created moment by moment in and around us by the heavenly maker, whose invention both enforces and enables our own.

Sidney's great gift as a poet is his impulse to wholeness, to an increasing and transforming field of vision that in his terms pushes outward toward the invention of Providence. His princes are heroes of a new sort insofar as they seek to imitate that invention, counterfeiting what they see only in part. Pyrocles practices this poetic vision when he says that "the course of my life hath a sport sometimes to poison me with roses, sometimes to heal me with wormwood" (*NA* 251), and when in Amphialus's dungeon he finds that he must accept not only suffering but also the joy beyond hope that Philoclea is alive. Like their poet-maker, the princes must choose not as Hercules at the crossroads between ease and action but between an inevitably false effort to fashion their lives on inadequate principles and an evitably uncertain effort to act in response to the complexity of experience. The work of invention begins in vision, and to see rightly—as any poet knows—is an exacting and fearful discipline, a moral act.

This invention is the work that Sidney's poetry requires of its readers.

5
Right Reading

> He cometh to you with words set in delightful proportion
> . . . and with a tale forsooth he cometh unto you, with a tale
> which holdeth children from play, and old men from the
> chimney corner. And pretending no more, doth intend the
> winning of the mind from wickedness to virtue.
>
> *A Defence of Poetry*

By resting his case for poetry on the claim that it moves us to virtue, Sidney rests his case on the reader. In the *Defence* he writes of poetry as doing work that changes the reader—*hoc opus, hic labor est*—enabling a self-knowledge that has the "end of well-doing and not of well-knowing only" (*DP* 83). I want to test this claim against the experience of reading the *New Arcadia*. My argument will be that "right reading" of this story involves us in a cycle of engagement and detachment that prompts us to act poetically—to invent. Right reading is then an inclusive term rather than an exclusive, meant to imply the fullest possible dialogue with the text.

Sidney sometimes represents as self-evident his declaration that poetry can move us to desire doing good: "Who readeth Aeneas carrying old Anchises on his back, that wisheth not it were his fortune to perform so excellent an act?" (*DP* 92). Such passages seem to assume that readers will be fully captivated by "the force of delight" in those tales holding them from play and chimney corners, so much so that even "hard-hearted evil men" will "steal to see the form of goodness (which seen they cannot but love) ere themselves be aware, as if they took a medicine of cherries" (*DP* 107, 93). This provocation to embrace "heart-ravishing knowledge" (*DP* 76) is the first move poetry makes in us, drawing us into that "learner-like admiration" that Sidney says he and Edward Wotton felt when listening to Pugliano's beguiling stories of horsemanship (*DP* 73).[1]

Yet the full argument of the *Defence* anticipates an active reader, conscious of fiction. We know a story is a story, Sidney says, a play a play: "What child is there, that, coming to a play, and seeing *Thebes* written in great letters upon an old door, doth believe that it is Thebes?" (*DP* 103). It is because the poet makes no effort to hide the literal untruth of his text that the reader, "looking but for fiction, . . . shall use the narration but as an imaginative ground-plot of a profitable invention" (*DP* 103). If poetry is to work "to make many Cyruses" from its image of one Cyrus, readers must "learn aright why and how that maker made him" (*DP* 79).

Engagement in the poet's fiction is then a necessary but not sufficient condition for poetry to do its work. Ignorance, perversity, or uncritical wonder can mislead the reader: "If I had not been a piece of a logician before I came to him," Sidney writes of the engaging Pugliano, "I think he would have persuaded me to have wished myself a horse" (*DP* 73). The merely admiring reader may, like Sidney's astronomer, fall into a moral or intellectual ditch (*DP* 82). In answering the charge that poetry arouses vice, Sidney insists that if this should happen, we must "not say that poetry abuseth man's wit, but that man's wit abuseth poetry" (*DP* 104).

The abuse of wit here may well be the reader's as the poet's. For lack of discernment a reader could fail to emulate Virgil's noble Aeneas, however much moved. Reading then requires an active wit, and this of necessity demands the detachment to recognize poetry as fiction made by writers operating within their own particular history. In other words, reading is as much a fully human enterprise as Sidney tells us poetry is when he rejects the neoplatonic "divine force" as the origin of fiction (*DP* 78–79, 109). If we are moved to wonder, we are likewise moved to think.

Reading describes a fluctuation between innocence and experience. In their innocence readers privilege the fiction, consenting to be moved by it in thought and emotion, not jealous of their own preconceptions. Such willing engagement demands a temporary resistance to the new historicist project of dissolving the literary text into its cultural context, however useful that may be elsewhere.[2] If we refuse to inhabit for a time the world a text has made, we risk learning nothing about the world from which it came but what we already know. In Sidney's fiction, we may miss (ironically enough) the way his text represents as inadequate hallowed Tudor formulations of just conduct.

But this choice of engagement in the text must be complemented by an equal regard for the reader's own mind and culture.[3] To move from innocence to experience is to remember that the text is an artifact, profoundly interwoven with the other productions of its culture, literary and not. This text cannot become the imaginative groundplot of the readers' profitable inventions unless they cast a cold eye on its assumptions, assessing them in light of those they bring (critically) to the text. Sidney's own employment of Petrarch in writing *Astrophil and Stella* and of the several pastoral and heroic sources for the *Old* and *New Arcadia* exemplifies a habit of reading that is "engaged" but also radically critical and innovative, as does his qualified praise in the *Defence* for such "poems" as More's *Utopia* and the *Amadis de Gaul* (*DP* 86, 92).

Sidney's *New Arcadia* becomes an occasion for this dialogic form of reading; his text both provokes and requires it, enabling what Susanne Woods calls an "elective poetics" and Alan Hager "retroactive reading."[4] For clarity's sake I will separate discussion of engaged and detached responses to the text even though they will rarely be so neatly distinct within particular readers.

Each section below begins with a parable of reading, the first from Sidney's text, the second from my own history of teaching it. The first section includes a review of Sidney's major fiction before the *New Arcadia*, tracing through the *Old Arcadia* and *Astrophil and Stella* a growing power to pull the reader into an "engaged" experience of disorientation that reflects the dilemma of Sidney's characters. The second section examines some of our own "detached" habits of reading Sidney, testing them against the complexity of his representation of gender, patriarchal rule, and the desires and desirability of the body. With this analysis completed, I can address more broadly the cultural liberty and constraint—the history—within which Sidney and his readers seek to construct an adequate model of experience.

I

In her attempt to convince the imprisoned Pamela to yield to her son, Cecropia presents the world as a text that Pamela can cast in her own image, a playground for her own pleasure and domination. Pamela says that the purse she embroiders as Cecropia enters her cell is "a very purse" (*NA* 356); it is not "a treasure itself," as Cecropia argues (*NA* 355) but a human work with a function. Pamela denies that beauty is "but a pleasant mixture of natural colours . . . without any further consequence" (*NA* 356): beauty has causes and effects. This skirmishing over the purse and whether it bears any relation to the surrounding world prefigures the major rhetorical battle of Book Three.

Under the cloak of sisterly frankness, Cecropia makes her two central moves. First she asserts that Pamela's womanly beauty has a magical force that exempts her from the ordinary rules of law and power:

the beautiful woman "is served and obeyed [by men] . . . not because the laws so command it, but because they become laws to themselves to obey her" (*NA* 356). This assertion leads to Cecropia's seductive claim that the external world need not be "read" at all, but simply seized for Pamela's own indulgence. Luxuriating in "natural felicity," Pamela is to "be wise, and that wisdom shall be a god unto thee"; she should ignore both the powers that govern nature ("if there be any such") and the scarecrows of interpretation that "great clerks" have posted to intimidate the weak and ignorant (*NA* 359, 358).

Pamela's indignant reply defends a providentially guided world where "we know that each effect hath a cause" (*NA* 359). Sidney's Protestant conception of an enigmatic but active Providence has been important to my argument in other chapters, but here I am concerned with the parable of reading available in this temptation scene. Cecropia conjures a scorn for the text of material existence, which she represents as a work without effect or cause except as strong minds devise it. Pamela is invited to play the same cynical role enacted by the "great clerks": she is to be exempt from "vulgar opinions" (*NA* 358), free to indulge in a radical aestheticism.[5] Yet readers can see that Pamela's willingness to see the text of nature as a valid teacher and mover grants her both greater self-knowledge and greater resistance to fantasy.

For Cecropia is a fantasy monger. She urges Pamela to disdain submission to God so that Pamela will submit to rape. This is the goal of Cecropia's persuasions: the princess is to give her body to her jailer Amphialus to buy her life. In fact, when her rhetoric fails, we find Cecropia "condemning . . . her son's overfeeble humbleness, and purposing to egg him forward to a course of violence" (*NA* 363). Cecropia herself proves at last to be a poor reader of the body of experience whose power she has mocked, fulfilling Pamela's prophecy that she will "know that power by feeling it" (*NA* 363). Pamela's willingness to acknowledge that power allows her to resist rape and to fashion in her reply a speaking picture of nature and nature's God that confirms rather than undermines her own human wit. The very structure of her discourse reveals that she must interpret and "imitate" the text of creation according to her own rational and image-making powers, not in a "divine fury" or by blind faith.

The kind of intelligent engagement with the text of nature practiced by Pamela is invited by the text of Sidney's revised *Arcadia*, and it is practiced by Sidney himself with the text of experience. His poetry from the *Old Arcadia* through the *New* is marked by a refusal to settle for false closure, by a willingness to extend the inventions of his culture until their limits plainly appear, by an unwillingness to deny the possibility of irony and the reality of contingency. Chronological review of Sidney's major fiction reveals an increasingly effective use of readers' "innocence," a more and more complete skill in enabling them to inhabit the fiction so that it can become, in time, the ground-plot of their own invention.

The *Old Arcadia* is a comedy that tests the humanist construct of justice.[6] Sidney devotes half of the fourth and all of the fifth act of this comedy to the ways in which radically biased figures seek to construct a "just" resolution of the erotic and political anarchy generated by their deceptions. By establishing the good ruler Euarchus as a fully impartial judge over all the lovers' biased constructions of truth, and by then undoing *his* judgment at the rising of the fool-king Basilius, Sidney invites readers irresistibly to play the game of judgment themselves. The invitation he makes *directly* in *The Lady of May*—which begins as the Lady's daughter comes to Queen Elizabeth "crying out for justice" (*LM* 21)—Sidney achieves *theatrically* here, drawing readers into the forensic drama, giving them a thoroughly scrupulous and thoroughly unsatisfactory settlement of the lovers' crimes and misdemeanors, and then giving them a happy ordering designed, we are told, "by the highest providence" (*OA* 416).

A. C. Hamilton calls this resolution a "trick," and assumes that Sidney would share his own dissatisfaction with it.[7] A trick it is, but a fitting end to Sidney's highly polished comedy. Of course all fiction is tricky—a counterfeiting by which an *analogy* of experience (an "opposing imitation" of things in words) is presented *as* experience. But the ending of the *Old Arcadia* calls attention to this gap between counterfeit and real and draws readers into it, never letting them forget that they *are* playing a game there. Sidney's trick is a transparent one, which accounts for its great charm, like a display of sprezzatura that makes us wonder at its seeming effortless grace even as we know it is a human invention, a work. "This is a story," the trick ending announces, "a story in which the conventions of justice will not be mocked but will not override the conventions of comic narrative."

In the *Old Arcadia*, the fateful power of the oracle, linked explicitly to "the highest providence," and the overwhelming relief of Euarchus himself allow us to accept and savor this trick without believing that the "sacred righteousness" Euarchus defended is violated (*OA* 416, 411). If the limits of human justice are revealed—and they are—we have been prepared for that throughout the story by the indulgent narrator's voice and by the story's comic form. Comedy tolerates no forms of rigidity, not even rigidity of virtue. Readers of the *Old Arcadia* can accept the text's invitation, assured that whatever may happen to any character's judgments, no shock will arise to betray their own judgment of comic form. They come into the text like volunteers into a magic show—flattered, intrigued, but always conscious that sooner or later they will be freed with everything but their own certainty intact.

What the *Old Arcadia* does comically with justice, *Astrophil and Stella* does tragically with the invention of eros. I do not intend to sketch any structure of rising action through catastrophe; instead I suggest that the sequence is a poem in which the gap between experience ("loving in truth") and attempting to make a satisfactory analogy of it in words ("faine in verse my love to show") remains unresolved—and unrelieved by the charm and comic distancing of an Arcadian game (*AS* 1.1).

Among many other things, Sidney's sonnet sequence serves as a critique of the tradition of eros examined above in relation to the *New Arcadia*.[8] Petrarch is the definitive figure of that tradition in which surrender to the will and interest of the beloved becomes, paradoxically, a means to control. For Petrarch, as David Kalstone has explained, the lover's pained devotion wins for him the compensation of vision, of poetic power, of fame's laurel.[9] But for Astrophil (as opposed to his maker) the gains never come. Astrophil seeks to close the gap between loving and feigning so that he can become, can inhabit, his own fiction: "I am not I, pitie the tale of me" (*AS* 45.14). But Stella will never accept the analogy, the tale, for the lover himself. The Petrarchan apparatus, transforming erotic pain into victory, cannot be made to work.

Astrophil so continually writes of his own struggle to "feign in truth" that Sidney's readers are pulled deep into questions of voice and purpose. How much is Astrophil Sidney? Is Sidney writing about love or writing about writing? Is this sequence a display of "impure persuasion" aimed directly at Penelope Rich; a Christian representation of the perils of just such impurity; or—something quite different—an Aristotelian poem rejecting the neoplatonic vision of inspired composition?[10] The reader cannot avoid such controversy; he or she is drawn into a rift between Astrophil's construction of experience and Sidney's, parallel but not identical to the distance between the real and the fictional that Astrophil strives to close but never can. Here there is no worldly-wise narrator to put us at ease, inviting us to enjoy a ladies' and gentlemen's game; nor is there the reassuring structure of comic "acts" to count on, only the uncertain rhythms of what C. S. Lewis called this "prolonged lyrical meditation."[11] What Sidney achieves here is to make us more than game players: insofar as we inhabit the poem, we live a version of Astrophil's experience, becoming ourselves reader-poets who must struggle in our own gap between the constructed and the real.

Astrophil and Stella moves within the gulf that separates Petrarchan and neoplatonic dreams of power from their achievement in the waking realm of a poet's experience. The sonnets on night and sleep (*AS*

31–33, 38–40) are poignant because in Astrophil's experience even the world of dreams gives him no respite: ironically, he must bribe healing Sleep to come by offering a glimpse of that very image that denies him sleep—"*Stella's* image," before him without end (*AS* 39.14). As a poem so much about itself, facing so unrelievedly the distance between the word and its fulfillment, the sequence runs deep but not wide. Those who have moved in Renaissance courses from Sidney's sequence to Shakespeare's will recall the sense of having entered a much larger (and less carefully plotted) space. One yellow leaf falling on Astrophil's introspection—always egocentric even when playful—would radically obscure its focus. In this sense only I agree with Richard Lanham's claim that *Astrophil and Stella* reveals a less than "capacious soul."[12] But that soul—angular and powerful, like a lightning stroke—is Astrophil's, not Sidney's. Or rather it is only one aspect in the zodiac of Sidney's wit. Sidney moved outward into a larger sphere—abandoning nothing but generously including much more—when he crossed over the comic circle of the *Old Arcadia* and fashioned the heroic plenitude and mystery of the *New*.

How does form in this story imitate the contingency of experience and seize upon the reader? The imitation appears in the sudden shifts or catastrophes of the plot, where what I have been calling the gaps between human constructs and deconstructive experience become apparent. It is in these breakdowns that Sidney's story seems most "real," most compelling. Sidney's language—schematic, metaphorical, almost centrifugal in its fullness—declares the story's artifice; the sudden turns in the plot surprise us as lifelike. As the ending of the *Old Arcadia* and the "surprise" structure within Astrophil's sonnets (with their striking last-line reversals) attest, Sidney's imitative genius is chiefly Aristotelian: it lies in structure, in plot. These apparent plot

Iris Murdoch has written that "form in art is properly the simulation of the self-contained aimlessness of the universe."[13] Replace "aimlessness" with "contingency" or "mystery," and this would make a good epigraph for Sidney's *New Arcadia*. This last and best of his poems puts justice on trial, like the first version; it puts eros on trial, like the sonnet sequence; but it also tests invention itself, and with it the experience of confronting the "endless overthrow" (*NA* 136) of our contingent, unsettled, mortal life. Here the gap between the real and the fictional, between experience and the analogy of experience in language becomes *itself* the subject or "groundplot" of Sidney's art. His *New Arcadian* characters live in this gap, and his readers find themselves within it too. The story describes the "endless" human need to construct experience even as we discover the limits of past constructions. The *New Arcadia* enacts the human work it represents.

breakdowns constitute the verisimilar in the *New Arcadia*: they have the evocative power of recognized experience.

The *New Arcadia* achieves this texture of lived experience by betraying the familiarity of the fictional. After the initial, formulaic invocation of spring, readers enter the pastoral convention of Strephon and Claius's lament for their beloved Urania. No sooner do they become accustomed to this form of fiction adapted from Montemayor than, like the shepherds', their meditations are broken by the sudden appearance of "a thing which floated" in the waves—the body of Musidorus (*NA* 5). This introduces the shipwreck, the fishermen, and the pirates. No sooner do readers adjust to these wonders of Greek romance—adapted from Heliodorus—than the plot turns to the military strategy and deliberative rhetoric that mark the princes' settlement of the helots' rebellion. No sooner do they grow to admire Musidorus as a shrewd tactician and Pyrocles as a brilliant orator than the latter disappears and returns— via the *Amadis de Gaul*—as an Amazon, and the former becomes a shepherd in the service of an Arcadian bumpkin.[14]

Eight such shifts displace the reader in the *New Arcadia*'s first twelve chapters, eight again in Book Two, though two of these—Musidorus's five-chapter narration of the princes' past and Pyrocles' seven-chapter account—are much longer. In Book Three there is only one major turn, the kidnapping of Zelmane and the princesses, directing the story away from *Amadis*-inspired love pursuits toward captivity and civil war. But this single catastrophe generates a series of narrative aftershocks: the deaths of Argalus and then Parthenia, the apparent death of Philoclea, the sudden end of Cecropia, the attempted suicide of her son.

Readers cannot guess where Sidney's narrative will go, only that they will be still more entangled in it. As the princes fall in love and into a disorientation both erotic and moral, so readers fall into a fiction that continually compels them to adjust to a plot that turns not only by shifting events but also by shifting genres in ways they cannot predict or control. As soon as we begin to "trust" one form, it proves unstable and is invaded by another. Sidney circles back to his broken narratives and abandoned genres, but their relation to the inbreaking actions and modes is almost never apparent at the time. How are we to take the Amazon Zelmane, who was the helots' masterful captain and before that "some god begotten between Neptune and Venus" astride a fallen mast in a bloody sea (*NA* 8)? Is he a joke, this Hercules in drag? Is he what his device claims—"Never more valiant" (*NA* 69)?

Victor Skretkowicz writes that in Sidney's story "Events become related not in the usual sequence of expectation and fulfillment, but rather through loose repetitions which connect them in retrospect."[15] We cannot at first apprehend the story's plot breakdowns as design: we face a narrative disorientation parallel to the princes' loss of the powerful conventions of humanist justice and to their inability to command the compensations promised by the tradition of eros. The gap between language and experience that Sidney employed as a flattering game to conclude his *Old Arcadia* and as an image of Astrophil's poetic-erotic frustrations now compels us to participate in the reality of contingent human experience that is both the subject and the form of the *New*.

In *Astrophil and Stella* readers cannot forget the distance between the "tale" of Astrophil and his own radically flawed experience. Nevertheless, that distance remains a constant, obsessive focus for reader and fictional poet alike, their only joy and annoy (*AS* 108.14). In the *New Arcadia* the gaps themselves change, not only in the series of genre invasions just recounted but also in individual scenes and grand catastrophes. Looking out from his cell in Amphialus's castle one morning, Pyrocles sees the severed head of Philoclea in a golden bowl. For him this reveals not contingency but final, irrevocable chaos: "O tyrant heaven! Traitor earth! Blind providence! No justice? How is this done? How is this suffered? Hath this world a government?" (*NA* 431).

Readers, whether they "identify" with Pyrocles or not, must also be disconcerted. This was not expected. Like the death of Shakespeare's Cordelia, which undoes the comic movement that began at her reunion with Lear in Act 4, Philoclea's murder breaks the convention of romance by which the heroine (whose restoration will surely end the story) cannot die. Yet

> toward the dawning of the [next] day, he heard one stir in his chamber by the motion of garments, and he with an angry voice asked who was there.
>
> "A poor gentlewoman," answered the party, "that wish long life unto you."
>
> "And I, soon death to you!" said he, "for the horrible curse you have given me." (*NA* 433–34)

When the distracted prince at last sees in this gentlewoman "the very face of Philoclea," he thinks her an angel until she assures him that she is his beloved indeed (*NA* 435). What looked like utter ruin turns out to be contingency once more, for character and reader alike. As Skretkowicz notes, Sidney eschews here his typical code of devices and symbols that signal the outcome of events, intensifying the surprise.[16] And *unlike* Pyrocles, the reader may be just as disoriented by this *joyous* catastrophe as by its sorrowful counterpart: what next?

In fact Sidney is not done with us in this scene. What looks like a miraculous resurrection is not so at all. Philoclea's death was a fiction, the work of a decidedly human intrigue—almost a vaudevillian trick. Cecropia's minions forced the princess to stand on tiptoe beneath the apparent execution platform and stick her head through a hole in the golden basin. (This show was for Pamela's benefit—to force her to yield to marriage with Amphialus—as a similar mock killing of Pamela was staged for her sister.) If after this Pyrocles "knew not to what key he should tune his mind" (*NA* 438), what of the reader? For that reader, even contingency becomes contingent when unsettling wonders turn out to be plots. Cecropia's plot, the fiction she stages to bend events her way, fails. What can Sidney's plot be?

In its unfinished state the *New Arcadia* incorporates two decisive disasters: the shipwreck that initiates the princes' Arcadian experience and the capture of Pyrocles and the princesses by Cecropia. If readers believe the story would have ended once again with a trial, as I do, there would have been three, providing an Aristotelian beginning, middle, and end.[17] These major catastrophes do not so much shock readers as underscore the *New Arcadian* theme that even the most careful designs can be undone—as are Plexirtus's plot to kill the princes at sea, leading to the wreck and their rescue; Cecropia's scheme to win her son a wife and a kingdom, leading to her own death; and—if we posit another trial—Euarchus's carefully weighed judgments, becoming suddenly irrelevant. The reader is both moved about by the plot and moved by the plot to distrust the finality of plotting. As with the princes' attempts to impose the constructions of eros and justice on their "endless overthrow," so acts of mere interpretive domination, efforts not attuned to the shifting voices of the text, will fail.

The form of Sidney's narrative is synonymous with its foreconceit of heroic action as an unceasing response to the uncertainty of our mortal life. To use Murdoch's language, the reader's experience of contingency in Sidney's *New Arcadia* imitates the contingency in human life itself,[18] and form in his final and most moving work counterfeits the self-contained contingency of the cosmos. Arthur Heiserman's description of the structure governing Heliodorus' *Æthiopian History* applies to Sidney's book as well:

> The syntax of the action . . . , which has unfolded like an enormous periodic sentence, . . . has released information to the characters and to us in ways that may be said to imitate the involuted ways through which men discover and work out their destinies.[19]

In the *New Arcadia* that destiny, for reader as well as character, is the reality of an "unfolding" that will not cease, always necessitating the act of invention. For reader and character, *New Arcadian* experience is always *novel.* Sidney's relentless undoing of formal conventions, compelling readers continually to step out of generic and other cultural boxes, composes his central legacy to the rise of English prose fiction.

II

I remember well finding among a set of Renaissance literature exams the declaration that "most of the women Sidney peoples his work with are bloodthirsty and manipulative bitches." If we add "lustful" and "reckless," this complaint will cover not only Andromana, Dido, Cecropia, Artaxia, and Gynecia, but also Erona and Helen. It leaves out Pamela and Philoclea, but they figure principally not as women who instigate action but as potential victims who *resist* it—the "only form of heroism," Anne Shaver quips, that "women [in Renaissance romance] can practice and still survive."[20] Parthenia is driven by neither blood nor lust, but she initiates her act as Knight of the Tomb only to die a la Shaver and join Argalus.

If we turn from amorous and political adventure to maternal care, the landscape looks equally bleak. Gynecia envisions her daughter / rival's death; Cecropia employs her wretched son to sate her own ambition; Parthenia's mother tries to barter her to an arrogant sadist; Andromana plots against her stepson and former lover, and her lust for the two princes leads to the death of her own child. Good mothers are either nameless and absent from the action, like Musidorus's, or nameless and dead, like Pyrocles'. The work of Margaret Mary Sullivan identifies a correspondingly grim pattern in the fate of Arcadian daughters Erona, Dido, and Zelmane: "daughter leaves father's house—resides in woman's house—departs to pursue a course of action—dies."[21]

Such readings (from amateur and professional scholars both) are not the work of "innocent" engagement; they are detached, "experienced" responses dependent on personal and cultural convictions readers bring to the text. These responses are the kind that Sidney's *New Arcadia* can and in fact should engender. Readers' engagement in an experience of contingency analogous to that of Sidney's main characters heightens their consciousness not only of those Tudor models of conduct that Sidney calls into question—justice, eros—but also of those he does not. Pulled into the labyrinth of story, the reader will follow its narrative inventions until their limits appear, forcing the reader to question them and to wonder about other paths as well. Readers' "innocent" entanglement in the fiction draws to their attention the historicity of Sidney's own assumptions, making these premises subject to the same sort of scrutiny Sidney regularly practiced as a reader himself.

I want to return briefly to Sidney's *Defence* to look at a few phrases I passed over before. In his account of poetry's narrative and imagistic power to move the reader to goodness, Sidney represents the poet as captivating children and old men with a tale and *"pretending no more,* doth intend the winning of the mind from wickedness to virtue—even as the child is often brought to take most wholesome things *by hiding them* in such other as have a pleasant taste" (*DP* 92, emphasis added). So, although the poet is not a liar, he does intend more than he pretends; he presumes to change the reader as he (the poet) knows best, and he no doubt "hides" notions of right conduct so deeply interfused in his own culture that he does not consciously intend them at all. Of course this is the practice of any accomplished teacher, however "dialogic" in style: "Delight them and win them," wrote Thomas Wilson; "weary them, and you lose them forever."[22] But because fiction both by intention and by cultural habit inscribes notions of great moral, political, and psychological force, it incites and requires a "detached" response. This must accompany engagement if Sidney's fiction is to become the groundplot of the reader's invention.

At this remove in time we are as apt to stumble over what Montaigne would call the "smooth paths" in the text as over those plainly problematic for Sidney.[23] Presently, we will most likely trip on Sidnean assumptions about gender and class. The *New Arcadia* represents in courtesy book fashion the education of male readers, making it what has been called a "drama of beset manhood."[24] In the chapters before this last I have written chiefly about male figures in the *New Arcadia* because I think Sidney's design is to reveal both the value and the limits of the dominant, male codes by which his Tudor culture sought to manage experience.

But does Sidney take to task that culture's fundamental assumption that the fulfillment of male ambition is the purpose of culture? The unsurprising answer is no. Professors Hamilton and Lawry rightly suggest that the limits of a male chivalric code appear in Amphialus's vain battles,[25] but this does not address what is from our perspective a striking absence. Writing of women as authors in the *New Arcadia*, Mary Ellen Lamb notes the "high quality" of their verse, but asserts that women's stories are restricted in length and in audience (told only to other women), and "permeated by guilty sexuality."[26] And considering the sinister motives and wretched consequences of women's more adventurous initiatives within the *New Arcadia*, Mary Margaret Sullivan has a case for dubbing the story "a handbook for turning queens into wives."[27]

Given the ways in which Sidney's narrative enforces such gender restrictions, the work at its margins merits a closer look. Indeed the virtues of detached reading suggest that it is exactly at the point where we seize passionately upon a cultural injustice or blindness that we should take care not to oversimplify the text at hand. In chapter 3 I noted Sidney's rejection of the neoplatonic tradition that sought to make love, even love for women, an all male affair. The man instructed by Castiglione's Bembo is to renounce the beloved woman's impurity (her physical nature) for the image of beauty engendered by his own soul. Yet for all its vaunted idealism, the *New Arcadia*'s opening exchange between Strephon and Claius sets this aside.[28] Sidney's clearly chosen focus on "this too much loved earth" (*DP* 78), consistent with his opening bow to the womanly earth adorned for the advent of her lover, tends to move his fiction away from what his culture would have regarded as the male hierarchy of abstract judgment and toward the "female" involvement with the body.

A second curious pattern is that within the patriarchal culture of Arcadia patriarchy does not fare well. Each of the "bloodthirsty and manipulative bitches" that so appalled my exam writer operates in the void left by a king/father or prince/son who confuses extreme self-indulgence with the legitimate exercise of power. Andromana both prospers and dies under the eye of the lecherous dupe who rules Iberia; Artaxia has perhaps met her match in Plexirtus, but she keeps hold of Erona through the besotted ambition of Antiphilus; Gynecia's evil thoughts about Philoclea grow in the fool's paradise established by King Basilius; and Cecropia—the most depraved figure in the story— hatches her plot during Basilius's ill-considered retreat and tortures the princesses while her son indulges his chivalric vanity outside their prison cells. No wonder even the dutiful Pamela grows restless under her father's rule and decides to "trust something to my own judgement" (*NA* 155). Does Sidney imply that if patriarchs and princes would take care of their proper business Arcadia would suffer no unruly mothers and wives? I think not, in part because the pattern of failed patriarchs is too thorough to function simply as a call for more effective male dominance. But there is another reason.

In the cross-dressing of Pyrocles and in the ironic consequences of Amphialus's efforts to dominate the women who govern his dreams and waking life, Sidney indicates that masculine codes alone cannot sustain his male characters. Pyrocles' defense of women and Amphialus's self-destructive attempts to subjugate them display the reality of what the once derisive Musidorus called a "womanish" presence in the male psyche (*NA* 70). It is true that the girl Zelmane's experience of cross-dressing intrigues Sidney less than that of the prince who takes her name: the real Zelmane has no leisure and no friend with whom to debate the value of the masculine in the female. Nor do the machinations of Andromana move Sidney to record her dreams as he does Amphialus's vision of Mira. Sidney is more interested in exploring complementarity within men than women.

Nonetheless, the *New Arcadia* finds repeated occasions to balance Sidnean "doing and suffering" among men and women: Zelmane's active service becomes the new model for Pyrocles' conduct; Argalus impresses us more in the patience of his courtship than in the rage of his final battle; Plangus remains a figure of passive endurance while his counterpart in unrequited love, Queen Helen, refuses to smile at grief and continually chooses to act. Noting that Sidney never leaves "misogyny . . . uncorrected," Katherine Duncan-Jones sees an "unusually sympathetic and attentive" representation of women in his work, attributing it to his "being surrounded from birth by sophisticated women who had enjoyed the benefit . . . of a humanist education."[29]

But most telling is Sidney's acknowledgment—how conscious I cannot tell—that the human act of invention involves crossing the borders of gender. Pyrocles' experience as a woman who sees the world more clearly and with wider sympathy, as one who finds more than "the familiarity of excellent men in learning and soldiery" (*NA* 49) to live for, implies that Sidney's image of a distaff Hercules is more than a joke. It also suggests that Xenophon's myth of Hercules—a male hero at the crossroads of feminized easy pleasure and stern virtue—oversimplifies the actions that for Sidney define the heroic life and the role that femininity plays in it. Sustained through virtually the whole narrative, Pyrocles' experience as Zelmane suggests that a truer construction of the male self requires more than a recognition of "valour of mind" and "virtue" in women, as Pyrocles tells Musidorus in their second debate (*NA* 73). Pyrocles' distaff life also implies that Sidney sees in men a potential, "female" awareness that the self is defined and extended through responsible relationship with the surrounding world as much as through "male" quests for political and erotic victory and domination over that world. Spenser was to imply the same awareness in Book Three of *The Faerie Queene;* Shakespeare was to make it the theme of his great comic heroines and his tragic, widowed queens. But Sidney opened the way before them.

I have noted that Sidney is remarkable for using the act of feigning to interrogate the constructs of his own patrician class. But his aim was to educate that same class rather than to enfranchise any other. This exemplifies the now familiar notion that power contains and uses the subversive voices within it, although even at the Elizabethan court such power was created collectively—it was not monolithic.[30] Plainly enough, the courtier who warned Elizabeth against "lenity" to the Irish rebels because they "choose rather all filthiness, than law"[31] and the poet who makes the slaughter of the artisans who rebel against the befuddled Basilius an occasion for mirth (*NA* 281–82) cannot be styled a modern democrat. Not only England but also Europe and America were, in his mind, the proper field of aristocratic ambition.

But for us, if not for Sidney himself, the striking incompetence of all the *Arcadia's* monarchs except Euarchus discloses the same class structural weakness as the killing of kings in Shakespeare. There is more than a little irony in the attribution of Pamela's prayer to King Charles on the scaffold.[32] The very form of the revised *Arcadia* inscribes a conceit of ever-reforming invention that runs directly counter to the patrician ambitions Sidney shared. The *New Arcadia* is an aristocratic fiction that habitually questions the claims of hierarchy: no "just" construct and no set genre can fully manage experience within this text.

Even in condensed form, these thoughts on gender and class in the *New Arcadia* reveal the need to shift from complete engagement in Sidney's text if it is to prompt us as makers of our present culture. If we approach his text critically, we find that Philip Sidney's vision of his culture was complex, at once reinscribing its assumptions and prophetic of change. One final category worth inquiry is Sidney's representation of the body. I have suggested that Sidney's Protestantism was of the sort that found in the *sola gratia* gospel a means to confirm earthly action. This faith also validates the human body by which such action is completed, as in Luther's 1522 defense of the "Estate of Marriage," where even fatherly diaper washing is redeemed.[33] Yet Sidney is no poet of married life, nor in the *New Arcadia* of consummated love. His insistence on continual counterfashioning in response to unsettling change does not extend to the invention of a full domestic life in which great princes must compromise their freedom to wander about resisting temptation and doing good.

But once more there are narrative discontents. In their misdirected efforts to regain a "just" self, freed from the constraints of deception and desire, Pyrocles and Musidorus continually stumble over the pleasures and clumsiness of the body, as I have noted in chapter 4. Even the pristine daughters of Basilius are not immune. After the love-distracted Philoclea has gone by night to retract the vows of chastity she once etched in marble, after she has acknowledged to herself the "unresistable violence" of those "unlawful desires" she feels for Zelmane/Pyrocles, she flees to the pure, majestic Pamela for counsel (*NA* 149). But entering her sister's chamber, Philoclea

> found her (though it were in the time that the wings of night doth blow sleep most willingly into mortal creatures) sitting in a chair, lying backward, with her head almost over the back of it, and looking upon a wax candle which burnt before her, in one hand holding a letter [from Musidorus], in the other her handkerchief which had lately drunk up the tears of her eyes, leaving instead of them crimson circles, like red flakes in the element. (*NA* 150)

Philoclea is taken aback to see her supremely temperate sister emotionally undone, but what strikes us equally is the radiant material imagery of this scene as Sidney has painted it. The portrait of Pamela alone—in silence, erotically overwhelmed—has in its objects (chair, candle, letter, handkerchief) and its metaphors (dark wings that blow, crimson circles like flecks in an angry sky) the arresting physicality we might associate with mannerist painting, intensified here by the night and enclosed setting. Sidney's fiction compels its characters to live and move within the physical realm of bodily presence and desire, its readers to feel and to think within the arresting presence of his radiant text, and beyond it.

III

The kind of experience afforded the reader of Sidney's fiction accords with his practice as a poet. Engaged by the Tudor humanist legacy of justice, love, and representational power, he experienced within it the reality of contingency, the limits inherent in the constructs of human invention, the necessity of change. He could not of course detach himself from his own history to cross-examine it from some neutral ground any more than critical readers can separate themselves fully from the effects that a text has had on them. But culture is multiform and unstable, offering many angles from which to perceive and to represent experience. I have argued that within the constraints of his history Sidney both discovered and designed an early Protestant and late humanist model for criticizing cultural "inventions fine" and for sustaining a faith in the act of invention itself. Such a critical-poetic practice unites Sidney with Luther and Montaigne, who dismantle human paradigms even as they insist on the human prerogative and necessity of constructing new ones. This fits the *Defence of Poetry's* preference for the foreconceiving act over the work it yields, a work valued primarily as the groundplot for still further invention by the reader (*DP* 79,103).

In the *New Arcadia* Sidney tests the political and erotic inventions of Tudor culture by feigning the fullest possible images of them, extending them throughout his narrative until they can no longer manage the political, ethical, and emotional territory they seek to rule. Pyrocles and Musidorus discover their radically complex relation to the world and the limits of self-sufficient justice and single-minded eros. Falling from their confidence as "lords of truth" into the mystery of a providential design that feels like chance, they alternately make fictions of false assurance and truer images of themselves as makers responding to "endless overthrow." Sidney's representation of the princes makes plain that he knew his own fictions could involve falsifying too, his wit abusing poetry. But he remains convinced of the necessity and value of invention. His poetry acknowledges the need to see the self as made by history and as a maker of it.

Tudor poetry is populated by numerous aspiring princes who yearn to escape the body of history and its manifold burdens. Staring the power of history in the face as he surveys Henry Bullingbrook, the unkinged Richard Plantagenet cries, "O! that I were a mockery king of snow, / Standing before the sun of Bullingbrook, / To melt myself away in water-drops."[34] Drawn from innocent assurance into his own strange, eventful history, Hamlet longs for "this too too solid flesh [to] . . . melt / Thaw and resolve itself into a dew."[35] Some of these Renaissance princes endure to discover meaning within the body of history, some like Hamlet declaring history to move within the larger design of Providence; others fall further into confusion and self-ruin as they seek to maintain faith in the lost paradise of fixed ideals.

At the beginning of this study, I wrote of the debate between those who describe a Sidney able to fashion in his poetry a clear, stable image of the heroic life and those who represent a Sidney who fails to do so, overcome by the very cultural or aesthetic constraints he "rebels" against. As I noted then, this debate, extensive and useful though it has been, has effectively played itself out because both sides attribute to Sidney a static conception of the heroic life—a conception at odds with Sidney's effort to establish a dynamic conceit of "counterfeiting" in response to the shifting patterns of experience. A reconsideration of the nature of Sidney's "history" may now complement this alternative mode of reading his texts.

Those critics who champion a Sidney able to resolve the tensions of his culture and to represent an ideal of "heroic love" appear to regard him as an exemplar of humanist justice whose personal and political history is an object to be overcome. The struggle demands intense and sustained effort, but Sidney has the equipment to prevail. Those who find his poetry an inevitable reprise of political and personal frustrations appear to regard the culture and language that compose Sidney's history as a Heideggerian prisonhouse, howsoever comfortable or confining. It seems, in other words, that in this debate not only the goal of Sidney's quest but also the "history" that threatens or thwarts it is understood by both sides to be static. The culture in which he moves is either a mountain he can climb or a power structure that anticipates and organizes any attempts to reform it.

A different metaphor may be useful. It is possible to describe the body of history as an ecology within which we live *and* within which we have—like it or not—the responsibility of consciousness and reformation. History then becomes a system of interrelations that not only imply continuity but also allow for a degree of change over which we exercise a real though limited control. Within history so conceived, it is the discovery of those complex interrelations, exposing the confines of existing models of experience, that both enables and requires the act of invention. And if history is such an ecology of interrelations, we do wisely to read and interrogate its texts, making them the imaginative groundplot of profitable inventions. If we live in such a system, continuous yet not enclosed, then creative dialogue with such texts is possible. As Hans-Georg Gadamer writes in *Truth and Method,*

> the way we experience one another, the way we explore historical traditions, the way that we experience the natural givenness of our existence and our world, constitutes a truly hermeneutic universe, in which we are not imprisoned, as if behind insurmountable barriers, but to which we are opened.[36]

Sidney's friend and biographer Fulke Greville represented him as one who liberates his readers from the confines of their history. In the *Arcadia*, writes Greville, "his end . . . was not vanishing pleasure alone, but moral images and examples, as directing threads, to guide every man through the confused labyrinth of his own desires and life."[37] In praising Sidney as an image maker Greville reveals his grasp of Sidney's poetics and fictional praxis, but he errs in dividing that poetic faculty from the labyrinth of personal and cultural desire that composes our life. The maze of experience or history as Sidney conceived it functions as the groundplot of the thinking poet's invention; indeed, he participates in the re-formation of the labyrinth even as he is formed by it. A more Sidnean vision of human invention and its interrelation with the other "texts" of the culture in which he moves appears in Montaigne:

> It is a signe his wits grow short when he is pleased, or a signe of wearinesse. No generous spirit stayes and relies upon himselfe: he ever pretendeth and goeth beyond his strength. . . . His nourishment is admiration, questing, and ambiguity: Which Apollo declared sufficiently, always speaking ambiguously, obscurely, and obliquely unto us—not feeding, but busying and ammusing [*sic*] us. It is an irregular, uncertaine motion, perpetuall, patternelesse, and without end. His inventions enflame, follow, and enter-produce one another.[38]

Montaigne believed that "There is no end in our inquisitions. Our end is in the other World."[39] Sidney's theory and practice as a poet show that he would agree, that he understood history as the mysterious text of Providence, a world within which we have a limited but active and valid part to play. Sidney's fiction is itself such a world—human, historical, a labyrinth but not a prison cell—constrained by the culture of writer and readers alike, but dynamic and liberating in the vigor of its invention.

Notes

Unless otherwise indicated, citations of major works or collections of works by Sidney are noted in the text as shown below.

AS   *Astrophil and Stella.* In *Poems of Sir Philip Sidney.* Edited by William A. Ringler. Oxford: Clarendon Press, 1962.

DP   *A Defence of Poetry.* In *Miscellaneous Prose of Sir Philip Sidney.* Edited by Katherine Duncan-Jones and Jan van Dorsten. Oxford: Clarendon Press, 1973.

LE   *A Letter written to Queen Elizabeth, touching her marriage with Monsieur.* In *Miscellaneous Prose.*

LM   *The Lady of May.* In *Miscellaneous Prose.*

NA   *The Countess of Pembroke's Arcadia (The New Arcadia).* Edited by Victor Skretkowicz. Oxford: Clarendon Press, 1987.

OA   *The Countess of Pembroke's Arcadia (The Old Arcadia).* Edited by Jean Robertson. Oxford: Clarendon Press, 1973.

The epigraphs at the opening of each chapter are from the following sources: for chapter 1, William Shakespeare, *As You Like It* 3.3.19–20, *The Riverside Shakespeare,* ed. G. Blakemore Evans (Boston: Houghton Mifflin, 1974); for chapter 2, Cicero, *De Amicitia* 22.82, *De Senectute, De Amicitia, De Divinatione,* trans. William Armistead Falconer (London: William Heinemann, 1923); for chapter 3, Geoffrey Chaucer, *Troilus and Criseyde* 1.365–71, *The Riverside Chaucer,* ed. Larry D. Benson, 3d ed. (Boston: Houghton Mifflin, 1987); for chapter 4, Michel de Montaigne, *Of Repenting, The Essayes of Michael Lord of Montaigne,* trans. John Florio (1603) (London: Oxford University Press, 1924), 3:20; for chapter 5, Sir Philip Sidney, *A Defence of Poetry, Miscellaneous Prose,* 92.

Chapter 1. Right Poetry

1. See Martin Luther's *Treatise on Good Works,* in *Luther's Works,* general eds. Jaroslav Pelikan and Helmut T. Lehmann, vol. 44 (Philadelphia: Fortress, 1966), 15–114, especially 24 –27.

2. In *Dazzling Images: The Masks of Sir Philip Sidney* (Newark: University of Delaware Press, 1991), Alan Hager argues that Sidney adopts numerous masks or "personae . . . for a higher ironic or curative purpose . . . following the humanist prais-ers of folly" (9). This act of "serious jesting" has the effect of "catching his auditors up in their own foolery," compelling them to reconsider perspectives they initially find so appealing (9). And so like me Hager finds that Sidney "sets out to expose the dangers of the very idealisms with which he has been traditionally associated" (19). Hager's book opens our understanding of Sidney significantly by placing him in a praise of folly tradition that gives him considerably more room to maneuver as poet-critic within the Tudor humanist culture that several recent critics have deemed so con-fining. My own reading of Sidney finds him more experimental in his feigning than Hager does, more "exploratory," as Joan Rees writes in *Sir Philip Sidney and Arcadia* (Rutherford, N.J.: Fairleigh Dickinson University Press, 1991), 8. Hager sees a writer more detached, more fully calculating of the effects of his work than I, and finally more hidden behind his ironic masks. In her recent *The Mistress-Knowledge: Sir Philip Sidney's* Defence of Poesie *and Literary Architectonics in the English Renaissance* (Nashville, Tenn.: Vanderbilt University Press, 1991), M. J. Doherty also suggests that modern readers have imposed on Sidney a "topos," in this case a "central self," more ours than his (xx), and she has noted that in poems such as Sidney's, "verbal formu-las regularly break down, giving way to a surpassing understanding" (xxvii).

3. Theodore Spencer, "The Poetry of Sir Philip Sidney," in *Essential Articles for the Study of Sir Philip Sidney,* ed. Arthur F. Kinney (Hamden, Conn: Archon, 1986), 58.

4. In *Dazzling Images,* Alan Hager notes that critical "factions . . . have alter-nately suggested that Sidney is either a case of perfect self-creation . . . or that he is a self-fashioned rebel . . . , albeit unsuccessful" (8–9).

5. Letter of 25 March 1578, quoted in Malcolm William Wallace, *The Life of Sir Philip Sidney* (1915; rpt. New York: Octagon, 1967), 208.

6. E. M. W. Tillyard, *The English Renaissance: Fact or Fiction?* (Baltimore: Johns Hopkins University Press, 1952), 111; C. S. Lewis, *English Literature in the Sixteenth Century, Excluding Drama* (Oxford: Clarendon Press, 1954), 339.

7. Lewis, 337, 339, 325.

8. Tillyard, 109.

9. For a list of past and present images of Sidney, see Gary Waller, *English Poet-ry of the Sixteenth Century* (London and New York: Longman, 1986), 139. For a study of Sidney as English gentleman, see John Gouws, "The Nineteenth-Century Develop-ment of the Sidney Legend," *Sir Philip Sidney's Achievements,* ed. M. J. B. Allen, Dominic Baker-Smith, and Arthur Kinney, with Margaret M. Sullivan (New York: AMS Press, 1990), 251–60.

10. See *The Prose Works of Fulke Greville,* ed. John Gouws (Oxford: Clarendon Press, 1986), 134.

11. A. C. Hamilton, *Sir Philip Sidney: A Study of His Life and Works* (Cambridge:

Cambridge University Press, 1977), 169, 168. See also Kenneth Myrick, *Sir Philip Sidney as a Literary Craftsman,* 2d ed. (Lincoln: University of Nebraska Press, 1965) on Sidney as a serious humanist poet, 3–45, and on Sidney's *New Arcadia* as a teaching poem, 242–97.

12. Quotation from Jon S. Lawry, *Sidney's Two* Arcadias: *Pattern and Proceeding* (Ithaca and London: Cornell University Press, 1972), 247. For Turner, see Myron Turner, "The Heroic Ideal in Sidney's Revised *Arcadia,*" *Studies in English Literature* 10 (1970): 71; for Hamilton, see 163.

13. Lawry, 166.

14. Richard Helgerson, *The Elizabethan Prodigals* (Berkeley: University of California Press, 1976), 155, 154.

15. Helgerson, 154.

16. Richard McCoy, *Sir Philip Sidney: Rebellion in Arcadia* (New Brunswick, N.J.: Rutgers University Press, 1979), x and 214. For McCoy's use of Stone, see 5–6. McCoy continues his argument in *The Rites of Knighthood: The Literature and Politics of Elizabethan Chivalry* (Berkeley: University of California Press, 1989), where he writes that though Sidney as courtier shared many of his characters' "youthful energy, passionate activism, and high ideals," in seeking to act upon them he "found himself entangled in intractable difficulties and conflicts with authority" (73).

17. McCoy, *Sidney,* 214.

18. John Carey, "Structure and Rhetoric in Sidney's *Arcadia,*" *Sir Philip Sidney: An Anthology of Modern Criticism,* ed. Dennis Kay (Oxford: Clarendon Press, 1987), 252. Carey sees in Sidney's *New Arcadia* a fiction governed by a union of "Sophoclean fatalism" and a Calvinism that asserted "the irretrievable wrongness of human reason" (249).

19. Annabel Patterson, " 'Under . . . Pretty Tales': Intention in Sidney's *Arcadia,*" *Essential Articles for the Study of Sir Philip Sidney,* ed. Arthur F. Kinney (Hamden, Conn: Archon, 1986), 359 and 371–72.

20. Ronald Levao, *Renaissance Minds and Their Fictions: Cusanus, Sidney, Shakespeare* (Berkeley: University of California Press, 1985), xxi.

21. Levao, 216.

22. Levao, 248. Michael McCanles also sees Sidney inventing an enclosed rhetorical world, though he does not dwell on its futility as Levao does. In "Oracular Prediction and the Fore-Conceit of Sidney's *Arcadia*" (*Essential Articles for the Study of Sir Philip Sidney,* ed. Arthur F. Kinney [Hamden, Conn.: Archon, 1986]), he examines the "interplay" between the freedom of a "transcendent perspective" and the determinism of the story's "fore-conceit," concluding that for "author, reader, and fictive character alike" these angles of vision are illusory and "finally self-cancelling" (387–88). This view is consistent with McCanles' more recent *The Text of Sidney's Arcadian World* (Durham, N.C.: Duke University Press, 1989), where he writes that the *New Arcadia*'s highly figured style, complex plots, and mingled genres "are all presented to the reader as human modes of creating the self and world, outside of which there is neither self nor world" (14).

23. Edmund Spenser, *The Faerie Queene* 2.7.2, in *The Works of Edmund Spenser: A Variorum Edition,* ed. Edwin Greenlaw, Charles Grosvenor Osgood, and Frederick Morgan Padelford (Baltimore: Johns Hopkins University Press, 1932–45).

24. I agree with Susanne Woods' placement of Sidney in a "rising humanist meritocracy [that] tended . . . to be subversive of stated assumptions about hierarchy and governance" and would extend Sidney's critical liberty to other cultural constructs as well. See "Freedom and Tyranny in Sidney's *Arcadia,*" *Sir Philip Sidney's Achievements,* 166 – 67.

25. *Of Repenting, The Essayes of Michael Lord of Montaigne,* trans. John Florio (1603) (London: Oxford University Press, 1924), 3:20.

26. Montaigne, *Of the Inconstancie of Our Actions, Essayes,* 2:10.

27. See Sidney's letters to Hubert Languet, 1 March 1578, in *The Correspondence of Sir Philip Sidney and Hubert Languet,* trans. Stewart A. Pears (London: William Pickering, 1845), 143; to Edward Denny, 22 May 1580, printed by James M. Osborn, *Young Philip Sidney, 1572–1577* (New Haven and London: Yale University Press, 1972), 537; and to his brother Robert, 18 October 1580, in Pears, 202.

28. Greville, 24.

29. Hager, *Dazzling Images,* 29. See also Hager, "The Exemplary Mirage: Fabrication of Sir Philip Sidney's Biographical Image and the Sidney Reader," *Essential Articles,* 24, and S. K. Orgel, "Sidney's Experiment in Pastoral: *The Lady of May,*" *Essential Articles,* 63.

30. See Hamilton, 27–28, for commentary on Sidney's failure to follow strictly the "humanist code" of obedient service to one's sovereign.

31. Hamilton, 2–3, 27–28.

32. Letter probably written in 1566, quoted by Wallace, 68– 69.

33. Letter of 25 March 1578, quoted by Wallace, 208.

34. For dates, see Katherine Duncan-Jones' introductions in *Miscellaneous Prose of Sir Philip Sidney,* ed. Katherine Duncan-Jones and Jan van Dorsten (Oxford: Clarendon Press, 1973), 13, 33–34.

35. Hamilton, 24 –26.

36. Hager, *Dazzling Images,* sees in Rombus a "wise fool," a Sidnean persona who raises fundamental questions about "love and rule" (46, 51).

37. Orgel, 69; for Sidney's criticism of pastoral categories, see 64 – 69.

38. William Ringler, *The Poems of Sir Philip Sidney* (Oxford: Clarendon Press, 1962), writes that Elizabeth's choice of the shepherd may be a rejection of the Leicester faction's lobbying for English military intervention in the Netherlands, though he believes that the final song of Espilus and Therion "was ingeniously devised to be appropriate to whichever suitor" the Queen chose (362– 63).

39. See Orgel, 70; see also Robert F. Kimbrough, *Sir Philip Sidney* (New York: Twayne, 1971), 64 – 66.

40. Hager, *Dazzling Images,* 23. See 42–52 for his full discussion of the masque.

41. Robert E. Stillman, "Justice and the 'Good Word' in Sidney's *The Lady of May,*" *Studies in English Literature* 24 (1984): 36, 38.

42. For the former claim, see Richard A. Lanham, "Sidney: The Ornament of His Age," *Southern Review* 2, no. 4 (1967): 327; Wallace, 219, implies the latter.

43. See Languet's 22 October 1580 letter in Pears, 187, as well as Wallace, 213; Osborn, 503; and Duncan-Jones, *Miscellaneous Prose,* 35.

44. The word is Gary Waller's, 142.

45. The Duke of Northumberland, Philip's maternal grandfather, tried to estab-

lish Lady Jane Grey, wife to his son Guilford, as queen after the death of Edward VI. Northumberland was executed in 1553 and his son and daughter-in-law early in 1554, the year of Philip's birth. See Wallace, 10 –13. Sidney's maternal greatgrandfather, Edmund Dudley, had been executed for treason by Henry VII in 1510.

46. See Duncan-Jones' commentary in *Miscellaneous Prose,* 37, and in her *Sir Philip Sidney: Courtier Poet* (New Haven: Yale University Press, 1991), 162– 63.

47. Letter of 12 June 1575, quoted by Osborn, 309, and cited in Duncan-Jones, *Miscellaneous Prose,* 37. Hager suggests in *Dazzling Images* that "posterity" can mean "the political progeny of England"—Elizabeth's subjects—as well as any actual children she might bear (55).

48. See Duncan-Jones, *Miscellaneous Prose,* 37.

49. Duncan-Jones, *Miscellaneous Prose,* 38–39.

50. Letter of 22 October 1580, in Pears, 187; cited in Duncan-Jones, *Miscellaneous Prose,* 33.

51. For the probable time of Sidney's first meeting with Languet, see Wallace, 118, and Osborn, 53.

52. Letters of 7 and 28 January 1574 and 11 June 1574, quoted by Osborn, 129, 139, 204.

53. Letter of 3 December 1575, quoted by Osborn, 390.

54. On Sidney's gratitude to Languet, see letter of 15 April 1574, quoted by Osborn, 163: "I have benefited more from my acquaintance with you than from all other experiences combined during my time on the Continent."

55. Letter from Sidney to Languet 1 March 1578, Pears, 143–44.

56. Letter from Languet to Sidney 2 May 1578, Pears, 147.

57. On dates of composition for the *Old Arcadia,* see Jean Robertson, xv–xix, in *The Countess of Pembroke's Arcadia (The Old Arcadia),* ed. Jean Robertson (Oxford: Clarendon Press, 1973) and Hamilton, 32–33.

58. Neil Rudenstine, *Sidney's Poetic Development* (Cambridge: Harvard University Press, 1967), 293.

59. Letter to Edward Denny, 22 May 1580, printed by Osborn, 537.

60. Letter of 24 March 1586, in *The Prose Works of Sir Philip Sidney,* ed. Albert Feuillerat (Cambridge: Cambridge University Press, 1912–26), 3: 166.

61. F. J. Levy, noting that Sidney's political frustrations were "representative of his generation" of highminded Protestant courtiers, argues that this circle "broadened the range of permissible [aristocratic] activities. The point of Sidney's *Defence of Poesie* was to make poetry a respectable form of work for a member of the ruling class, because poetry, more than any other kind of writing, taught morality and right action." See "Philip Sidney Reconsidered," in Kinney, 10.

62. In " 'The Poets Only Deliver': Sidney's Conception of *Mimesis,*" in Kinney, 141– 42, John Ulreich suggests that the debate over whether Sidney's theory of poetry owes more to Aristotle or Plato obscures the fact that in both formulations mimesis is dynamic. For Aristotle, imitation is "the activity (*energia*) by which matter is realized in form"; for Plato, mimesis is not "the external copy of an object, but . . . an internal reproducing of those vital energies which have engendered Nature." In both instances, "what the poet imitates is not *Natura Naturata,* . . . the objects visible to sense, but *Natura naturans,* the invisible working of nature revealed to [what Sidney

calls] our 'inward reason.'" In the *Timaeus* Plato is not writing about *mimesis* in the poet but in the demiurge.

63. Here I use the text printed for William Ponsonby in 1595 (London), Clv.

64. Unpublished translation by S. K. Heninger, Jr., used here with his permission. I am delighted to acknowledge the debt my understanding of the *Defence* owes to Professor Heninger's 1984 Folger Library seminar on "Sidney's Program for Poetry." For other Renaissance Italian critics who find verse essential to poetry, see Kenneth Myrick, *Sir Philip Sidney as a Literary Craftsman,* 2d ed. (Lincoln: University of Nebraska Press, 1965), 118.

65. Heninger translation.

66. Plato, *The Republic,* trans. Paul Shorey (London: William Heinemann, 1946), bk. 4: sect. 12.

67. See S. K. Heninger, Jr., *Sidney and Spenser: The Poet as Maker* (University Park and London: Pennsylvania State University Press, 1989), 128ff.

68. Levao, 104.

69. Aristotle, *Poetics,* in *Criticism: The Major Texts,* ed. Walter Jackson Bate (New York: Harcourt, Brace, Jovanovich, 1970), 20, 25, 23.

70. Johann Wolfgang von Goethe, *Faust,* ed. R-M. S. Heffner, Helmut Rehder, and W. F. Twaddell (Boston: D. C. Heath, 1955), line 11, 936.

71. I follow the Ponsonby text in using *incredulous* and take the passage to mean that those who doubt the Fall need to consider why we cannot fully follow the way revealed by the "erected wit." In his edition of *An Apology for Poetry* (London: Nelson, 1965), 159, Geoffrey Shepherd cites Calvin's point that the wit "is not so blockish, but that it tasteth also some little of the higher things."

72. See Augustine, *The City of God against the Pagans,* trans. Philip Levine, 7 vols. (Cambridge: Harvard University Press, 1957–72), vol. 4, bk 12, chap. 14.

73. John Calvin, *Institutes of the Christian Religion,* ed. John T. McNeill, trans. Ford Lewis Battles, 2 vols. (Philadelphia: Westminster, 1960), Book 1: chap. 16: Sections 1 and 3, and Chapter 17: Section 4.

74. Robert D. Knudsen, "Calvinism as a Cultural Force," in *John Calvin: His Influence in the Western World,* ed. W. Stanford Reid (Grand Rapids, Mich.: Zondervan, 1982), 28.

75. Francois Wendel, *Calvin: Origins and Development of His Religious Thought,* trans. Philip Mairet (Durham, N.C.: Labyrinth, 1987), 177. On p. 177n., Wendel cites Luther's commentary on the first article of the Creed in the *Small* and *Large Catechism.* He also notes a parallel with Zwingli's sermon *De Providentia Dei.*

76. Eric Gritsch, *Martin—God's Court Jester: Luther in Retrospect* (Philadelphia: Fortress, 1983), 99.

77. Martin Luther, *Large Catechism,* pt 2: sect. 19, in *The Book of Concord: The Confessions of the Evangelical Lutheran Church,* trans. and ed. Theodore G. Tappert, in collaboration with others (Philadelphia: Fortress, 1959).

78. Eric W. Gritsch and Robert Jenson, *Lutheranism: The Theological Movement and Its Confessional Writings* (Philadelphia: Fortress, 1976), 160.

79. Luther, *Large Catechism,* 2: 58.

80. Thomas Wilson, *Arte of Rhetorique* (1553), ed. Thomas J. Derrick (New York and London: Garland, 1982), 31–32.

81. Joel B. Altman, *The Tudor Play of Mind: Rhetorical Inquiry and the Development of Elizabethan Drama* (Berkeley: University of California Press, 1978), 52.

82. Quintillian, *Institutio Oratoria,* trans. H. E. Butler, 4 vols. (Cambridge: Harvard University Press, 1953), bk 8: preface: sect. 14; on Bacon, see Lisa Jardine, *Francis Bacon: Discovery and the Art of Discourse* (Cambridge: Cambridge University Press, 1974), 6.

83. Murray Wright Bundy, " 'Invention' and 'Imagination' in the Renaissance," *Journal of English and Germanic Philology* 29 (1930): 539–45.

84. See Ringler's commentary on this sonnet, 458.

85. In *Miscellaneous Prose,* 189, Jan van Dorsten writes that the use of "Invention" as "Nature's child" in this sonnet contrasts with "invention" in the *Defence* as a faculty that enables the poet to exceed nature. For van Dorsten the former sense "ties the artist to the phenomenal [natural] world," while the latter "introduces a very different, primarily Christian-platonist argument." But this reasoning assumes that what the poet imitates in nature is "things" rather than the activity of making—that he draws from *Natura naturata* rather than counterfeiting *natura naturans.* As I argue throughout, Sidney is part of a Reformation culture that rejected neoplatonic claims of direct access to heavenly "ideas."

86. See Andrew Weiner, *Sir Philip Sidney and the Poetics of Protestantism* (Minneapolis: University of Minnesota Press, 1978), especially the preface and first chapter. I cannot agree with Weiner that Sidney is a Calvinist ideologue, but he is right to insist that Reformation thought is fundamental to Sidney's poetic theory and practice.

87. Waller, 142.

88. Luther, *Works,* 37: 361, 365.

89. Luther, *Works,* 37: 361, 366.

90. See Heiko A. Oberman, *Luther: Man between God and the Devil,* trans. Eileen Walliser-Schwarztbart (New Haven: Yale University Press, 1989), 179: "Whereas good works had once been done for God's sake, to comply with His high righteousness, they were now [in the Reformation] redirected to earth for the sake of man. . . ." Oberman writes on p. 192 that in Luther's conception of faith "Good works are not repudiated, but their aim and direction have been radically 'horizontalized': they have been moved from Heaven to earth. . . ." See also 74–80.

91. Luther, *Works,* 44: 24.

92. Weiner, 48–50.

93. See Calvin, 3.24.4–7.

94. Philipp Melanchthon, *Apology of the Augsburg Confession,* article 18: sect. 4, in *The Book of Concord:* "Since human nature still has reason and judgment about the things the senses can grasp, it also retains a choice in these things, as well as the liberty and ability to achieve civil righteousness." For Luther, see Jenson's excellent discussion of reason as "the whole effort of man to deal with the circumstances of his life," *Lutheranism,* 150–51. Calvin writes that reason can act to some use in "earthly things," in which he includes "government, household management, all mechanical skills, and the liberal arts" (2: 2.13). In *The Mistress-Knowledge,* M. J. Doherty argues that in the creative act of "poesie," the male "architect-poet" and the female "mistress-knowledge" (defined as the knowledge of the human conscience given by God) unite, and that their union enables the poet's work to participate in the "graced

'light of Christ'" to lift the poet and his readers out of human limitation and toward God (261, 259). See also pp. xxiii–xxviii. I think this reading, though underwritten by substantial scholarship on Augustinian Platonism, is at odds with Sidney's Protestant insistence on the division between human and divine work, however analogous the two may be. Sidney, like Luther and Calvin, is strict in observing this division, because for them it is the fact of God's freely given, unassisted grace that liberates us to undertake "earthly learning" (*DP* 83) and earthly action for their own sake—because they are in themselves virtuous and good. Sidney is an orthodox sixteenth-century Protestant when he tells us that the poet is not a co-producer in the drama of salvation.

95. Calvin, 3.19.4–5.

96. Weiner, 50, argues eloquently that poetry imparts sufficient self-knowledge for us to know that we need the gospel of God's saving mercy. In other words, poetry acts in the same manner as the reformers say the law does. I think this is probably right, but I suggest that Sidney conceives of poetry as acting also in a way like the gospel: "to lead and draw us to as high a perfection as our degenerate souls, made worse by their clayey lodgings, can be capable of" (*DP* 82). For specific discussion of Sidney's place in the spectrum of Reformation religion see below, pp. 139–47.

97. Luther, *Works,* 48: 281–82.

98. Montaigne, *Of Repenting, Essayes,* 3: 20.

99. Luther, *Works,* 44: 366.

100. Levao, 234.

Chapter 2. The Invention of Justice

1. Letter probably written in 1566, quoted by Malcolm William Wallace, *The Life of Sir Philip Sidney* (Cambridge: Cambridge University Press, 1915), 68–69.

2. The interest in controlled self-development will be familiar to students of the Renaissance. The most famous literary expression of it appears in Spenser's *Letter to Raleigh,* prefaced to *The Faerie Queene,* where he writes that his poem is designed "to fashion [to represent and to form] a gentleman or noble person in virtuous and gentle discipline" (Edmund Spenser, *The Works of Edmund Spenser: A Variorum Edition,* ed. Edwin Greenlaw, Charles Grosvenor Osgood and Frederick Morgan Padelford [Baltimore: Johns Hopkins University Press, 1932–45], 1:167). This interest engendered the great education and courtesy book tradition found in Elyot's *Gouernour* (1531), Ascham's *Scholemaster* (1570), and in foreign works like Castiglione's *Courtier* (1529; trans. Hoby, 1561) and Erasmus's *Institutio Principis Christiani* (1516). It has been the subject of study in Thomas Greene's "The Flexibility of the Self in Renaissance Literature," in *The Disciplines of Criticism: Essays in Literary Theory, Interpretation, and History,* ed. Peter Demetz, Thomas M. Greene, and Lowry Nelson, Jr. (New Haven: Yale University Press, 1968), 241–64, and in Stephen Greenblatt's influential *Renaissance Self-Fashioning from More to Shakespeare* (Chicago: University of Chicago Press, 1980). Greene, 249, quotes Erasmus: "Homines non nascuntur, sed finguntur."

3. Plato, *Republic,* trans. Paul Shorey (London: William Heinemann, 1946), Section 588 C–D.

4. Plato, *Republic,* 500C.

5. Plato, *Republic,* 443D.

6. Plato, *Republic,* 443E.

7. Plato, *Republic,* 589, 589D.

8. Cicero, *De Officiis,* trans. Walter Miller (London: William Heinemann, 1961), bk 1, pt 6, sect. 19, and pt 7, sect. 20.

9. Cicero, *De Officiis,* 1.4.13.

10. Cicero, *De Officiis,* 1.20.67, 1.27.96.

11. Cicero, *De Officiis,* 1.20.66, 1.29.102.

12. Cicero, *De Officiis,* 2.2.5.

13. Plato, *Republic,* 387E.

14. Plato, *Timaeus,* in *Plato,* vol. 7, trans. R. G. Bury (Cambridge: Harvard University Press, 1952), Section 33.

15. Seneca, *Ad Lucilium Epistulae Morales,* trans. Richard M. Gummere, 3 vols. (London: William Heinemann, 1917–25), *Epistle* 9, sect. 15.

16. I have turned around Aristotle's simile in *The Nicomachean Ethics,* trans. H. Rackham (London: William Heinemann, 1962), bk. 9, pt. 8, sect. 6. He writes that just as "in the state it is the sovereign that is held in the fullest sense to *be* the state," so it is with the sovereign of the soul: "the intellect is the man himself."

17. Plato, *Republic,* 428E.

18. Cicero, *De Officiis,* 2.12.41.

19. A. C. Hamilton, *Sir Philip Sidney: A Study of His Life and Works* (Cambridge: Cambridge University Press, 1977), 2.

20. Desiderius Erasmus, *The Education of a Christian Prince,* trans. Lester K. Born (New York: Octagon, 1965), 189.

21. Sir Thomas Elyot, *The Boke Named the Gouernour,* ed. Henry Herbert Stephen Croft, 2 (London: Kegan Paul, Trench, 1883): 373.

22. Elyot, 2: 201, 187.

23. Pierre de la Primaudaye, *The French Academie* (1586), trans. T. B[owes]., (Hildesheim, West Germany, and New York: Georg Olms, 1972), 52–53.

24. Primaudaye, 391–92.

25. Primaudaye, 390. In *Sidney's Poetic Justice:* The Old Arcadia, *Its Eclogues, and Renaissance Pastoral Traditions* (Lewisburg, Pa.: Bucknell University Press, 1986), Robert E. Stillman notes from Dutch Calvinist Andraeus Rivetus a description of justice—in this case the "justitia originalis" of humankind before the Fall—similar to Primaudaye's: a virtue "produced in the whole man by the order of his parts and the best disposition of his faculties" (198).

26. In the *Defence* Sidney reveals his familiarity with the *Republic* and other works. See S. K. Heninger, Jr., "Sidney and Serranus' Plato," *English Literary Renaissance* 13 (1983), 146–61; see also Irene Samuel, "The Influence of Plato on Sidney's *Defense of Poesie," MLQ* 1 (1940): 383–84. While on his tour of the Continent, Sidney told Languet that he sought a "perfect understanding of Aristotle" and when he was finishing the *Old Arcadia* recommended the *Nicomachean Ethics.* See letters of 4 February 1574 and 22 May 1580, in James M. Osborn's *Young Philip Sidney, 1572–1577* (New Haven: Yale University Press, 1972), 142, 538. To Denny he also advised that next to Scripture, "let Tully be for *that* [moral] matter your foundation"; he says that *De Officiis* is the equal of Aristotle's *Ethics* and is among moral studies "truly for you

& my selfe beyond any." Denny is to make both the Bible and *De Officiis* his daily study (22 May 1580 letter, in Osborn, 538–40). In a letter of 18 October 1580, Sidney warns his brother Robert to avoid "Ciceronianisme the chief abuse of Oxford" (Osborn, 81), but this is the standard warning against slavish imitation of Cicero's style. Languet tempered his commendation of Cicero with the same caution (see letter of 1 January 1574, in Osborn, 126). There can be no doubt that Sidney admired Plato (whom "of all philosophers I have ever esteemed most worthy of reverence," *DP*, 107), studied Aristotle, and found in Cicero's work a guide to moral and political courage.

27. Roger Ascham, *The Scholemaster* (1570), ed. John E. B. Mayor (New York: AMS Press, 1967), 56.

28. A. C. Hamilton writes in *Sir Philip Sidney* that the stories the princes tell in Book Two are "to serve the reader even as stories of princes served them during their early education" (152). As this chapter and the two which follow indicate, I also think they serve the reader, but in a less direct way, for they glorify the code of justice only to reveal its inadequacy in the princes' Arcadian dilemma. As I noted in my introduction, Professor Hamilton himself writes very well about Philip Sidney's ambivalence toward the "humanist code" endorsed by his father and by Languet, 27–28.

29. Spenser, 6.3.2.

30. Courtesy books obviously stress nurture, but they acknowledge the necessity of privileged birth: there is a genetic as well as a learned code for gentlemen. Hoby's translation of the *Courtier* (1561) declares that "nature in every thing hath depely sowed the privie sede, which giueth a certaine force and propertie of her beginning, unto whatsoever springeth of it, and maketh it lyke unto her selfe" (Baldassare Castiglione, *The Book of the Courtier*, trans. Sir Thomas Hoby [London: David Nutt, 1900], 44–45). Elyot cites Plato to argue that wisdom grows from seeds naturally planted in the soul, noting that Socrates likens himself to a midwife, bringing out of his pupils "that which was all redy in them" (*Gouernour* 2: 364).

31. Xenophon, *Cyropaedia*, trans. Walter Miller, 2 vols. (London: William Heinemann, 1914), bk 1, chap. 6, pts. 5–6. For Sidney's admiration of this "heroic" work, see *DP*, 79, 81, 86, 88, 92, 98, and 103. For other Renaissance tributes, see Richard Mulcaster's *Elementarie* (1582), ed. E. T. Compangnae (Oxford: Clarendon Press, 1925), 17, where the London schoolmaster extols Cyrus "as the best boy for a patern to bring vp, & the best pri~ce for a preside~t to princes." Mulcaster's work was dedicated to Sidney's uncle, the Earl of Leicester. Castiglione (83), Elyot (1: 84), and Ascham (33 and 52) also praise the book. They may all be following Cicero, who cites Xenophon with praise in *De Officiis* (1.32.118, also 2.24.87) and in *De Senectute*, in *De Senectute, De Amicitia, De Divinatione*, trans. William Armistead Falconer (London: William Heinemann, 1923), pt. 9.30, 14.46, 17.59, and 22.79–81.

32. Euarchus establishes an educational program like that recommended by Erasmus in *The Education of the Christian Prince*: "It is not enough to hand out precepts; they must be impressed, crammed in, inculcated, and in one way and another be kept before him [the prince], now by a suggestive thought, now by a fable, now by analogy, now by example, now by maxims, now by a proverb" (144–45).

33. Aristotle, *Ethics*, 9.8.6.

34. Elyot, 2: 288–89.

35. Xenophon, 8.7.6.

36. Plato, *Republic*, 575, 576B, 579D.

37. See also Plato's *Menexenus*, where the warriors about to go into battle say that for a friend they wish to have a man "who makes all that concerns his welfare depend upon himself" and so is not subject to fortune (*Plato*, vol. 7, trans. R. G. Bury [Cambridge: Harvard University Press, 1952], sect. 248). In the *Ethics*, Aristotle explains that true friendship rests on each man's independent love of the good, so that one loves his friend for the same reason he loves himself: a recognition of the divinity of intellect within (9.4.2–3, 9.8.2).

38. In Cicero, *De Senectute, De Amicitia, De Divinatione*, trans. Falconer, pt. 9, sect. 30. See also Seneca, Epistle 9, section 12 "if friendship is to be sought for its own sake, he may seek it who is self-sufficient."

39. Cicero, *De Amicitia*, 13.46, 8.27.

40. Cicero, *De Amicitia*, 6.21.

41. Elyot, 2.128.

42. Aristotle, *Ethics*, 8.5.3; Primaudaye, 138.

43. It is in this spirit that Cicero says that "real friendships are eternal" (*De Amicitia* 9.32).

44. Cicero, *De Officiis*, 3.10.45.

45. Cicero, *De Amicitia*, 17.64. Compare Seneca in Epistle 9, section 10: "For to what purpose, then, do I make a man my friend? In order to have someone for whom I may die."

46. Cicero, *De Amicitia*, 13.47, 16.59.

47. Nancy Lindheim notices a likeness between the brothers' misplaced service and Pyrocles' promise to Plexirtus's dying daughter (Zelmane) that he will rescue her undeserving father. See "Retrospective Narrative," *Studies in Philology* 64 (January 1967): 176–77, and her *The Structures of Sidney's* Arcadia (Toronto: University of Toronto Press, 1982), 100. Hamilton, citing Lindheim, makes the same point in *Sir Philip Sidney*, 154. Both stress the increasing moral complexities in the Asia Minor experiences recounted by Pyrocles. But the differences between Pyrocles' promise and the loyalty of Tydeus and Telenor to Plexirtus are greater than the likenesses. The brothers have "knit their minds unto" Plexirtus, who is "crafty enough either to hide his faults or never to show them, but when they might pay home" (*NA* 184). Pyrocles acts to save Plexirtus knowing keenly the ambiguity of his situation; nor are the pardon and help that Pyrocles is asked to give the evil king the same as the advancement of Plexirtus's plots, in which the brothers play a willing part.

48. This Tudor commonplace is quoted from Mulcaster's *First Elementarie*, 13: those who "serue in publick function do turn their learning to publick vse, which is the naturall vse of all learning."

49. Elyot, 2.186.

50. Cicero, *De Officiis*, 3.6.32.

51. See *Miscellaneous Prose of Sidney*, ed. Katherine Duncan-Jones and Jan van Dorsten (Oxford: Clarendon Press, 1973), 6.

52. Cicero, *De Amicitia*, 14.50.

53. This triumphant departure may echo Edmund Campion's report of Sir Henry Sidney's departure from Ireland in 1571: "He was honoured . . . with such resource,

pomp, music, shows and interludes as no man remembereth the like. He took ship towards England at the key of Divelin [Dublin] in Lent following, accompanied to sea with the Estates and Worshipful of Ireland with innumerable hearty prayers, and with that wish of his return whereof but few Governors in these last sixty years have held possession" (quoted in Wallace, 87). This was one of the few happy occasions in Sir Henry's long and unprofitable service as Lord Deputy of Ireland, and Sidney may have recalled it as he wrote of the princes' departure from their great service away from their native land.

54. That Plexirtus stands among the well-wishers at Pontus does not negate the princes' victories, nor does it reveal any loss of identity or purpose within them. Their inner assurance and public striving for justice remain unchanged until they fall in love with King Basilius's daughters. As Nancy Lindheim notes, in Pyrocles' stories of their adventures the princes face a world more complex than in those told by his cousin, a world that requires unsettling and sometimes unsatisfying choices. Yet Lindheim says rightly that within these episodes "the princes themselves do not change" (*Structures*, 94). Pyrocles decides to leave his battle with Anaxius to rescue the wretched Dido, an act that reveals that he knows saving a woman from death to be more just than preserving his reputation with a braggart. He is embarrassed that onlookers call him coward, but he remains resolute: "Anaxius, . . . I neither fear thy force nor thy opinion" (*NA* 242). On Pyrocles' rescue of Plexirtus I have already commented. But now we need to recall that shortly before he undertakes this distasteful task, he and Musidorus "brought to good end a cruel war long maintained between the king of Bythinia and his brother," so that there is "as great peace between themselves, as love towards us for having made the peace" (*NA* 261–62). And it is after Plexirtus is saved from the monster that the princes achieve the brilliant resolution of the helots' rebellion: events alter, offering some choices and challenges more disturbing than others, but before they fall in love the princes do not alter. Facing moral dilemmas is not confusion; in fact it is entirely in the spirit of the *De Officiis*, which Sidney commended to his own friend, Edward Denny. Nor is an inability to eradicate evil, as with Plexirtus, proof of moral weakness. When Sidney later shows the princes compromised and confused in love, he makes their loss of justice plain enough. For a contrasting reading of the princes in Asia Minor, see Richard McCoy, *Sir Philip Sidney: Rebellion in Arcadia* (New Brunswick, N.J.: Rutgers University Press, 1979), 141–60.

55. See chapter 5 in Lindheim's *Structures*, especially 88–89, for distinctions between the kind of experience recounted in the two princes' stories. The terms *ethic* and *politic* are from Sidney's *DP*, 83.

56. Erasmus, 147.

57. The Ciceronian rhetorics present the orator as a man of comprehensive knowledge and moral integrity whose work is crucial to the stability of the state. *De Oratore* declares rhetoric to be the supreme use of man's definitive intellect, through which faculty the orator can unify citizens in "peace and tranquility." See Cicero, *De Oratore*, trans. E. W. Sutton, intro. H. Rackham, 2 vols. (Cambridge: Harvard University Press, 1942), bk. 1, pt. 8, sect. 30–31. For the ancients this skill is by nature moral, so that Quintillian can say that "no man can speak well who is not good himself" (*Institutio* 1.15.34). The art developed from the work of court and forum; all its

divisions and figures are subordinate to the end of establishing justice. That is why Cicero and Quintillian alike stress flexibility, the ability to adapt to circumstance that comes not only from practice but also from inner moral strength (*De Oratore* 1.32.144ff.; *Institutio* 2.13.2).

The humanist rhetorical tradition is familiar in its aims and methods. Perhaps the best essay on the subject is Hannah H. Gray's "Renaissance Humanism: The Pursuit of Eloquence," in *Renaissance Essays*, ed. Paul Oskar Kristeller and Philip P. Wiener (New York: Harper and Row, 1968), 199–216. For medieval and Renaissance considerations of rhetoric in England, see Wilbur Samuel Howell, *Logic and Rhetoric in England, 1500–1700* (Princeton: Princeton University Press, 1956). Philip Sidney's training in rhetoric may have begun during his study under Thomas Ashton at Shrewsbury School, though most of the boys' time there was spent in the study of grammar (language). Wallace's *Life* details the curriculum on p. 42. Richard Carew found Sidney a daunting opponent in the public disputations at Oxford, where Sidney enrolled at Christ Church (see Osborn, 23). John Stowe's *Annals* (1592) attest to Sidney's rhetorical skills employed before the daring and successful night raid against the town of Axel in July, 1586: Sidney exhorted his soldiers to remember their noble cause and their honor as Englishmen, "Which oration of his did like the minds of the people that they desired rather to die in that service than to live in the contrary" (quoted by Wallace, 370).

58. Aristotle, *The "Art" of Rhetoric*, trans. John Henry Freese (London: William Heinemann, 1926), bk. 1, pt. 3, sect. 2–3. For Sidney's translation of this work, see John Buxton, *Sir Philip Sidney and the English Renaissance* (New York: St. Martin's Press, 1964), 146.

59. Aristotle, *Rhetoric*, 1.3.4, 1.4.7.

60. Aristotle, *Rhetoric*, 1.2.3.

61. Aristotle, *Rhetoric*, 1.5, 1.6–7, 1.8.

62. For Sidney's use of this seven-part structure in the *Defence* see Kenneth Myrick, *Sir Philip Sidney as a Literary Craftsman*, 2d ed. (Lincoln: University of Nebraska Press, 1965), 46–83.

63. Aristotle, *Rhetoric*, 3.13.4.

64. The importance of a plain and direct manner in establishing the orator's character (the ethical proof) obtains particularly in deliberative oratory, whose "style is exactly like a rough sketch, for the greater the crowd, the further off is the point of view; wherefore . . . too much refinement is a superfluity and even a disadvantage" (Aristotle, *Rhetoric*, 3.12.5).

65. Aristotle, *Ethics*, 8.1.4.

66. Cicero, *De Amicitia*, 22.82.

67. The fiasco at the Ladon takes place in the afternoon (after the princesses' "sober dinner," "while the heat of the day lasted," *NA* 188). This does not seem to fit with the later statement that the dream of Mira took place at night (*NA* 346). But it is possible that the dream that "waked" Amphialus at the riverside is the same one he dreamed the night before, or that, exhausted from his flight after killing Philoxenus, he slept well into the day, until awakened by the swimmers at the river. Of course the dream that afternoon could have been a different dream from the one of Mira; perhaps

it was about Helen and Philoxenus, since the dream "not obscurely signified that he felt the smart of his own doings" (*NA* 198). Yet the fact that in waking, Amphialus saw "that whereof he dreamed" (*NA* 198) does suggest the dream was about Mira/Philoclea. The signals are contradictory, and so it is likely that in taking the dream from the *Old Arcadia* Sidney did not fully reconcile the details with its new function.

68. For Philisides' story, see the *The Countess of Pembroke's Arcadia (The Old Arcadia)*, ed. Jean Robertson (Oxford: Clarendon Press, 1973), 334–41. The quotations are from 334 and 341. For the identification of Philisides with Philip Sidney, see *The Poems of Sir Philip Sidney*, ed. William A. Ringler (Oxford: Clarendon Press, 1962), 418. With Amphialus Sidney shares not only some misfortune in love but also the experience of losing the inheritance of an uncle through the unexpected birth of a direct heir. In 1581, Leicester's wife (the widow of Essex) gave birth to a son and heir. See Hamilton, 3.

69. Compare Astrophil's "Thou my Wit, and thou my Vertue art" (*AS* 64, line 14). See also *AS* 19, lines 12–14, and *AS* 26.

70. Carl Jung would call such a self the *anima* in a man. See *The Collected Works of C. G. Jung*, trans. R. F. C. Hall, ed. Sir Hubert Rod and others (Princeton: Princeton University Press, 1954–73), vol. 9, pt. 1, paragraph 66. Jung shares with Sidney, and with other Renaissance reformers like Luther and Montaigne, the experience of discovering a traditional model of the psyche to be not only insufficient to the fullness of human nature but also destructive of it. More specifically, he shares with Sidney an interest in the feminine within the masculine soul—a point that Thelma Greenfield makes in her analysis of Pyrocles' transformation into Zelmane—and with the dangers of denying its power. See Thelma Greenfield, *The Eye of Judgment: Reading the New Arcadia* (Lewisburg, Pa.: Bucknell University Press, 1982), 61–62.

71. See Maurice Evans, ed., *The Countess of Pembroke's Arcadia* (1593) (Harmondsworth, England: Penguin, 1977), 861.

72. See Jon S. Lawry, *Sidney's Two Arcadias: Pattern and Proceeding* (Ithaca: Cornell University Press, 1972), 263–75. See also Hamilton, 163, and David Kalstone, *Sidney's Poetry, Contexts and Interpretations* (New York: Norton, 1970), 98–99.

73. Elyot, 1: 182, 181.

74. Sidney was aware of chivalry as a more elaborate game of mastery through his participation in the pageantry of Elizabeth's court. For his role in 1581 Whitsuntide tournament, see John Nichols, *The Progresses of Queen Elizabeth* (London: John Nichols and Son, 1823), 2: 314ff. For Elizabeth's use of chivalric pageantry as a display of power, see Francis Yates, *Astraea: The Imperial Theme in the Sixteenth Century* (London: Routledge and Kegan Paul, 1975); see also Stephen Greenblatt, *Renaissance Self-Fashioning*, 166–69. In "The Exemplary Mirage," *Essential Articles for the Study of Sir Philip Sidney*, ed. Arthur F. Kinney (Hamden, Conn.: Archon, 1986), 20–21, Alan Hager notes the way in which after Sidney's death, Elizabeth used his chivalric role as Shepherd Knight to manipulate Essex; see also Hager's *Dazzling Images: The Masks of Sir Philip Sidney* (Newark: University of Delaware Press, 1991), 24–25.

75. This is Sir Henry Sidney's praise of Philip, found in his letter of 25 March 1578, quoted by Wallace, 208.

Chapter 3. The Invention of Eros

1. Geoffrey Chaucer, *Troilus and Criseyde* 1.1079–80, *The Riverside Chaucer,* ed. Larry D. Benson, 3d ed. (Boston: Houghton Mifflin, 1987).

2. On courtly love, see the bibliography in *The Riverside Chaucer;* on the relation of Sannazaro's *Arcadia* and Petrarch's *Rime* to love in Sidney's poetry, see David Kalstone, *Sidney's Poetry: Contexts and Interpretations* (Cambridge: Harvard University Press, 1965), 9–39, 105–32; see A. C. Hamilton, *Sir Philip Sidney: A Study of His Life and Works* (Cambridge: Cambridge University Press, 1977), 43–45 on Sannazaro; 47–49 and 129–31 on Heliodorus's *Æthiopian History;* and 126–29 on Montemayor's *Diana.* See also Dorothy Connell, *Sir Philip Sidney: The Maker's Mind* (Oxford: Clarendon Press, 1977), 9–33 for an essay on "Sidney's Conception of Love."

3. *The Poems of Sir Philip Sidney,* ed. William A. Ringler, Jr. (Oxford: Clarendon Press, 1962), 154–55, lines 30–34.

4. Petrarch, Sonnet 61.12–13, *Petrarch's Lyric Poems,* trans. and ed. Robert M. Durling (Cambridge: Harvard University Press, 1976).

5. Kalstone, 105.

6. Hamilton, 109.

7. Sannazaro, *Arcadia and Piscatorial Eclogues,* ed. Ralph Nash (Detroit: Wayne State University Press, 1966), 20. The link between love and death in pastoral predates the Renaissance. See E. Panofsky, "Et in Arcadia Ego," *Philosophy and History: Essays Presented to Ernst Cassirer,* ed. Raymond Klibonsky and H. J. Paton (New York: Harper and Row, 1963), 227–28: "At the very moment when this new Arcadia was created [by Virgil] a dissonance made itself felt between its preternatural perfection and the fundamental limitations of human nature as such: even in Arcadia there existed the two fundamental tragedies of human life, inextricably connected with one another: frustrated love and death."

8. *A Critical Edition of Yong's Translation of George of Montemayor's* Diana *and Gil Polo's* Enamoured Diana, ed. Judith Kennedy (Oxford: Clarendon Press, 1968), 102 and 103.

9. On Sidney's doubts about neoplatonism, see also Alan Hager, *Dazzling Images: The Masks of Sir Philip Sidney* (Newark: University of Delaware Press, 1991), where Hager attributes this skepticism to Sidney's distrust of abstraction and "pure contemplation" because they take one out of "an immediate social structure" (115); and Ake Bergvall writes in his doctoral thesis, *The "Enabling of Judgement": Sir Philip Sidney and the Education of the Reader* (Uppsala: Acta Universitatis Upsaliensis, 1989), that "Sidney reacted against the premises of Florentine neoplatonism," though Bergvall sees an "Augustinian synthesis of Platonism and Christianity" in Sidney's work (abstract).

10. Castiglione, *The Book of the Courtier,* trans. Sir Thomas Hoby (1561), intro. Walter Raleigh (London: David Nutt, 1900), 360.

11. See Katherine Duncan-Jones, "Sidney's Urania," *Review of English Studies,* ns 17 (1966): 123–32. My reading of the dialogue between Strephon and Claius is influenced by Dorothy Connell's commentary on these two shepherds as they are found in *Other Poems* 4 (Ringler, *Poems,* 242–56). See Connell, 117–25. See also analysis by

Nancy Lindheim in *The Structure of Sidney's* Arcadia (Toronto: University of Toronto Press, 1982), 17–19.

12. Castiglione, 353, 343. See also Marsilio Ficino, *Commentary on Plato's Symposium,* trans. Sears Jayne, *University of Missouri Studies* 19 (1944): 146 – 47.

13. See Lindheim, 18, for the parallel with the Song of Songs.

14. Ficino, 213.

15. The Florentines did not introduce Plato's thought to English humanists. Neoplatonic thought had long been influential through Augustine, Boethius, and Pseudo-Dionysius. On Sidney's knowledge of the Latin translation of Plato's works by Jean de Serres (1578), see S. K. Heninger, Jr., "Sidney and Serranus' Plato," *English Literary Renaissance,* 13 (1983): 146 – 61. In "Ficino and the Platonism of the English Renaissance," *Comparative Literature* 4 (1952): 214 –38, Sears Jayne argues that most English "platonic" literature is inspired by French poetry from the court of Marguerite of Navarre and is only superficially given to the pursuit of Ficino's higher love, being far more Petrarchan in manner and matter. But Jayne suggests that some Tudor writers, including Colet, Raleigh, Spenser, and Chapman, did go *ad fontes.* Sidney's use of Ficino is less certain, but he knew Hoby's *Courtier* and probably other *trattati d'amore.* I assume that he understood neoplatonism sufficiently to distinguish it from the Petrarchan sonnet tradition.

16. Here is the passage:

Venus is two-fold: one is certainly that intelligence which we said was in the Angelic Mind; the other is the power of generation with which the World-Soul is endowed. Each has as consort a similar Love. The first, by innate love is stimulated to know the beauty of God; the second, by its Love, to procreate the same beauty in bodies. The former Venus first embraces the Glory of God in herself, and then translates it into the second Venus. The latter Venus translates the sparks of divine glory into earthly matter. (Ficino, 142)

17. Thomas Greene, "The Flexibility of the Self in Renaissance Literature," *The Disciplines of Criticism: Essays in Literary Theory, Interpretation, and History,* ed. Peter Demetz, Thomas M. Greene, and Lowry Nelson, Jr. (New Haven: Yale University Press, 1968), 251.

18. Quoted in Paul Oskar Kristeller, *Renaissance Thought: The Classic, Scholastic, and Humanistic Strains* (New York: Harper and Row, 1961), 129.

19. Giovanni Pico della Mirandolla, *Oration on the Dignity of Man,* in *The Renaissance Philosophy of Man,* ed. Ernst Cassirer, Paul Oskar Kristeller, and John Herman Randall, Jr. (Chicago: University of Chicago Press, 1948), 225.

20. Pico, 225.

21. Giordano Bruno, *The Heroic Frenzies (De gl'heroci furori),* quoted in Frances Yates, *Giordano Bruno and the Hermetic Tradition* (Chicago: University of Chicago Press, 1964), 237 and 283.

22. See Jayne's notes 20 and 24 on Ficino's *Commentary,* 126 –27.

23. Plato, *Symposium,* in *Plato,* vol. 5, trans. W. R. M. Lamb (Cambridge: Harvard University Press, 1967), 206C–E, 208E–209E.

24. Ficino, 207.

25. Ficino, 211.

26. Castiglione, 353–54.

27. Castiglione, 358.

28. Pico, 229.

29. Martin Luther, *The Disputation Concerning Man, Luther's Works,* ed. Jaroslav Pelikan and Helmut Lehmann, vol. 34 (Philadelphia: Fortress [formerly Muhlenberg] Press, 1960), 143.

30. Ficino, 182.

31. Ficino, 182.

32. Connell, 9.

33. Kalstone, 153.

34. See Ringler's note on *Astrophil and Stella* 21 in *Poems,* 468.

35. See Rosemond Tuve, "Spenser and Some Pictorial Conventions: With Particular Reference to Illustrated Manuscripts," *Essays by Rosemond Tuve,* ed. Thomas P. Roche, Jr. (Princeton: Princeton University Press, 1970), 119. Tuve is writing about Spenser, but she cites illustrated manuscripts belonging to Sidney's family and friends, including John Dee. See pp. 112–15. Readers need only compare Tuve's account of Amazon pictures (120–24) with Sidney's description of Pyrocles as the Amazon Zelmane (*NA* 68–69) to see Sidney's familiarity with the pictorial tradition that Tuve describes.

36. See John Nichols for Henry Goldwell's account in *The Progresses of Queen Elizabeth* (London: John Nichols and Son, 1823), 2:314, 318, and 328. Ringler, *Poems,* 345–46, prints the two sonnets. On Sidney's role in designing this entertainment, see Malcolm William Wallace, *The Life of Sir Philip Sidney* (Cambridge: Cambridge University Press, 1915), 264. On the authorship of the two sonnets, see Ringler, 518–19, and James M. Osborn, *Young Philip Sidney, 1572–77* (New Haven: Yale University Press, 1972), 505.

37. Sannazaro, 42–44.

38. Montemayor, 142.

39. Jon S. Lawry, *Sidney's Two* Arcadias: *Pattern and Proceeding* (Ithaca: Cornell University Press, 1972), 156, 162.

40. See Lawry, 155, 268–89, and Hamilton, 163. Both champion an ideal of "feminine," passive heroism.

41. Lawry, 241.

42. Stephen Orgel, "Sidney's Experiment in Pastoral: *The Lady of May,*" in *Essential Articles for the Study of Sir Philip Sidney,* ed. Arthur F. Kinney (Hamden, Conn: Archon Books, 1986), 67, 64.

43. See Connell, 14.

44. Mark Lambert, "*Troilus,* Books I–III. A Criseydan Reading," *Essays on Troilus and Creseyde,* ed. Mary Salu (Cambridge: D. J. Brower, 1979), 108, 114, 117, 119.

45. Richard McCoy, *Sir Philip Sidney: Rebellion in Arcadia* (New Brunswick, N.J.: Rutgers University Press, 1979), 155.

46. McCoy, 157.

47. Lawry, 264; Hamilton, 163.

48. See Hamilton, 163.

49. See Maurice Evans, ed., *The Countess of Pembroke's Arcadia* (1593) (New York: Penguin, 1977), 862.

50. Evans, 859.

51. Pierre de la Primaudaye, *The French Academie,* trans. T. B[owes]., (Hildesheim, West Germany, and New York: Georg Olms, 1972), 479.

52. In the *Defence,* Aeneas is cited six times, Achilles five, Hercules four, Ulysses three.

53. William Shakespeare, *As You Like It* 4.1.106 – 08, *The Riverside Shakespeare,* ed. G. Blakemore Evans (Boston: Houghton Mifflin, 1974).

54. John Calvin, *Institutes of the Christian Religion,* ed. John T. McNeill, trans. Ford Lewis Battles, 2 vols. (Philadelphia: Westminster, 1960), bk. 4, sect. 12, chap. 24; Martin Luther, *The Estate of Marriage, Luther's Works,* vol. 45, ed. Walter I. Brandt (1962), 39.

55. Luther, 45:39.

56. Heinrich Bullinger, preface to *The Golden Boke of Christen Matrimonye,* trans. Miles Coverdale (London, 1543), Aii.

57. *The Prose Works of Fulke Greville,* ed. John Gouws (Oxford: Clarendon Press, 1986), 11.

Chapter 4. The Work of Invention

1. Cicero, *De Officiis,* trans. Walter Miller (London: William Heinemann, 1961), 1.32.118.

2. Xenophon, *Memorabilia,* in *Memorabilia and Oeconomics,* trans. E. C. Marchant (London: William Heinemann, 1923), 2.1.28.

3. See Erwin Panofsky, *Hercules am Scheidewege* (Leipzig and Berlin: B. G. Teubner, 1930). Plate 31 provides a good example.

4. Hallet Smith, *Elizabethan Poetry: A Study in Convention, Meaning, and Expression* (Cambridge: Harvard University Press, 1952), 324. For the full discussion of the choice of Hercules, see 294 –324. For the tradition of interpreting this choice, see Nancy Lindheim, *The Structures of Sidney's* Arcadia (Toronto: University of Toronto Press, 1982), 43ff. See also Eugene M. Waith, *The Herculean Hero in Marlowe, Chapman, Shakespeare and Dryden* (New York: Columbia University Press, 1962), 39–59, on Renaissance readings of Hercules.

5. See P. Albert Duhamel, "Sidney's Arcadia and Elizabethan Rhetoric," *Studies in Philology,* 45 (1948): 134 –50. For a different reading of the princes' debates, see Walter R. Davis, "A Map of *Arcadia,* Sidney's Romance in its Tradition," in *Sidney's Arcadia* (New Haven: Yale University Press, 1965), 69–72.

6. Plato, *Symposium,* in *Plato,* vol. 5, trans. W. R. M. Lamb (London: William Heinemann, 1925), 209B–C.

7. Sir Philip Sidney, *The Defence of Poesie* (London: William Ponsonby, 1595), C1v.

8. In Geoffrey Chaucer, *The Riverside Chaucer,* ed. Larry D. Benson and others (Boston: Houghton Mifflin, 1987), lines 1241– 42, p. 345.

9. Robert E. Stillman, *Sidney's Poetic Justice:* The Old Arcadia, *Its Eclogues, and Renaissance Pastoral Traditions* (Lewisburg, Pa.: Bucknell University Press, 1986), 191–92.

10. Martin Luther, *Luther's Works*, ed. Jaroslav Pelikan and Helmut T. Lehmann, 44 (Philadelphia: Fortress Press, 1966): 34.

11. Luther, *Works*, 37:361–66.

12. John Calvin, *Institutes of the Christian Religion*, ed. John T. McNeill, trans. Ford Lewis Battles (Philadelphia: Westminster Press, 1960), 3.3.9. On Calvin's conception of "grace as power" see John H. Leith, *An Introduction to the Reformed Tradition: A Way of Being the Christian Community* (Atlanta: John Knox Press, 1977), 72–77, 101–102. Calvin sees a role for justified sinners in their own sanctification that Luther would not, but both see the necessity of human activity in imitation of God.

13. Calvin, 3.19.5. In "Sidney and the Active Life," *Sir Philip Sidney's Achievements,* ed. M. J. B. Allen, Dominic Baker-Smith, and Arthur Kinney, with Margaret M. Sullivan (New York: AMS Press, 1990), Peter Lindenbaum suggests Sidney's Calvinist belief in "man's recalcitrant nature" led to "view of life as a constant struggle . . . which impels Sidney to insist on constant adherence to the active life" and to reject "the contemplative ideal" (192). "Constant struggle" is right, but Lindenbaum does not acknowledge the Calvinist (and Lutheran) emphasis on God's grace, which liberates the redeemed but unfinished self to undertake a more potentially creative labor, including the "contemplative" struggle of writing poetry.

14. Calvin, 3.6.3.

15. Calvin, 1.10.2.

16. See A. G. Dickens, *The English Reformation* (New York: Schocken Books, 1964), 64–66.

17. For a theologian's use of this term, see Wilfried Jost, *Ontologie der Person bei Luther* (Gottingen: Vandenhoeck and Ruprecht, 1967), 233–74.

18. Luther, *Works*, 31: 365.

19. Luther, *Works*, 31: 371.

20. Calvin, 2.3.7, 3.19.4–5.

21. Calvin, 3.2.6.

22. Calvin, 3.19.8.

23. Leith, 72–77.

24. John T. McNeill, *The History and Character of Calvinism* (New York: Oxford University Press, 1967), 110–18.

25. Calvin, 2.2.10.

26. Luther, *Works*, 31: 358.

27. See Calvin's preface to the reader (1559) for *Institutes*, p. 4 in the McNeill edition, vol. 1, as well as McNeill's introduction, p. xxxv.

28. On this pamphlet, see Eric W. Gritsch, *Martin—God's Court Jester, Luther in Retrospect* (Philadelphia: Fortress Press, 1983), 197–98.

29. Dickens, 63, 251. On the White Horse Tavern group, see David H. Pill, *The English Reformation, 1529–58* (Totowa, N.J.: Rowman and Littlefield, 1973), 39–40. Readers interested in the development of reformist thought in England should consult such studies as A. G. Dickens (see note 15) and Horton Davies, *Worship and Theology in England,* 5 vols. (Princeton: Princeton University Press, 1961–75); those particularly interested in Lutheran influence in England can begin with the work of Gordon Rupp, *Studies in the Making of the English Protestant Tradition* (Cambridge: Cambridge University Press, 1966), and those with the Calvinist with that of John McNeill (see note 23).

30. Dickens, 197.

31. Dickens, 294; McNeill, 315, 313.

32. See M. Eugene Osterhaven, *The Spirit of the Reformed Tradition* (Grand Rapids, Mich.: Eerdmans, 1971), 171–76, on the meaning of "reformed"; for Elizabeth's letter, see Osterhaven, 173. Luther apologist Philipp Melanchthon makes a notable case for the difficulty of pinning down the exact nature of a reformed believer's faith in Sidney's century. Luther praised the first *Loci* as worthy of reception into the scriptural canon; in the *Augsburg Confession* (1530) and the subsequent *Apology* (1531) Melanchthon wrote the definitive statements of the Lutheran belief. Yet he was attacked later in life for his allowance of certain adiophora—things indifferent to salvation—and for his more Calvinist understanding of communion. See Clyde Leonard Manschreck, *Melanchthon: The Quiet Reformer* (1958; rpt. Westport, Conn.: Greenwood, 1975), 175–96, 240–42, and 277–92.

33. See Dickens, 316, on Puritanism among Elizabeth's advisors; Roger Lockyer, *Tudor and Stuart Britain, 1471–1714* (New York: St. Martin's Press, 1964), 180, on Antwerp.

34. See Katherine Duncan-Jones, *Miscellaneous Prose of Sir Philip Sidney*, ed. Duncan-Jones and Jan van Dorsten (Oxford: Clarendon Press, 1973), 155–57.

35. See James M. Osborn, *Young Philip Sidney, 1572–1577* (New Haven: Yale University Press, 1972), 5.

36. See Osborn, 47, 140. Ake Bergvall, *The "Enabling of Judgement": Sir Philip Sidney and the Education of the Reader* (Uppsala: Acta Universitatis Upsaliensis, 1989), 32–36, points out that Melanchthon's influence in northern Europe extended beyond theology to his proposals for academic curricula, especially his view of rhetoric as teaching good judgment through the reading of texts, and he notes that Sidney would have encountered Melanchthon's ideas not only from continental figures like Languet and Johann Sturm of Strasborg but also at Oxford.

37. Andrew D. Weiner, *Sir Philip Sidney and the Poetics of Protestantism: A Study of Contexts* (Minneapolis: University of Minnesota Press, 1978), 5. My general debt to Professor Weiner's 1978 study of Sidney's "Protestant poetics" is clear. But I cannot agree with his resolution there of the question of how poetry can be of spiritual or moral value if it is written by the sinful poet, burdened by an infected will. Weiner's solution is ingenious, but incorrect. Turning to Elizabethan faculty psychology, he argues that the imagination—as opposed to the reason, will, and senses—is less corrupted by the Fall and can work directly on the will, bypassing the clouded reason. See 36–40. This will not work. Sidney insists that making poetry is a matter of the human wit—the reason—something the poet has to *think* about, both in forming his "foreconceit" (*DP* 79) and in laboring to express it so as to move the reader (*DP* 91). Weiner then poses the equally difficult question of why the elect *need* poets and poetry since their justification is the work of God—not of authors (47). Weiner first answers this by noting, as I have, that Renaissance Protestantism recognized the human province of "civil righteousness," of legitimate action in those matters of less import than salvation (48–49). With this I have no quarrel, though I think Weiner underestimates its role. But he then closes the discussion with another, to my mind very striking, suggestion: poetry acts "as a possible handmaid to the church" by revealing to us our human limitations, driving us to realize that in our imperfection

we must cast ourselves on God (50). In Protestant terms, Weiner's argument is that poetry is like the rigors of the law: its revelation of our failure compels us to turn to the Gospel. I find this so attractive that I would like to endorse it, but it seems finally a backdoor attempt to claim that the human work of poetry can assist in salvation— work that the reformers insisted is God's alone. Poetry is neither law nor gospel, which are God's work and sufficient in themselves. It is a counterfeiting, the "eccentric" human.response to the eccentric work of God. It rests on the Reformation conviction that only when we stop trying to assume God's part can we begin our imitation of God's creative work.

38. Malcolm William Wallace, *The Life of Sir Philip Sidney* (Cambridge: Cambridge University Press, 1915), 27–34, 179. See Osborn, 507, on Sidney's Catholic friends in Europe.

39. Katherine Duncan-Jones, *Sir Philip Sidney: Courtier Poet* (New Haven: Yale University Press, 1991), 124 –27.

40. Dickens, 312.

41. Wallace, 173–94; Osborn, 511.

42. Osborn, 457, emphasis added.

43. The phrases are from Sidney's letter to Walsingham, 24 March 1586, found in *The Prose Works of Sir Philip Sidney,* ed. Albert Feuillerat (Cambridge: Cambridge University Press, 1962) 3:7 9.

44. *The Essayes of Michael Lord of Montaigne,* trans. John Florio (1603) (London: Oxford University Press, 1924), 3: 379.

45. Montaigne, *Of Repenting, Essayes,* 3: 20.

46. Montaigne, *Of Experience, Essayes,* 3: 367.

47. Montaigne, *Of Repenting, Essayes,* 3: 20.

48. Montaigne, *Of Experience, Essayes,* 3: 370 –71.

49. Montaigne, *Of Repenting, Essayes,* 3: 20.

50. For a useful discussion of genre, see the note in A. C. Hamilton's *Sir Philip Sidney: A Study of His Life and Works* (Cambridge: Cambridge University Press, 1977), 190 –91. See also Stephen Greenblatt, "Sidney's *Arcadia* and the Mixed Mode," *Studies in Philology* 70 (1973): 269–78, and Alan Hager, *Dazzling Images: The Masks of Sir Philip Sidney* (Newark: University of Delaware Press, 1991), 157– 66.

51. Jon S. Lawry, *Sidney's Two* Arcadias: *Pattern and Proceeding* (Ithaca: Cornell University Press, 1972), 155.

52. Heliodorus, *An Æthiopian History,* trans. Thomas Underdowne (1569) (London: David Nutt, 1895), 93.

53. Castiglione, *The Book of the Courtier,* trans. Thomas Hoby (1561) (London: David Nutt, 1900), 357.

54. Hamilton, 159, 171.

55. Lawry, 247, 284.

56. For an extended discussion of the ending of the *New Arcadia* and its relations to the *Old,* as well as the 1593 composite, see my chapter 5, note 17, pp. 147–49.

57. C. L. Barber, *Shakespeare's Festive Comedy: A Study of Dramatic Form and its Relation to Social Custom* (Princeton: Princeton University Press, 1959), 193.

58. Walter Raleigh, *The History of the World* (1614), ed. C.A. Patrides (Philadelphia: Temple University Press, 1971), 125.

59. See Ringler, *Poems,* 372, and Skretkowicz, lxxx.

60. See Ringler's note to *OA* 62, p. 410.

61. Stillman, *Sidney's Poetic Justice,* 177.

62. Skretkowicz, following *OA* versions of the poem, prints *pains* rather the 1590 *tales.*

63. William Shakespeare, *Hamlet,* 5.1.8–ll, *The Riverside Shakespeare,* ed. G. Blakemore Evans (Boston: Houghton Mifflin, 1974).

64. Shakespeare, *Hamlet,* 5.1.48, 219–20.

65. This thought was influenced by Professor Ray Waddington's essay on "The Lutheran Hamlet," *English Language Notes* 27, no. 2 (1989): 27–42. Waddington writes that for Luther "the province of reason is firmly within the temporal kingdom, where it holds a worthy place in guiding the individual through the private and public activities of human life. It is only when it encroaches on the boundaries of the heavenly kingdom that the misapplication of reason exposes its limitations" (36).

66. Gritsch, *Martin,* 152.

67. Montaigne, *Of Experience, Essayes,* 3: 402.

Chapter 5. Right Reading

1. For an insightful reading of the teaching and moving role of delight in Sidney's poetics, see James A. Devereux, S. J., "The Meaning of Delight in Sidney's *Defence of Poesy,*" *Studies in the Literary Imagination* 15 (1982): 85–97. Devereux argues that for Sidney the delight of poetry arises primarily not from rhetorical ornament or "static" images but from narratives of "persons in action" (92).

2. For discussion of this new historicist assumption, see the introduction to *The Historical Renaissance: New Essays on Tudor and Stuart Literature and Culture,* ed. Heather Dubrow and Richard Strier (Chicago: University of Chicago Press, 1988), 3. See also Jean S. Howard, "The New Historicism in Renaissance Studies," in *Renaissance Historicism: Selections from English Literary Renaissance,* ed. Arthur F. Kinney and Dan S. Collins (Amherst: University of Massachusetts Press, 1987), 8.

3. For a full consideration of "dialogic" reading, see Tzvetan Todorov, *Literature and Its Theorists: A Personal View of Twentieth-Century Criticism,* trans. Catherine Porter (Ithaca: Cornell University Press, 1987), 155–68.

4. See Susanne Woods, "Freedom and Tyranny in Sidney's *Arcadia,*" *Sir Philip Sidney's Achievements,* ed. M. J. B. Allen, Dominic Baker-Smith, and Arthur Kinney, with Margaret M. Sullivan (New York: AMS Press, 1990), 174, and Alan Hager, *Dazzling Images: The Masks of Sir Philip Sidney* (Newark: University of Delaware Press, 1991), 130.

5. See Geoffrey Shepherd, ed., *An Apology for Poetry* (London: Nelson, 1965), 54.

6. See my discussion of justice above, in chapter 2. For a book length study of justice in the *Old Arcadia,* see Robert E. Stillman, *Sidney's Poetic Justice*: The Old Arcadia, *Its Eclogues, and Renaissance Pastoral Traditions* (Lewisburg, Pa.: Bucknell University Press, 1986).

7. A. C. Hamilton, *Sir Philip Sidney: A Study of His Life and Works* (Cambridge: Cambridge University Press, 1977), 125.

8. See above, chapter 3.

9. See David Kalstone, *Sidney's Poetry, Contexts and Interpretations* (New York: Norton, 1970), 15–23. See also Maureen Quilligan's analysis of Sidney's use of the strategies of "Petrarchan abasement" in "Sidney and His Queen," *The Historical Renaissance*, 185–89.

10. For these three diverse readings, see Richard A. Lanham, *"Astrophil and Stella:* Pure and Impure Persuasion," in *Essential Articles for the Study of Sir Philip Sidney*, ed. Arthur F. Kinney (Hamden, Conn.: Archon, 1986), 223–40; Thomas P. Roche, Jr., *"Astrophil and Stella:* A Radical Reading," *Spenser Studies* 3 (1982): 139–91; and S. K. Heninger, Jr., *Sidney and Spenser: The Poet as Maker* (University Park and London: Pennsylvania State University Press, 1989), 470–87.

11. C. S. Lewis, *English Literature in the Sixteenth Century, Excluding Drama* (Oxford: Clarendon Press, 1954), 327.

12. Lanham, 227.

13. Iris Murdoch, "On 'God' and 'Good,'" in *The Sovereignty of Good* (London: Ark, 1979), 86.

14. For discussion of the literary sources for Sidney's *New Acardia* see the Skretkowicz edition, xvii–xxiv, and Hamilton, *Sir Philip Sidney,* 126–31 and 42–50 (on sources for the *Old Arcadia*).

15. Skretkowicz, xxxiv.

16. Skretkowicz, xxxii.

17. My argument here is not dependent on the *New Arcadia*'s return to a judgment pronounced by Euarchus and then undone by the revival of Basilius. But I agree with Nancy Lindheim that "the trial scene is a fitting culmination of actions, attitudes, and themes central to Sidney's revision." See *The Structures of Sidney's* Arcadia (Toronto: University of Toronto Press, 1982), 163. No definitive resolution of this matter is to be found, though I see no evidence that Sidney quit in dismay at the new complexities introduced by Book Three. Those who favor this latter view include Richard Helgerson, 151–55; Richard C. McCoy, *Rebellion in Arcadia* (New Brunswick, N.J.: Rutgers University Press, 1979), 214; and Robert Kimbrough, *Sir Philip Sidney* (New York: Twayne, 1971), 142. In my defense I would cite both minor and major changes in Sidney's revision of the *Old Arcadia* that direct the *New* toward the trial.

In Book Two of the *New Arcadia*, Sidney adds a new and long rehearsal by Musidorus of how the young king Euarchus established justice in Macedon (*NA* 158–61), "making his life the example of his laws" and his rule a picture of "the whole art of government" (*NA* 160–61). This addition displays the character of the man who guided the education of the princes, but also it would serve to establish Euarchus's moral and political judgment in anticipation of the trial. Two revisions found in the 1593 conclusion to the unfinished story—revisions deemed to be Sidney's own by Ringler, Robertson, and Skretkowicz—indicate that there would be cause for such a trial. These references are to a second rebellion by the helots and to Pyrocles' hope that either Musidorus or these former comrades in arms could aid him in his flight with Philoclea. (See the 1593 variants on pp. 217 and 355–57 in Robertson's *Old Arcadia* for these changes. On their authority, see Robertson, lx–lxi; Ringler, 377–78; and Skretkowicz, lxxiv–lxxvi. All three editors assume these changes were made before Sidney wrote the substantially new Book Three. I agree, but I do not see that the story of Amphialus's rebellion or of the princesses' heroic resistance to rape invalidates the substance of such revisions.)

A. C. Hamilton argues that Pamela and Philoclea "could not be subject to the absurd masculine aggression" of an elopement guided by the princes after their rejection of Amphialus and his mother in the castle (*Sidney*, p. 171). But I think it likely that Sidney would represent this very experience as making the princesses, Pamela in particular, far less willing to brook their "absurd" forced retreat at the hands of their father and that the extremes of grief and joy endured by Philoclea and Pyrocles would confirm their devotion to the princes and their determination to outface all odds. In fact, even before the captivity Pamela grows restless under her parents' rule and tells Philoclea that "it is time for me to trust something to my own judgement" (*NA* 155).

More important than these minor indications are one passage retained from the *Old Arcadia*, one altered in the *New*, and one added to it. The passage retained is Gynecia's dream of seeing Zelmane on a hill only to reach it to find the body of Basilius, who embraces her and cries, "Gynecia, leave all, for here is thy only rest" (*NA* 277; *OA* 117; *NA* adds "leave all"). Placed late in the *New* Book Two, the dream commits Sidney at this point to the *Old* plot in which Pyrocles' efforts to hoodwink Gynecia and Basilius lead to the latter's apparent death. The altered passage is the Delphic oracle that first drove Basilius and his family into retreat. In the *New Arcadia*, the oracle— quoted near the end of Book Two—has three entirely new lines about the princesses and their suitors:

> Both they themselves unto such two shall wed,
> Who at the bier, as at a bar, shall plead
> Why thee (a living man) they had made dead.   (*NA* 296)

As Dorothy Connell points out in *Sir Philip Sidney: The Maker's Mind* (Oxford: Clarendon Press, 1977), these added lines "explicitly predict the trial and also point to its happy ending" (141). The new passage occurs very near the end of the revised Book Three in the *New Arcadia*, after Sidney has committed himself to the new material of the captivity. This is a second oracle, in which the king is told not to yield his daughters to Anaxius and his brothers and advised that he "should keep on his solitary course till both Philanax and Basilius fully agreed in the understanding of the former prophecy" (*NA* 457). Connell's judgment that in this second oracle "Sidney has committed himself to the task of forcing the action back" to the trial (140) makes sense. Robertson argues that we should not "deduce from this that Sidney intended to conclude his story with the *Old Arcadia* ending as it stood" (lx). She is no doubt correct, but this does not alter the likelihood of a revised trial in the *New*.

Unlike Robertson (lxii) and Ringler (379), I do not believe that Sidney would have tried the princes for the death of Basilius only, sparing them the indignity of the elopement charges. I think it probable that *three* princes—Pyrocles, Musidorus, and a revived Amphialus—would stand trial on charges that mingled love and politics. This would confirm the parallels between the cousins and Amphialus that the revised story is so careful to establish, and it would conclude with a flourish Sidney's fictional critique of male-dominated justice. Even the "plot" of the wise and powerful Euarchus would be subject to contingency and to re-formation.

But this is speculation. We do not know how Sidney would have concluded his great book. Perhaps he would have made changes in the already revised books and made all our arguments irrelevant. All we know is that he left the work unfinished at his death.

18. For Murdoch, see note 13 above.

19. Arthur Heiserman, *The Novel before the Novel: Essays and Discussions about the Beginnings of Prose Fiction in the West* (Chicago: University of Chicago Press, 1977), 194.

20. Anne Shaver, "Woman's Place in the *New Arcadia*," *Sidney Newsletter* 10, no. 2 (1990): 3.

21. Margaret Mary Sullivan, "Getting Pamela Out of the House: Gendering Genealogy in the *New Arcadia*," *Sidney Newsletter*, 9.2 (1988/89): 8.

22. Thomas Wilson, *Arte of Rhetorique* (1553), ed. Thomas J. Derrick (New York: Garland, 1982), 27. I have modernized the spelling; in Derrick's text the passage reads "Delight theim and wynne them; werie theim, and you lose theim for ever."

23. See *The Essayes of Michael Lord of Montaigne,* trans. John Florio (1603) (London: Oxford University Press, 1924), 3: 371.

24. I paraphrase the title of Nina Baym's "Melodramas of Beset Manhood: How Theories of American Fiction Exclude Women Authors," in *The New Feminist Criticism: Essays on Women, Literature, and Theory*, ed. Elaine Showalter (New York: Pantheon, 1985), 63–80.

25. See Hamilton, 163, and Jon S. Lawry, *Sidney's Two* Arcadias: *Pattern and Proceeding* (Ithaca: Cornell University Press, 1972), 268–69. Note also Myron Turner, "The Heroic Ideal in Sidney's Revised *Arcadia,*" *SEL* 10 (Winter 1970): 71, where "a well-planned shift away from the exclusively male hero" is noted.

26. Mary Ellen Lamb, *Gender and Authorship in the Sidney Circle* (Madison: University of Wisconsin Press, 1990), 73.

27. Sullivan, 3.

28. See above, chapter 3, pp. 55–57.

29. Katherine Duncan-Jones, *Sir Philip Sidney: Courtier Poet* (New Haven: Yale University Press, 1991), 2.

30. On this point, see Alan Sinfield, "Power and Ideology: An Outline Theory and Sidney's *Arcadia*," in *Essential Articles*, ed. Kinney, 391–410, especially 397: "We should . . . perceive the Elizabethan state not as a static totality whose power structure is revealed in the ideology of monarchy, but as diverse and changing, the site of profound contradictions."

31. Philip Sidney, *Irish Affairs*, in *Miscellaneous Prose of Sir Philip Sidney*, ed. Katherine Duncan-Jones and Jan van Dorsten (Oxford: Clarendon Press, 1973), 11.

32. See John Milton, *Eikonoklastes, John Milton: Complete Poems and Major Prose,* ed. Merritt Y. Hughes (Indianapolis: Odyssey Press, 1957), 793.

33. Martin Luther, "The Estate of Marriage," trans. Walter I. Brandt, in *Luther's Works*, 45, pt. 2, ed. Walter I. Brandt, general ed. Helmut T. Lehmann (Philadelphia: Muhlenberg Press, 1962), 39. For Luther's rejection of a false "spiritualization" of human nature, his delight in God-given bodily pleasures, see Heiko Oberman, *Luther: Man between God and the Devil*, trans. Eileen Walliser-Schwarztbart (New Haven: Yale University Press, 1989), 274–89.

34. William Shakespeare, *The Tragedy of King Richard the Second* 4.1.260–62, *The Riverside Shakespeare*, ed. G. Blakemore Evans (Boston: Houghton Mifflin, 1974).

35. Shakespeare, *Hamlet*, 1.2.129–30.

36. Hans-Georg Gadamer, *Truth and Method*, 2d ed. (New York: Seabury Press, 1975), xiv.

37. *The Prose Works of Fulke Greville*, ed. John Gouws (Oxford: Clarendon Press, 1986), 134.

38. Montaigne, *Of Experience, Essayes* 3: 372.

39. Montaigne, *Of Experience, Essayes* 3: 372.

Bibliography

Allen, M. J. B., Dominic Baker-Smith, and Arthur Kinney, eds., with Margaret M. Sullivan. *Sir Philip Sidney's Achievements*. New York: AMS Press, 1990.

Altman, Joel B. *The Tudor Play of Mind: Rhetorical Inquiry and the Development of Elizabethan Drama*. Berkeley: University of California Press, 1978.

Aristotle. *The "Art" of Rhetoric*. Translated by John Henry Freese. London: William Heinemann, 1926.

———. *The Nicomachean Ethics*. Translated by H. Rackham. Cambridge, Mass.: Harvard University Press, 1968.

———. *Poetics. Criticism: The Major Texts*. Edited by Walter Jackson Bate. New York: Harcourt, Brace, Jovanovich, 1970.

Ascham, Roger. *The Scholemaster* (1570). Edited by John E. B. Mayor. 1863. New York: AMS Press, 1967.

Augustine. *The City of God against the Pagans*. 7 vols. Translated by George E. McCracken and others. Cambridge: Harvard University Press, 1957–72.

Baldwin, T. W. *William Shakespeare's Small Latine & Lesse Greeke*. 2 vols. Urbana: University of Illinois Press, 1944.

Barber, C. L. *Shakespeare's Festive Comedy: A Study of Dramatic Form and its Relation to Social Custom*. Princeton: Princeton University Press, 1959.

Baym, Nina. "Melodramas of Beset Manhood: How Theories of American Fiction Exclude Women Authors." In *The New Feminist Criticism: Essays on Women, Literature, and Theory*, edited by Elaine Showalter. New York: Pantheon, 1985.

Bergvall, Ake. *The "Enabling of Judgement": Sir Philip Sidney and the Education of the Reader*. Uppsala: Acta Universitatis Upsaliensis, 1989. (Doctoral Thesis at Uppsala University, 1989.)

Bullinger, Heinrich. Preface to *The Golden Boke of Christen Matrimonye*. Translated by Miles Coverdale. London: n.p., 1543.

Bundy, Murray Wright. " 'Invention' and 'Imagination' in the Renaissance." *Journal of English and Germanic Philology* 29 (1930): 539–45.

Buxton, John. *Sir Philip Sidney and the English Renaissance*. New York: St. Martin's Press, 1964.

Calvin, John. *Institutes of the Christian Religion*. Edited by John T. McNeill, translated by Ford Lewis Battles, 2 vols. Philadelphia: Westminster, 1960.

Carey, John. "Structure and Rhetoric in Sidney's *Arcadia.*" In *Sir Philip Sidney: An Anthology of Modern Criticism*, edited by Dennis Kay. Oxford: Clarendon Press, 1987.

Castiglione, Baldassare. *The Book of the Courtier* (1529). Translated by Sir Thomas Hoby (1561). Introduction by Walter Raleigh. London: David Nutt, 1900.

Chaucer, Geoffrey. *The Riverside Chaucer*. Edited by Larry D. Benson. 3d ed. Boston: Houghton Mifflin, 1987.

Cicero. *De Officiis*. Translated by Walter Miller. London: William Heinemann, 1961.

———. *De Oratore*. Translated by E. W. Sutton. Completed with introduction by H. Rackham. Cambridge: Harvard University Press, 1942.

———. *De Senectute, De Amicitia, De Divinatione*. Translated by William Armistead Falconer. London: William Heinemann, 1923.

———. *Memorabilia. Memorabilia and Oeconomics*. Translated by E. C. Marchant. London: William Heinemann, 1923.

Connell, Dorothy. *Sir Philip Sidney: The Maker's Mind*. Oxford: Clarendon Press, 1977.

Davies, Horton. *Worship and Theology in England*. 5 vols. Princeton: Princeton University Press, 1961–75.

Davis, Walter. "A Map of Arcadia." *Sidney's Arcadia*. New Haven and London: Yale University Press, 1965.

Devereux, James A., S.J. "The Meaning of Delight in Sidney's *Defence of Poesy.*" *Studies in the Literary Imagination* 15 (1982): 85–97.

Dickens, A. G. *The English Reformation*. New York: Schocken Books, 1964.

Doherty, M. J. *The Mistress-Knowledge: Sir Philip Sidney's* Defence of Poesie *and Literary Architectonics in the English Renaissance*. Nashville, Tenn.: University of Vanderbilt Press, 1991.

Dubrow, Heather and Richard Strier, eds. *The Historical Renaissance: New Essays on Tudor and Stuart Literature and Culture*. Chicago: University of Chicago Press, 1988.

Duhamel, P. Albert. "Sidney's Arcadia and Elizabethan Rhetoric." *Studies in Philology* 45 (1948): 134–50.

Duncan-Jones, Katherine. "Sidney's Urania." *Review of English Studies* n.s. 17 (1966): 123–32.

———. *Sir Philip Sidney: Courtier Poet*. New Haven: Yale University Press, 1991.

Elyot, Sir Thomas. *The Boke Named the Gouernour* (1531). Edited by Henry Herbert Stephen Croft. 2 vols. London: Kegan Paul, Trench, 1883.

Erasmus, Desiderius. *The Education of a Christian Prince* (1516). Translated with introduction by Lester K. Born. New York: Octagon, 1965.

Ficino, Marsilio. *Commentary on Plato's Symposium*. Translated by Sears Jayne. *University of Missouri Studies* 19 (1944).

Gadamer, Hans-Georg. *Truth and Method*. 2d ed. New York: Seabury Press, 1975.

Goethe, Johann Wolfgang von. *Faust*. Edited by R-M. S. Heffner, Helmut Rehder, and W. F. Twaddell. Boston: D. C. Heath, 1955.

Gouws, John. "The Nineteenth-Century Development of the Sidney Legend." *Sir Philip Sidney's Achievements*. Edited by M. J. B. Allen, Dominic Baker-Smith, and Arthur Kinney with Margaret M. Sullivan. New York: AMS Press, 1990.

Gray, Hannah H. "Renaissance Humanism: The Pursuit of Eloquence." *Renaissance Essays*. Edited by Paul Oskar Kristeller and Philip P. Wiener. New York: Harper and Row, 1968.

Greenblatt, Stephen. *Renaissance Self-Fashioning from More to Shakespeare*. Chicago: University of Chicago Press, 1980.

———. "Sidney's *Arcadia* and the Mixed Mode." *Studies in Philology* 70 (1973): 269–78.

Greene, Thomas. "The Flexibility of the Self in Renaissance Literature." *The Disciplines of Criticism: Essays in Literary Theory, Interpretation, and History*. Edited by Peter Demetz, Thomas Greene, and Lowry Nelson, Jr. New Haven and London: Yale University Press, 1968.

Greenfield, Thelma. *The Eye of Judgment: Reading the* New Arcadia. Lewisburg, Pa.: Bucknell University Press, 1982.

Greville, Fulke, Lord Brooke. *The Prose Works of Fulke Greville*. Edited by John Gouws. Oxford: Clarendon Press, 1986.

Gritsch, Eric W. *Martin—God's Court Jester: Luther in Retrospect*. Philadelphia: Fortress, 1983.

———, and Robert Jenson. *Lutheranism: The Theological Movement and Its Confessional Writings*. Philadelphia: Fortress, 1976.

Hager, Alan. *Dazzling Images: The Masks of Sir Philip Sidney*. Newark: University of Delaware Press, 1991.

———. "The Exemplary Mirage: Fabrication of Sir Philip Sidney's Biographical Image and the Sidney Reader." *English Literary History* 48 (1981): 1–16. Reprinted in *Essential Articles for the Study of Sir Philip Sidi ?y*, edited by Arthur F. Kinney. Hamden, Conn.: Archon, 1986.

Hamilton, A.C. *Sir Philip Sidney: A Study of His Life and Works*. Cambridge: Cambridge University Press, 1977.

Heiserman, Arthur. *The Novel before the Novel: Essays and Discussions about the Beginnings of Prose Fiction in the West*. Chicago: University of Chicago Press, 1977.

Helgerson, Richard. *The Elizabethan Prodigals*. Berkeley: University of California Press, 1976.

Heliodorus. *An Æthiopian History*. Translated by Thomas Underdowne (1569). London: David Nutt, 1895.

Heninger, S. K., Jr. "Sidney and Boethian Music." *Studies in English Literature* 23 (1983): 37–46.

———. "Sidney and Serranus' Plato." *English Literary Renaissance* 13 (1983): 146–61.

———. *Sidney and Spenser: The Poet as Maker*. University Park and London: Pennsylvania State University Press, 1989.

Howard, Jean S. "The New Historicism in Renaissance Studies." *Renaissance Historicism: Selections from English Literary Renaissance*, edited by Arthur F. Kinney and Dan S. Collins. Amherst: University of Massachusetts Press, 1987.

Howell, Wilbur Samuel. *Logic and Rhetoric in England, 1500–1700*. Princeton: Princeton University Press, 1956.

Jardine, Lisa. *Francis Bacon: Discovery and the Art of Discourse*. Cambridge: Cambridge University Press, 1974.

Jayne, Sears. "Ficino and the Platonism of the English Renaissance," *Comparative Literature* 4 (1952): 214 –38.

Jost, Wilfried. *Ontologie der Person bei Luther*. Gottingen: Vandenhoeck and Ruprecht, 1967.

Jung, C. G. *The Collected Works of C. G. Jung*. 17 vols. Edited by Sir Hubert Rod and others, translated by R. F. C. Hall. Princeton: Princeton University Press, 1954 –73.

Kalstone, David. *Sidney's Poetry, Contexts and Interpretations*. New York: Norton, 1970.

Kimbrough, Robert. *Sir Philip Sidney*. New York: Twayne, 1971.

Knudsen, Robert D. "Calvinism as a Cultural Force." In *John Calvin: His Influence in the Western World*, edited by W. Stanford Reid. Grand Rapids: Zondervan, 1982.

Kristeller, Paul Oskar. *Renaissance Thought: The Classic, Scholastic, and Humanistic Strains*. New York: Harper and Row, 1961.

Lamb, Mary Ellen. *Gender and Authorship in the Sidney Circle*. Madison: University of Wisconsin Press, 1990.

Lambert, Mark. "*Troilus*, Books I-III. A Criseydan Reading." In *Essays on Troilus and Creseyde*, edited by Mary Salu. Cambridge: D. J. Brower, 1979.

Lanham, Richard A. "*Astrophil and Stella*: Pure and Impure Persuasion." *English Literary Renaissance* 2 (1972): 100 –115. Reprinted in *Essential Articles for the Study of Sir Philip Sidney*, edited by Arthur F. Kinney. Hamden, Conn.: Archon, 1986.

———. "Sidney: The Ornament of His Age." *Southern Review* 2, no. 4 (1967): 319–40.

Lawry, Jon S. *Sidney's Two* Arcadias: *Pattern and Proceeding*. Ithaca and London: Cornell University Press, 1972.

Leith, John H. *An Introduction to the Reformed Tradition: A Way of Being the Christian Community*. Atlanta: John Knox Press, 1977.

Levao, Ronald. *Renaissance Minds and Their Fictions: Cusanus, Sidney, Shakespeare*. Berkeley: University of California Press, 1985.

Levy, F. J. "Philip Sidney Reconsidered." *English Literary Renaissance* 2 (1972): 5–18. Reprinted in *Essential Articles for the Study of Sir Philip Sidney*, edited by Arthur F. Kinney. Hamden, Conn.: Archon, 1986.

Lewis, C. S. *English Literature in the Sixteenth Century, Excluding Drama*. Oxford: Clarendon Press, 1954.

Lindenbaum, Peter. "Sidney and the Active Life." In *Sir Philip Sidney's Achievements*, edited by M. J. B. Allen, Dominic Baker-Smith, and Arthur Kinney, with Margaret M. Sullivan. New York: AMS Press, 1990.

Lindheim, Nancy. "Sidney's *Arcadia*, Book II: Retrospective Narrative." *Studies in Philology* 64 (1967): 159– 86.

———. *The Structures of Sidney's Arcadia.* Toronto: University of Toronto Press, 1982.

Lockyer, Roger. *Tudor and Stuart Britain, 1471–1714.* New York: St. Martin's Press, 1964.

Luther, Martin. *Large Catechism. The Book of Concord: The Confessions of the Evangelical Lutheran Church.* Translated and edited by Theodore G. Tappert, in collaboration with others. Philadelphia: Fortress, 1959.

———. *Luther's Works.* 55 vols. Edited by Jaroslav Pelikan (vols. 1–30) and Helmut T. Lehmann (vols. 31–55). St. Louis: Concordia; Philadelphia: Fortress, 1955–86.

Manschreck, Clyde Leonard. *Melanchthon: The Quiet Reformer.* 1958. Westport, Conn.: Greenwood, 1975.

McCanles, Michael. "Oracular Prediction and the Fore-Conceit of Sidney's *Arcadia.*" *English Literary History* 50, no. 2 (1983): 233–44. Reprinted in *Essential Articles for the Study of Sir Philip Sidney,* Edited by Arthur F. Kinney. Hamden, Conn.: Archon, 1986.

———. *The Text of Sidney's Arcadia World.* Durham, N.C.: Duke University Press, 1989.

McCoy, Richard C. *The Rites of Knighthood: The Literature and Politics of Elizabethan Chivalry.* Berkeley: University of California Press, 1989.

———. *Sir Philip Sidney: Rebellion in Arcadia.* New Brunswick, N.J.: Rutgers University Press, 1979.

McNeill, John T. *The History and Character of Calvinism.* New York: Oxford University Press, 1967.

Melanchthon, Philipp. *Apology of the Augsburg Confession. The Book of Concord: The Confessions of the Evangelical Lutheran Church.* Translated and edited by Theodore G. Tappert, in collaboration with others. Philadelphia: Fortress, 1959.

Milton, John. *Eikonoklastes.* In *John Milton: Complete Poems and Major Prose,* edited by Merritt Y. Hughes. Indianapolis, Ind.: Odyssey Press, 1957.

Montaigne, Michel de. *The Essayes of Michael Lord of Montaigne.* Translated by John Florio (1603). 3 vols. London: Oxford University Press, 1924.

Montemayor, George. *A Critical Edition of Yong's Translation of George of Montemayor's* Diana *and Gil Polo's* Enamoured Diana. Edited by Judith Kennedy. Oxford: Clarendon Press, 1968.

Mulcaster, Richard. *Mulcaster's Elementarie.* Edited by E. T. Compangnae. Oxford: Clarendon Press, 1925.

Murdoch, Iris. "On 'God' and 'Good.'" In *The Sovereignty of Good.* London: Ark, 1979.

Myrick, Kenneth. *Sir Philip Sidney as a Literary Craftsman.* 2d ed. Lincoln: University of Nebraska Press, 1965.

Nichols, John. *The Progresses of Queen Elizabeth.* London: John Nichols and Son, 1823.

Oberman, Heiko. *Luther: Man between God and the Devil.* Translated by Eileen Walliser-Schwarztbart. New Haven: Yale University Press, 1989.

Orgel, Stephen K. "Sidney's Experiment in Pastoral: *The Lady of May.*" *Journal of the Wartburg and Courtald Institutio* 26 (1963): 198–203. Reprinted in *Essential Articles for the Study of Sir Philip Sidney,* edited by Arthur F. Kinney. Hamden, Conn.: Archon, 1986.

Osborn, James M. *Young Philip Sidney, 1572–1577.* New Haven and London: Yale University Press, 1972.

Osterhaven, M. Eugene. *The Spirit of the Reformed Tradition.* Grand Rapids, Mich.: Eerdmans, 1971.

Panofsky, Erwin. "Et in Arcadia Ego." In *Philosophy and History: Essays Presented to Ernst Cassirer,* edited by Raymond Klibonsky and H. J. Paton. New York: Harper and Row, 1963.

———. *Hercules am Scheidewege.* Leipzig and Berlin: B. G. Teubner, 1930.

Patterson, Annabel M. " 'Under . . . Pretty Tales': Intention in Sidney's *Arcadia.* " *Studies in the Literary Imagination* 15, no. 1 (1982): 5–21. Reprinted in *Essential Articles for the Study of Sir Philip Sidney,* edited by Arthur F. Kinney. Hamden, Conn.: Archon, 1986.

Pears, Stewart A., trans. *The Correspondence of Sir Philip Sidney and Hubert Languet.* London: William Pickering, 1845.

Petrarch, Francis. *Petrarch's Lyric Poems.* Translated and edited by Robert M. Durling. Cambridge: Harvard University Press, 1976.

Pico della Mirandola, Giovanni. *Oration on the Dignity of Man.* In *The Renaissance Philosophy of Man,* edited by Ernst Cassirer, Paul Oskar Kristeller, and John Herman Randall, Jr. Chicago: University of Chicago Press, 1948.

Pill, David H. *The English Reformation, 1529–58.* Totowa, N.J.: Rowman and Littlefield, 1973.

Plato. *Menexenus. Plato.* Vol. 7. Translated by R. G. Bury. Cambridge: Harvard University Press, 1952.

———. *The Republic.* 2 vols. Translated by Paul Shorey. London: William Heinemann, 1946.

———. *Symposium. Plato.* Vol. 5. Translated by W. R. M. Lamb. London: William Heinemann, 1925.

———. *Timaeus. Plato.* Vol. 7. Translated by R. G. Bury. Cambridge: Harvard University Press, 1952.

Primaudaye, Peter de la. *The French Academie* (1586). Translated by T. B[owes]. Hildesheim, West Germany, and New York: Georg Olms Verlong, 1972.

Quilligan, Maureen. "Sidney and His Queen." In *The Historical Renaissance,* edited by Heather Dubrow and Richard Strier. Chicago: University of Chicago Press, 1988.

Quintillian. *Institutio Oratoria.* Translated by H. E. Butler. 4 vols. Cambridge: Harvard University Press, 1953.

Raleigh, Walter. *The History of the World* (1614). Edited by C. A. Patrides. Philadelphia: Temple University Press, 1971.

Rees, Joan. *Sir Philip Sidney and* Arcadia. Rutherford, N.J.: Fairleigh Dickinson University Press, 1991.

Roche, Thomas P., Jr. "*Astrophil and Stella:* A Radical Reading." *Spenser Studies* 3 (1982): 139–91.

Rudenstine, Neil. *Sidney's Poetic Development.* Cambridge: Harvard University Press, 1967.

Rupp, E. G. *Studies in the Making of the English Protestant Tradition.* Cambridge: Cambridge University Press, 1966.

Samuel, Irene. "The Influence of Plato on Sidney's *Defense of Poesie.*" *Modern Language Quarterly* 1 (1940): 383–91.

Sannazaro. *Arcadia and Piscatorial Eclogue.* Translated by Ralph Nash. Detroit: Wayne State University Press, 1966.

Seneca. *Ad Lucilium Epistulae Morales.* 3 vols. Translated by Richard M. Gummere. London: William Heinemann, 1917–25.

Shakespeare, William. *The Riverside Shakespeare.* Edited by G. Blakemore Evans. Boston: Houghton Mifflin, 1974.

Shaver, Anne. "Woman's Place in the *New Arcadia.*" *Sidney Newsletter* 10, no. 2 (1990): 3–15.

Sidney, Sir Philip. *An Apology for Poetry.* Edited by Geoffrey Shepherd. London: Nelson, 1965.

———. *The Complete Works of Sir Philip Sidney.* Edited by Albert Feuillerat. 4 vols. Cambridge: Cambridge University Press, 1912–26.

———. *The Countess of Pembroke's Arcadia.* Edited by with introduction by Maurice Evans. Harmondsworth, England: Penguin, 1977.

———. *The Countess of Pembroke's Arcadia (The New Arcadia).* Edited by Victor Skretkowicz. Oxford: Clarendon Press, 1987.

———. *The Countess of Pembroke's Arcadia (The Old Arcadia).* Edited by Jean Robertson. Oxford: Clarendon Press, 1973.

———. *A Defence of Poesie.* London: William Ponsonby, 1595.

———. *Miscellaneous Prose of Sir Philip Sidney.* Edited by Katherine Duncan-Jones and Jan van Dorsten. Oxford: Clarendon Press, 1973.

———. *The Poems of Sir Philip Sidney.* Edited by William A. Ringler, Jr. Oxford: Clarendon Press, 1962.

Sinfield, Alan. "Power and Ideology: An Outline Theory and Sidney's *Arcadia.*" *English Literary History* 52 (1985): 259–77. Reprinted in *Essential Articles for the Study of Sir Philip Sidney,* edited by Arthur F. Kinney. Hamden, Conn.: Archon, 1986.

Smith, Hallet. *Elizabethan Poetry: A Study in Conventions, Meaning, and Expression.* Cambridge: Harvard University Press, 1952.

Spencer, Theodore. "The Poetry of Sir Philip Sidney." *English Literary History* 12 (1945): 251–78. Reprinted in *Essential Articles for the Study of Sir Philip Sidney,* edited by Arthur F. Kinney. Hamden, Conn.: Archon, 1986.

Spenser, Edmund. *The Works of Edmund Spenser, A Variorum Edition.* Edited by Edwin Greenlaw, Charles Grosvenor Osgood, and Frederick Morgan Padelford. 11 vols. Baltimore: Johns Hopkins University Press, 1932–45.

Stillman, Robert E. "Justice and the 'Good Word' in Sidney's *The Lady of May.*" *Studies in English Literature* 24 (1984): 23–38.

———. *Sidney's Poetic Justice: The Old Arcadia, Its Eclogues, and Renaissance Pastoral Traditions.* Lewisburg, Pa.: Bucknell University Press, 1986.

Sullivan, Margaret M. "Getting Pamela Out of the House: Gendering Genealogy in the *New Arcadia.*" *Sidney Newsletter* 9, no.2 (1988/89): 3–18.

Tappert, Theodore G., with others, translators and editors. *The Book of Concord: The Confessions of the Evangelical Lutheran Church.* Philadelphia: Fortress, 1959.

Tillyard, E. M. W. *The English Renaissance: Fact or Fiction?* Baltimore: Johns Hopkins University Press, 1952.

Todorov, Tzvetan. *Literature and Its Theorists: A Personal View of Twentieth-Century Criticism.* Translated by Catherine Porter. Ithaca: Cornell University Press, 1987.

Turner, Myron. "The Heroic Ideal in Sidney's Revised *Arcadia.*" *Studies in English Literature* 10 (1970): 63–82.

Tuve, Rosemond. "Spenser and Some Pictorial Conventions: With Particular Reference to Illustrated Manuscripts." In *Essays by Rosemond Tuve.* Edited by Thomas P. Roche, Jr. Princeton: Princeton University Press, 1970.

Ulreich, John C., Jr. " 'The Poets Only Deliver': Sidney's Conception of *Mimesis.*" *Studies in the Literary Imagination* 15.1 (1982): 67–84. Reprinted in *Essential Articles for the Study of Sir Philip Sidney,* edited by Arthur F. Kinney. Hamden, Conn.: Archon, 1986.

Waddington, Raymond B. "Lutheran Hamlet." *English Language Notes,* 27.2 (December 1989): 27–42.

Wallace, Malcolm William. *The Life of Sir Philip Sidney.* Cambridge: Cambridge University Press, 1915. Reprinted. New York: Octagon, 1967.

Waller, Gary. *English Poetry of the Sixteenth Century.* London and New York: Longman, 1986.

Weiner, Andrew D. *Sir Philip Sidney and the Poetics of Protestantism: A Study of Contexts.* Minneapolis: University of Minnesota Press, 1978.

Wendel, Francois. *Calvin: Origins and Development of His Religious Thought.* Translated by Philip Mairet. Durham, N.C.: Labyrinth, 1987.

Wilson, Thomas. *The Arte of Rhetorique* (1553). Edited by Thomas J. Derrick. New York and London: Garland, 1982.

Woods, Susanne. "Freedom and Tyranny in Sidney's *Arcadia.*" *Sir Philip Sidney's Achievements.* Edited by M. J. B. Allen, Dominic Baker-Smith, and Arthur Kinney with Margaret M. Sullivan. New York: AMS Press, 1990.

Xenophon. *Cyropaedia.* 2 vols. Translated by Walter Miller. London: William Heinemann, 1914.

Yates, Francis A. *The Art of Memory.* Chicago: University of Chicago Press, 1966.

———. *Astraea: The Imperial Theme in the Sixteenth Century.* London: Routledge and Kegan Paul, 1975.

———. *Giordano Bruno and the Hermetic Tradition.* Chicago: University of Chicago Press, 1964.

Index